ADVANCED VISUAL BASIC 6
Projects

By

Ivan Bayross

bpb BPB PUBLICATIONS
B-14, CONNAUGHT PLACE, NEW DELHI-110001

FIRST INDIAN EDITION 2002

REPRINTED 2005

Distributors:

MICRO BOOK CENTRE
2, City Centre, CG Road,
Near Swastic Char Rasta,
AHMEDABAD-380009 Phone: 26421611

COMPUTER BOOK CENTRE
12, Shrungar Shopping Centre, M.G. Road,
BANGALORE-560001 Phone: 5587923, 5584641

MICRO BOOKS
Shanti Niketan Building, 8, Camac Street,
KOLKATTA-700017 Phone: 22826518, 22826519

BUSINESS PROMOTION BUREAU
8/1, Ritchie Street, Mount Road,
CHENNAI-600002 Phone: 28410796, 28550491

DECCAN AGENCIES
4-3-329, Bank Street,
HYDERABAD-500195 Phone: 24756400, 24756967

MICRO MEDIA
Shop No. 5, Mahendra Chambers, 150 D.N. Road,
Next to Capital Cinema V.T. (C.S.T.) Station,
MUMBAI-400001 Ph.: 22078296, 22078297

BPB PUBLICATIONS
B-14, Connaught Place, **NEW DELHI-110001**
Phone: 23325760, 23723393, 23737742

INFO TECH
G-2, Sidhartha Building, 96 Nehru Place,
NEW DELHI-110019
Phone: 26438245, 26415092, 26234208

INFO TECH
Shop No. 2, F-38, South Extension Part-1
NEW DELHI-110049
Phone: 24691288, 24641941

BPB BOOK CENTRE
376, Old Lajpat Rai Market,
DELHI-110006 PHONE: 23861747

NOTE: THE CD-ROM INCLUDED WITH THE BOOK HAS NO COMMERCIAL VALUE AND CANNOT BE SOLD SEPARATELY.

Copyright © BPB PUBLICATIONS

All Rights Reserved. No part of this publication can be stored in any retrieval system or reproduced in any form or by any means without the prior written permission of the publishers.

LIMITS OF LIABILITY AND DISCLAIMER OF WARRANTY

The Author and Publisher of this book have tried their best to ensure that the programmes, procedures and functions described in the book are correct. However, the author and the publishers make no warranty of any kind, expressed or implied, with regard to these programmes or the documentation contained in the book. The author and publishers shall not be liable in any event of any damages, incidental or consequential, in connection with, or arising out of the furnishing, performance or use of these programmes, procedures and functions. Product name mentioned are used for identification purposes only and may be trademarks of their respective companies.

All trademarks referred to in the book are acknowledged as properties of their respective owners.

Price : Rs. 195/-

ISBN 81-7656-675-6

Published by Manish Jain for BPB Publications, B-14, Connaught Place, New Delhi-110 001 and Printed by him at Pressworks, New Delhi.

PREFACE TO THE BOOK

FOREWORD

Visual Basic has always been perceived as a very simple programming environment. Most people who are starting out to program for the first time choose to learn Visual Basic because of this perception.

Nonetheless, Visual Basic has evolved over time and has become a very powerful programming environment with an excellent **I**ntegrated **D**evelopment **E**nvironment. Creating large, multi-user, commercial applications using the Visual Basic IDE is really quite simple because of all the built in visual tools.

Since Visual Basic is very popular, and used extensively, a large number of web sites make available excellent Visual Basic material, often for free. Download this material it will support your learning of programming in Visual Basic.

Most of these freebies are surprisingly very well documented. Code snippets use 'Rem' statements extensively. Many even have complete 'Help' files in HTML or PDF (Acrobat Reader files) format. Access to this will really make you fly.

In this material the general concepts of creating good commercial applications are built using simple language. Careful attention has been paid on how to write tight, well documented code. A separate section has been included on project management and quality assurance. I hope that this really helps in creating good quality, repeatable code blocks. Believe me, finding a programmer capable of delivering good quality code consistently, is really as difficult as finding a needle in a haystack. The ability to create high quality code consistently, is a skill that can always be sold to the highest bidder.

A CD-ROM is enclosed has the complete code base used in the book. Use the way the code is structured to assist you when you are trying your own code snippets.

This foreword would not be complete without my thanking the many people who encouraged me and put up with my many revisions and updation of the material with patience and tolerance.

My sincere thanks goes to first my publisher Mr. Manish Jain who has grown into my close friend and mentor. Thanks Manish I'm getting better each day.

To Ms. Ashwini Joshi, honestly this book would have never made it without you and the TLC you gave it. For the long hours you put in coding and testing each example. Especially for putting up with my Visual Basic coding demands, which often times must have given you high blood pressure. Thank you.

Mr. Hansel Colaco, whose attention to detail ensures the page numbering, Index and Table of contents, header, footers of the manuscript are first class. Authors simply cannot make it without people like you, who take care of the thousands of tiny issues that make a manuscript perfect for publishing. Thank you.

Mr. Deepak Sharma who worked on the PIM project. There was a lot of TAPI code spec that actually happened simply because you took a lot of interest.

The many trainees / students will read this book, each time you found a mistake and suggested a correction you helped me towards perfection, a very big thank you to each and every one of you.

The many programmers who read this book I would welcome your brickbats or bouquets. Without you I would not be an author. You can contact me via my publisher Mr. Manish Jain at BpB New Delhi.

Finally and most importantly to my wife Cynthia who always encouraged me whenever I thought that I would never get this manuscript ready for publishing. You've always helped keep my feet planted firmly on the ground, with you I'm truly blessed.

Ivan N. Bayross

TABLE OF CONTENTS

TABLE OF CONTENTS

1. CONNECTIVITY IN VB 6 USING ODBC AND ADO 5

DATA STORAGE 5
Creating A Database/Table In M.S. Access 5
Testing To See Whether The Table Created Exists 11
CONNECTING TO A DATABASE USING ODBC 12
Middle Ware Technology 13
CONNECTING TO A DATABASE USING ADO 18
ActiveX Data Objects 18
Data Providers 20
Data Consumers 20
Service Components 20
Accessing Data Via A Visual Basic Form 20
Binding ADO To A Visual Basic Form 21
USING ADO PROGRAMMATICALLY 22
Creating A RecordSet Object In Memory 24
MASTER DETAIL CONCEPTS 25
Technique Used 26
DATA GRID CONCEPTS 26
Setting the ADODC's Properties: 26
Binding The Data Grid To The ADODC Control 30
Inserting Table Data Via The Data Grid 30
Viewing Table Data Via The Data Grid 31
Updating Table Data Via The Data Grid 32
Deleting Table Data Via The Data Grid 32

2. AN APPLICATION'S TOOLBAR LOGIC 39

GENERATING A TRUTH TABLE TO CONTROL A TOOLBAR 40
Toolbar Status During The No Mode 41
Toolbar Status During The Insert Mode 42
Toolbar Status During The View Mode 43
Toolbar Status During The Update Mode 45
Toolbar Status During The Delete Mode 45
THE DETAIL SECTION 48
Insert Mode in Details section 48
Update Mode in details section 49
Delete Mode in details section 49
Save Mode In Detail Section 51

PRACTICAL VB 6 PROJECTS

    MASTER-DETAIL TOOLBAR BUTTON INTERACTION 52
    MASTER FORM COMMAND BUTTON'S TRUTH TABLE 56
    DETAILS SECTION COMMAND BUTTON'S TRUTH TABLE 58

3. A PERSONAL INFORMATION MANAGER: A PLAN 65

    PROJECT SCOPE 65
    ENTITY RELATIONSHIP DIAGRAM FOR THE P. I. M. 67
    TABLE DEFINITIONS – P.I.M 68
    TABLE DATA VALIDATION RULES 74
    MICRO HELP FOR TABLE FIELDS 76
    TEST DATA FOR THE P. I. M. 78

4. A PERSONAL INFORMATION MANAGER: THE WORKING 93

    ADDITIONAL COMPONENTS AND REFERENCES 98
    PROJECT CODE FOR FRMCARDBOOK.FRM 99
    PROJECT CODE FOR FRMDIAL.FRM 173
    PROJECT CODE FOR FRMEMAIL.FRM 185
    PROJECT CODE FOR FRMSEARCH.FRM 193
    PROJECT CODE FOR MODULE1 197

5. A COMMERCIAL BANKING SYSTEM: THE PLAN 203

    PROJECT SCOPE 203
    ENTITY RELATION DIAGRAM FOR THE BANKING SYSTEM 207
    TABLE DEFINITION – BANKING SYSTEM 208
    TABLE DATA VALIDATION RULES 215
    MICROHELP 218
    TEST RECORDS FOR THE BANKING SYSTEM 221

6. A COMMERCIAL BANKING SYSTEM: THE WORKING 231

    ADDITIONAL COMPONENTS AND REFERENCES 240
    PROJECT CODE FOR FRMMAIN.FRM 241
    PROJECT CODE FOR MODBNKSYS.BAS 249
    PROJECT CODE FOR FRMOPENFRM.FRM 266
    PROJECT CODE FOR FRMEMPMSTR.FRM 268
    PROJECT CODE FOR FRMCLNTMSTR.FRM 280
    PROJECT CODE FOR FRMSLCTCLNT.FRM 301
    PROJECT CODE FOR FRMACCTMSTR.FRM 304
    PROJECT CODE FOR FRMTRANSMSTR.FRM 318

TABLE OF CONTENTS

7. CREATING REPORTS IN VB 6 341
Microsoft Data Reports *341*
Crystal Reports *342*
When To Use Microsoft Data Reports *343*
When To Use Crystal Reports *343*
CREATING A REPORT USING MICROSOFT DATA REPORTS 344
Understanding Microsoft Data Report *354*
AN ADODB'S RECORDSET VS A DATA ENVIRONMENT 357
PROJECT CODE FOR FRMSHOWRPRT.FRM 358
PROJECT SOURCE CODE FOR RPTSTATEMENT.DSR 371
PROJECT SOURCE CODE FOR RPTACCHOLDERINFO.DSR 373

8. BASICS OF PROJECT MANAGEMENT AND QUALITY ASSURANCE 379
An Introduction *379*
THE PROJECT MANAGEMENT PROCESS 380
Beginning A Software Project *381*
Measures And Metrics *382*
Estimation *382*
Risk Analysis *383*
Project Scheduling *383*
Project Tracking and Control *384*
THE QUALITY ASSURANCE PROCESS 386
STANDARDS FOR MASTER DATA ENTRY FORMS 387
CHECKLIST FOR MASTER D/E FORM AESTHETICS 389
NON-CONFORMITIES OF THE MASTER DATA ENTRY FORM 390
Data Entry – Aesthetics *390*
INTRODUCING QUALITY TO CODEBASE 392
QA Techniques *392*
A Recommended Structure For A .frm File *392*
The Form Opening Section *393*
The Database Connection Section *393*
The Data Navigation Section *393*
The Data Manipulation Section *393*
The Data Validation Section *394*
Documenting The Codebase *394*
In Conclusion *399*

PRACTICAL VB 6 PROJECTS

1. CONNECTIVITY IN VB 6 USING ODBC AND ADO

DATA STORAGE

Commercial Applications require that business data is stored using any system that can both store and locate the data quickly on demand. This caused the rapid growth of **d**ata **b**ase **m**anagement **s**ystems (**DBMS**), which are-- specifically designed to managed business data at very high speed and with great efficiency. Access is one such data base management system from Microsoft's stable.

Prior the use of database systems business data was stored as **flat files** (Plain ASCII text) on the hard disk. Flat files are very inefficient in both data storage and retrieval.

The projects described in this material use M.S. Access as their data base management system for modeling. M.S. Access can be replaced by any other data base management system (Oracle, SQL Server, Sybase and so on) simply by changing the middleware used to the appropriate ODBC driver or ADODC data provider for the DBMS.

Both ODBC and ADODC are used in the projects contained in this material. Each middleware system has been given brief but intensive coverage sufficient to develop all the necessary skills to use them confidently.

Creating A Database/Table In M.S. Access

Load the MS Access executable in memory by clicking on **Start → Programs → MS Access**, as shown in diagram 1.1.1.

When MS Access loads successfully in memory, the screen as shown in diagram 1.1.2 is displayed on the VDU.

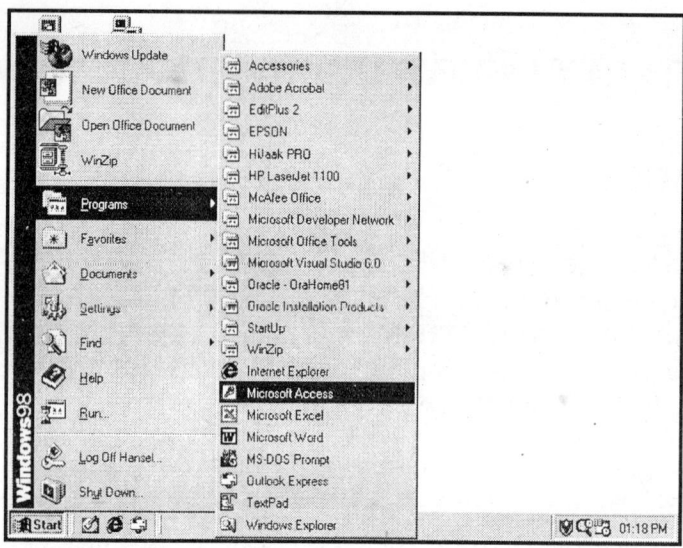

Diagram 1.1.1: Starting a session of MS Access

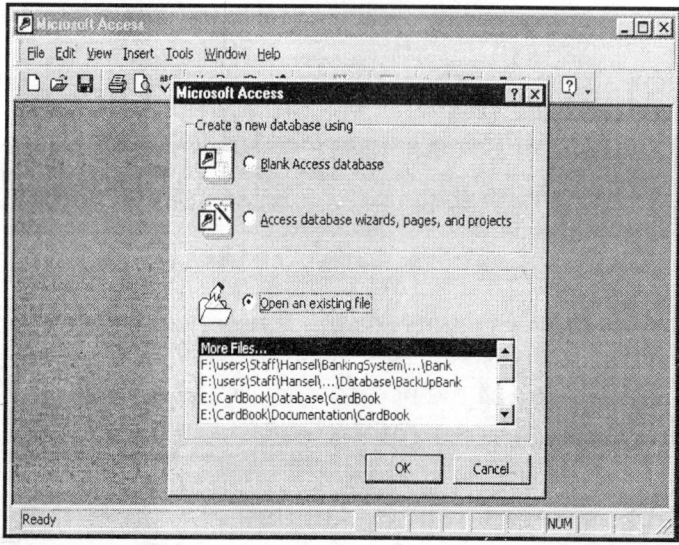

Diagram 1.1.2: Dialog box to open a file in MS Access

The dialog box provide different options to open a '**.mdb**' file. Select the first option, '**Blank Access database**' and click '**OK**'.

In the **Open** dialog box, as shown in diagram 1.1.3, specify the path and file name for storing the file on the HDD. Click **Create** to create a new '.mdb' file

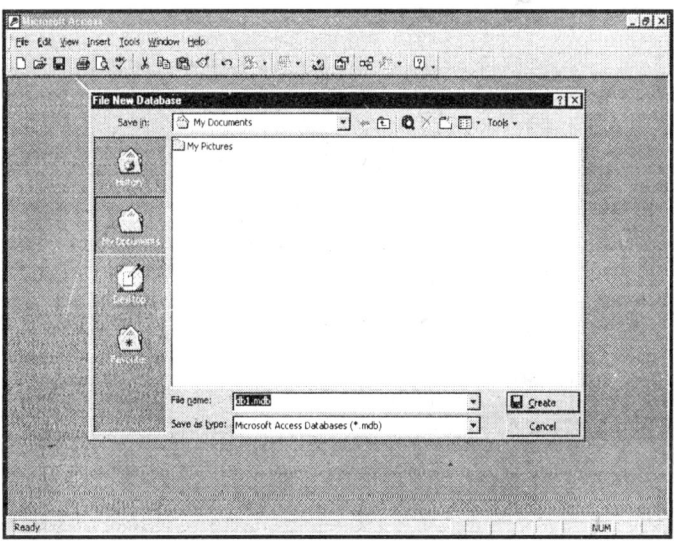

Diagram 1.1.3: An Open dialog box in MS Access

After the new '.mdb' file is create and stored on the HDD, MS Access opens it by listing the objects stored in it. Since the file is just created, the list only show shortcuts used to activate different application wizards. Refer to diagram 1.1.4.

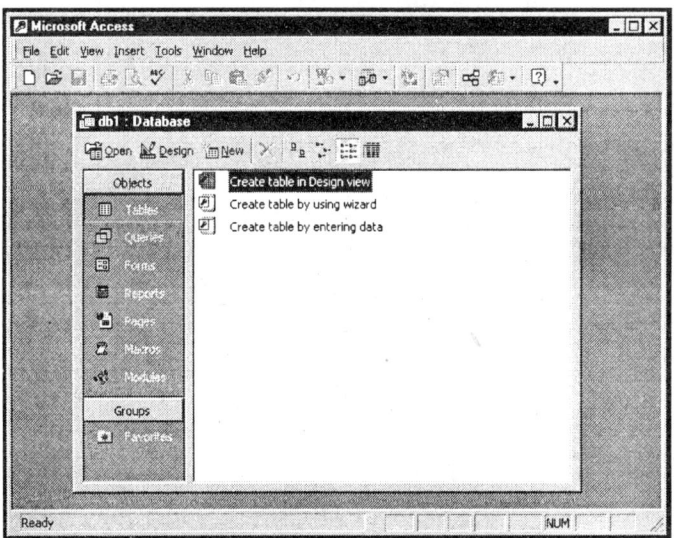

Diagram 1.1.4: List of objects stored within a '.mdi' file

Double click **'Create table in Design View'**. Immediately the table structure definition response window opens, as shown in diagram 1.1.5.

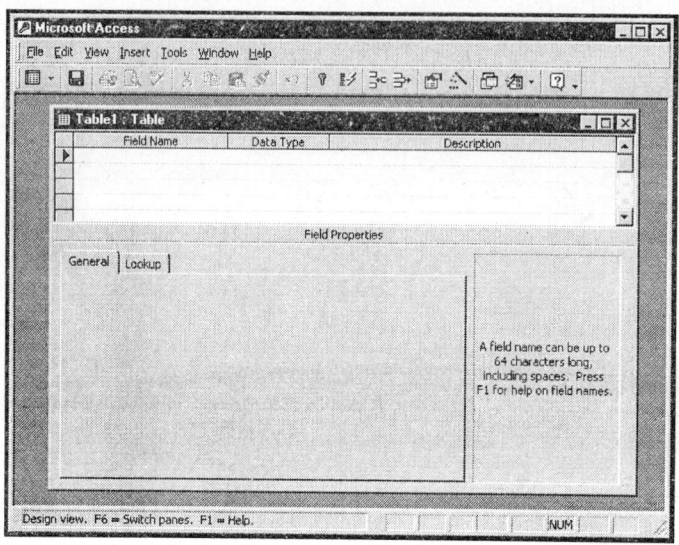

Diagram 1.1.5: Table's Design View in MS Access

This interface permits the creation of a table to hold the application information and binds this table to the database created earlier.

The interface has **three** columns:

- The first accepts the **name** of a table column.

- The second, a drop down list box, permits choosing of an appropriate **data type** that the column will hold. Refer to diagram 1.1.6.

- The last column permits a **brief description** to be entered of the data being held in the table column. Entering a brief description of the column data is optional.

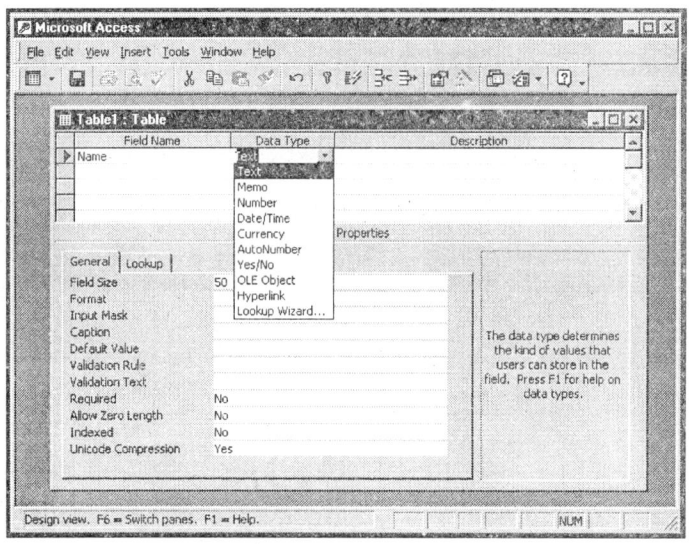

Diagram 1.1.6: Column data types in MS Access

The notebook object at the bottom of the screen in diagram 1.1.6 has two pages. The first labeled **General** the second labeled **Lookup**.

Using the **General** tab, other table column attributes can be entered such as the width of the column, whether it is a mandatory column or not, and so on.

Once complete, click on **File → Save**. A response window, as shown in diagram 1.1.7, opens that allows the entry of the table name.

Diagram 1.1.7: Dialog box accepting a name for the new table

Enter the table name and click **OK**. The table creation tool will then request for a primary key for the table. Select **Yes**. Refer to diagram 1.1.8.

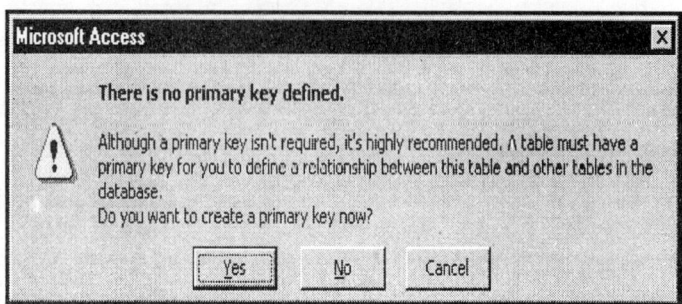

Diagram 1.1.8: Confirmation to create a primary key

If **Yes** is selected MS Access will **automatically** add another column to the table which it will use as the table's primary key.

If the primary key has to be user created, then select the appropriate column of the table by clicking on it. In the **General** tab at the bottom of the screen enter the column attributes as shown in Table 1.1.1.

Column Attribute	Value loaded
Required	Yes
Allow Zero Length	No
Indexed	Yes (No Duplicates)

Table 1.1.2

Caution

Be especially careful when creating table columns in M.S. Access. Ensure that the **Allow Zero Length** column attribute for the table columns is set appropriately. **No** is the **default** setting for this column attribute. This will ensure that the cell cannot be left blank.

Another column attribute that has to be set correctly is the **Required** attribute. Making the Required attribute of a table column to **Yes** indicates that the cell cannot be left blank.

Setting these table column attributes will force the database to perform some table data validation automatically. This approach helps reduce form-based coding.

Once all table columns have been created and all table column attributes set as indicated, click 'File' → 'Save'. The table structure then gets created and saved into the database.

The table is an empty shell, but it is ready to accept records being passed backwards for storage by an appropriate data capture (and validation) form.

Testing To See Whether The Table Created Exists

Close and Re-Start MS Access.

Click **File** → **Open**. Navigate to the sub directory where the database (**.mdb**) file has been saved. Select the **.mdb** file by clicking on it and then click '**Open**'.

Double click the recently created table, form the response window that displays all the table names contained within the database selected.

An empty structure of the table is displayed. This proves that the table has been created and saved correctly. This table is now ready for usage on demand.

CONNECTING TO A DATABASE USING ODBC

ODBC is a Microsoft specific technology. Hence, both Microsoft as well as the makers of the database engine can provide ODBC drivers. These drivers will be installed under the explicit control of the M.S. Windows operating system.

To make use of the ODBC drivers installed the operating system (M.S. Windows) provides an interactive tool via which three different types of **D**ata **S**ource **N**ames (DSN) can be created. The most extensively used DSN on a database server is a **System DSN**. The system DSN offers a few **distinct advantages** over File and User DSNs.

Using the operating system's interactive tool
- An appropriate system DSN will be created
- This DSN will be bound to a database specific ODBC driver
- The ODBC driver will be in turn bound to a specific database on the hard disk

The DSN will then be a unique **named** object that knows
- The ODBC driver to be used

And
- Where the database to which the driver needs to connect is located on the ++hard disk

This System DSN is often referred to a **Middleware** in a Client Server based application. This is because the system DSN sits between the Visual Basic form and the database/table in which application data is stored for manipulation.

Middle Ware

The Focus is to create a named, 32-bit ODBC driver (**i.e.** Middleware), via which a Visual Basic form (**i.e.** the GUI) will communicate with an M.S. Access database/table.

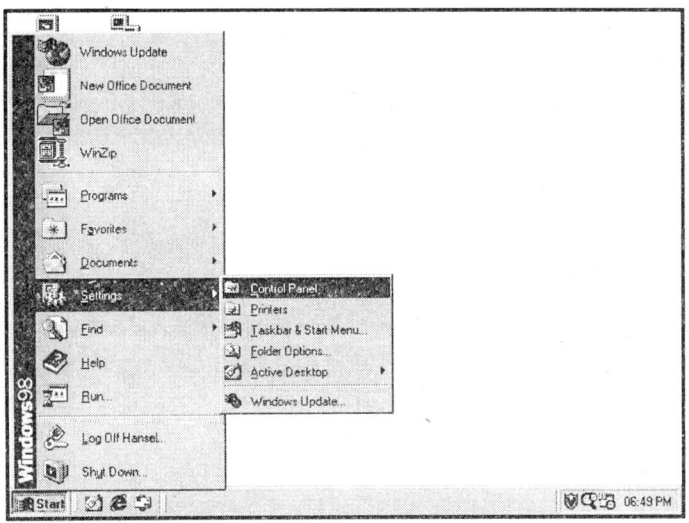

Diagram 1.2.1: Opening the Control Panel window

Click on **Start → Settings → Control Panel**, as shown in diagram 1.2.1. The screen as shown in diagram 1.2.2 will appear.

Diagram 1.2.2: The Control Panel window

Select the **ODBC Data Source (32bit)** from the **Control Panel**. When this is done the **ODBC Data Source Administrator** interface will open as shown in diagram 1.2.3.

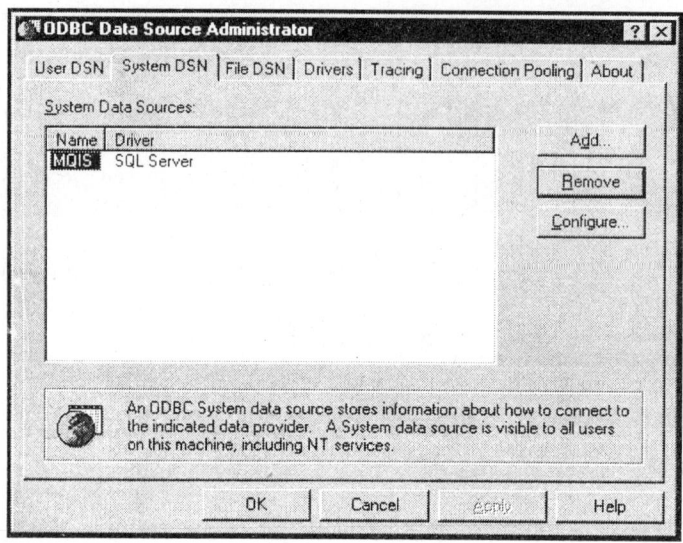

Diagram 1.2.3: The ODBC Data Source Administrator's dialog box

The ODBC data source administrator allows the creation of **several types** of **named** Data Sources. Select **System DSN** from the tabbed notebook as shown in diagram 1.2.3 (**i.e.** the second tab from the left hand side).

Once the System DSN page is selected in the tabbed notebook, click **Add...** in the interface (**i.e.** on the right hand side of the interface).

This will open up another interface, which will display **all** the ODBC drivers installed with the operating system on the computer. Each ODBC driver will communicate effectively only with the database for which the driver was built.

Select the appropriate driver. In this case, **Microsoft Access Driver [.mdb]** will be selected as shown in diagram 1.2.4.

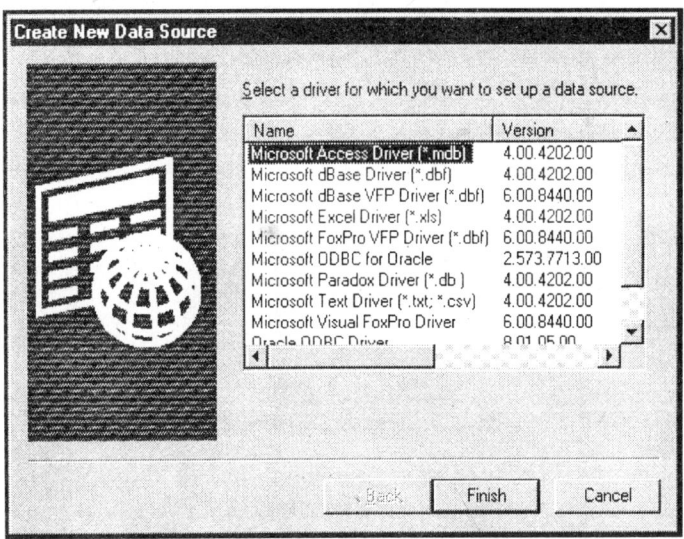

Diagram 1.2.4: Selecting a driver to set up a data source

Once the Microsoft Access Driver [.mdb] ODBC driver has been selected as the driver of choice, click **Finish** on the interface to complete creating the system DSN. The interface as shown in diagram x.1.5 will appear.

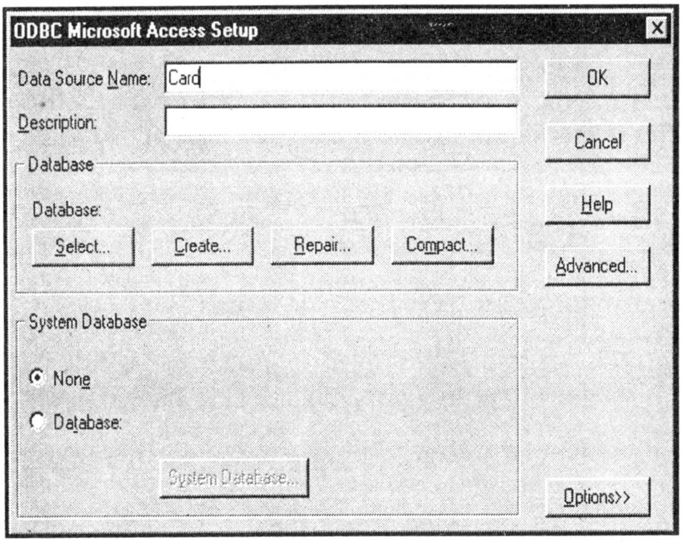

Diagram 1.2.5: Naming the new System DSN

This interface allows the user to give a **unique name** to the system DSN being created. Fill in the **D**ata **S**ource **N**ame field on the interface. In this case the name given is **Card**. Refer to diagram 1.2.5.

Once done this (**named**) system DSN needs to know location at which the database resides on the computer's HDD.

The technique of doing this is described in diagram 1.2.6.

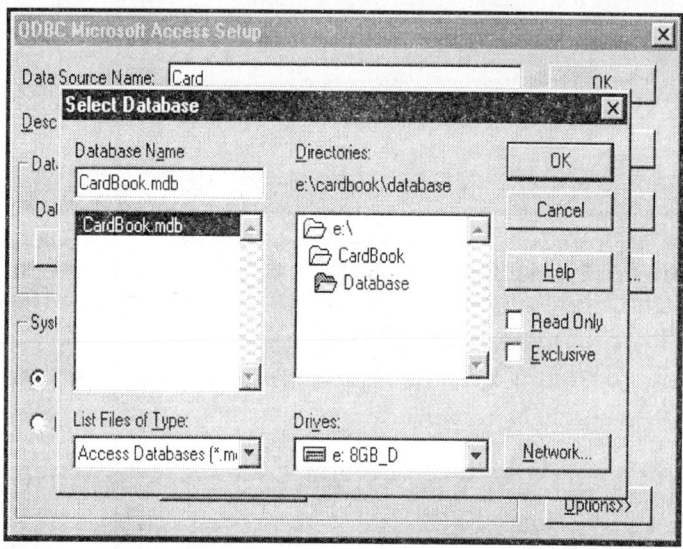

Diagram 1.2.6: Selecting a .mdb file

Use the **Select** button on the interface (held within the **Database** frame) and select the Access database by browsing through the directory tree structure of the hard disk until the appropriate Access **.mdb** file is located. As shown in diagram 1.2.6.

When this is correctly done the absolute path to the M.S. Access database will be visible in the interface, (within the Database frame) as shown in diagram 1.2.7.

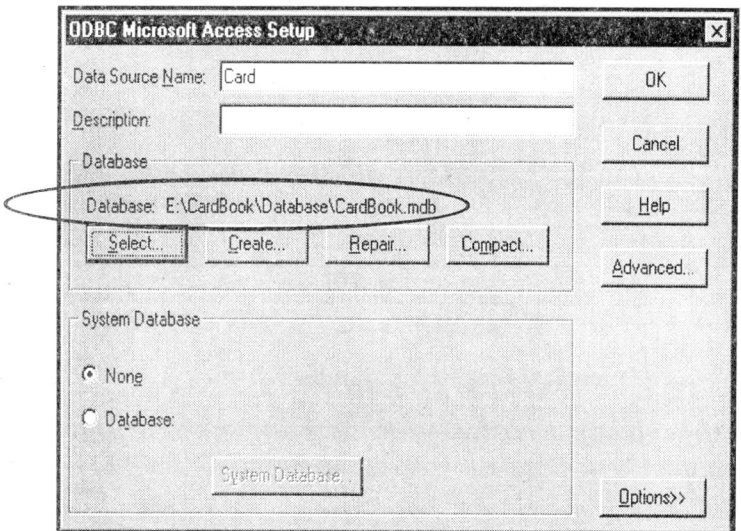

Diagram 1.2.7: Path and filename for the selected database

Once these steps are completed, a 32-bit ODBC, named Data Source (**i.e. Card** the named ODBC driver) is created and registered with the operating system M.S. Windows. The system DSN **Card** now exists. Notice the Path visible next to the label **Database** in the Database frame in diagram 1.2.7.

This system DSN **Card**, knows where the MS Access database ClientMaster.mdb is located on the hard disk and can communicate with any tables held within it.

All that remains is that this user created **middleware** (32-bit ODBC, DSN **Card**), has to be bound to the Visual Basic form in some way so that the form can establish communication with the M.S. Access database **CardBook.mdb**, to manipulate or navigate through any of its table's data.

CONNECTING TO A DATABASE USING ADO

ActiveX Data Objects

Microsoft **A**ctiveX **D**ata **O**bjects (ADO) is an object oriented database access technology. It is part of Microsoft's Universal Data Access initiative, which seeks to make all data sources generic in the way that, currently, all relational data sources are generic by virtue of ODBC.

Because ADO is provided in the form of an ActiveX library ADO can be used in a Visual Basic application with no problem. In many ways it is easier to connect to a client/server database using ADO than any of the other techniques offered by Microsoft such as DAO and RDO. ADO's performance today in connecting to client/server databases is much better than RDO.

ADO technology uses middleware built around OLE DB technology. Middleware built around this technology is called an **OLE DB data provider**.

Conceptually the OLE DB data provider sits between the ADO interface and a database. Programmers interact with the ADO interface, the ADO interface interacts with the OLE DB data provider and the OLE DB data provider in turn interacts with the database **to which it is bound**. This means that there is a specific OLE DB data provider for a specific database.

Note

In case there is no OLE DB data provider for a database bound to a commercial application a workaround is to use the OLE DB data provider that is bound to ODBC, which is currently available.

In this case the ADO interface connects to the OLE DB ODBC data provider, which interfaces with the ODBC driver, which in turn interfaces with an ODBC compliant database. Please refer to diagram 1.3.1.

Often this combination provides better performance than ODBC alone when connecting to the database.

CHAP 01 — CONNECTIVITY IN VB 6 USING ODBC AND ADO

OLE DB is Microsoft's strategic, system-level programming interface to access data across an organization. **O**pen **D**ata**B**ase **C**onnectivity (ODBC) is designed to allow access to relational data, OLE DB is an **open standard** designed to allow access to **all kinds** of data.

OLE DB has three types of components:

| Data providers | Data Consumers | Service Components |

Diagram 1.3.1 provides and overview of OLE DB architecture.

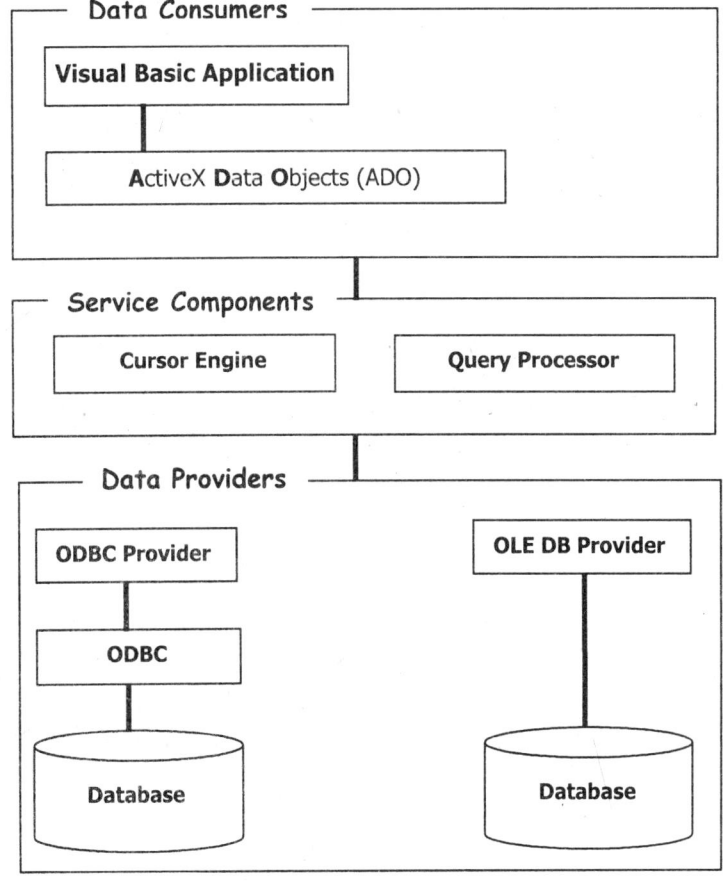

Diagram 1.3.1

Data Providers

Data Providers are applications such as MS SQL Server, MS Exchange, Operating System components such as the file system that have data that other applications may need to access.

These **data providers** expose OLE DB interfaces that **service components** or **data consumers** can access directly. There is also an OLE DB provider for ODBC. This provider makes any ODBC data available to OLE DB data consumers.

Data Consumers

Data consumers are applications that use the data exposed by the data providers. **A**ctiveX **D**ata **O**bjects (ADO) is a programmatic interface for using OLE DB data. Any application that uses ADO is an OLE DB data consumer.

Service Components

Service components are components of OLE DB that process and transport data. These components include query processors and cursor engines. Architecturally, OLE DB is separated into components so data providers do not need to have the inbuilt ability to provide data in a way that ADO can understand.

These service components give ADO the ability to consume OLE DB data from providers that do not inherently offer handling of result sets or interpretation of SQL queries.

Accessing Data Via A Visual Basic Form

ActiveX **D**ata **O**bjects is the data access method that Microsoft recommends for new applications. ADO is an evolution if the **R**emote **D**ata **O**bject (RDO) and **D**ata **A**ccess **O**bject (DAO) architecture and replaces them with one robust, easy to use interface.

RDO and DAO were limited to using ODBC and Jet compliant data providers. ADO, however provides quick, high-performance access to all of the types of data and information that are available through OLE DB, while maintaining a low overhead on system resources.

Before beginning to work with ADO in a Visual Basic application it must be installed on the computer. ADO is installed as part of the normal install of Visual Basic 6.0.

> The latest version of ActiveX Data Objects is available as a free download from the Microsoft web site at:
>
> `http://www.microsoft.com /data/ado`
>
> As Microsoft releases additional capabilities to ADO this can be downloaded from the web. Remember, ADO works with any development environment that can deal with ActiveX/COM objects.

If ADO is installed on a computer it can be used in any Visual Basic application by making a **reference** to the ADO library.

Binding ADO To A Visual Basic Form

- In the Visual Basic project IDE, choose **Project → References**
- The **References** dialog box appears
- Click on the **check box** on the left hand side of **Microsoft Data Objects 2.0 library**
- Click **OK**

ADO can now be used in the project's code.

> Do not inadvertently make a reference to the **Microsoft ActiveX Data Objects 2.0 Recordset** library. This is a lightweight library designed for use on the client side of a client/server application.

The Visual Basic RAD, IDE, has a tool that allows a programmer to rapidly connect to a database source. This is the Data Environment Designer.

An example of how to use the Data Environment Designer to connect to a database follows immediately.

USING ADO PROGRAMMATICALLY

Once a reference has been set between a VB project and the **Microsoft ActiveX Data Object 2.7** library, the ADODB typed objects can be instantiated and used in the project programmatically.

The Approach
In the **OPTION EXPLICIT** section of the form declare memory variables that will be used to hold ADODB's Connection and Recordset objects.

```
Dim gConnect As ADODB.Connection
Dim gMstrRs As ADODB.Recordset
```

Whenever the form has to be bound to a database table then:

```
Set gConnect = New ADODB.Connection
Set gMstrRs = New ADODB.Recordset
```

Once done the memory variables **gConnect** and **gMstrRs** will hold appropriate ADODB type objects, whose methods can be accessed when required.

The ADODB connection object's **provider** needs to be passed two bits of information.
1. The name of the ADODB provider to be used to connect to the database
2. The location of the database on the hard disk drive

This can be done as follows:

```
gConnect.Provider = "Microsoft.Jet.OLEDB.4.0; _
                DataSource = Absolute Path to the .mdb file"
```

Caution

The **problem** with hard coding the absolute path and passing this as a value to the **DataSource** parameter is if the database is ever moved to another location on the hard disk the absolute path will have to be recoded right across the application.

The way to overcome this problem is to take the following approach.

Ensure that the Database subdirectory that holds the actual database is one level below the application.

eg.   Application's ROOT
                Database
                        .mdb file

In the above directory tree the **root** directory holds all the Visual Basic files required to run the application. Below **root** directory is a subdirectory **Database** which holds the M.S. Access database that in turn holds all the tables.

When the VB application is run from the **Banking** directory the path to the Banking directory is registered with the application. Using App.Path a handle can be obtained to where the application ran from.

Now rewriting the DataSource value as follows:

   **SavAcctMastCN.Provider = "Microsoft.Jet.OLEDB.4.0; _
                DataSource = " & App.Path & "\Database\.mdb filename"**

Will ensure that wherever the database is changed to on the Hard disk drive the application will run successfully.

Tip

Using this technique **ensures** when an application is deployed on a client's hard disk there will be no errors thrown up when database tables need to be accessed.

Once the ADODB connection object knows which provider to use and which is its DataSource a RecordSet object can be created in memory to hold records retrieved from the database table.

Creating A RecordSet Object In Memory

    gConnect.Open

Ensures that the **gConnect** connection object instantiated in memory will setup a connection to the M.S. Access database.

Once a connection is opened to a database standard ANSI SQL can be used to extract an appropriate set of records from a database table to be held in an ADODB RecordSet object in memory.

One way of doing this is to store to standard ANSI SQL query in a memory variable and then pass the memory variable to the Open method of the RecordSet object instantiated in memory earlier on.

    mSqlStr = "SELECT * FROM <Table name>"

To create the RecordSet in memory and populate it with records the following approach can be taken.

    gMstrRS.Open mSqlStr, gConnet, adOpenDynamic, adLockOptimistic

- The ADODB RecordSet object is passed
- The ANSI SQL query
- Given a handle to the ADODB Connection object
- Instructed on what kind of cursor to open in memory
- Instructed on what kind of lock to apply to the database table to ensure appropriate concurrency control

This exposes a **collection** of all the all records held in the M.S. Access database table into the RecordSet in memory. Once exposed the data can be appropriately manipulated when required.

Once the records of the table are exposed in the RecordSet they can be bound to data display items on a Visual Basic form via the setting of appropriate data display item **attributes or** by program code and thus made visible on the U.I..

MASTER DETAIL CONCEPTS

The saving bank account, data capture system, requires the capture of a customer's contact numbers such as residence or office telephone numbers and mobile, pager or fax numbers.

The relationship between a customer and their contact information may be **one** to **many** (**i.e.** One customer may have multiple contact numbers). In a commercial application this situation is always handled by creating**:**

1. A **pair** of **related** database/tables
2. A Master/Detail data capture form that works against these tables

Consider that the related tables are placed within the Access database **CardBook.mdb**. Also, that the **master** table's name **is Contact_Master** and the **detail** table's name is **Contact_TelNo**.

Since the tables are related, **data** stored in the **primary key** column of the table Contact_Master must be automatically **/** programmatically transferred to the **foreign key** column of the table Contact_TelNo.

This **guarantees** that all records held in the **detail** table Contact_TelNo **will** be bound to a corresponding record in the **master** table.

Under no circumstances can a record be inserted into the detail table **without** a corresponding record existing in the master table.

A **single** occurrence of a value held in the master table's Primary Key field, can have **multiple** occurrences of the same value as the detail table's Foreign Key field. The two sets of records, in their individual tables, are therefore permanently related.

Manipulating Data In The Detail Table – An Approach

The data stored in the Detail table needs to be manipulated independently. Table data manipulation is always done via a form. A form bound to the master table could be used to manipulate data in the detail table as well. A details, data capture system, has to be added to the form used to capture master table information.

Alternatively, a separate form can be created that will be called from the form associated with the master table. The detail table's data can then be manipulated via this form.

Technique Used

Each time a record is created to be stored in the details table, the **contents** of the form field, holding the master table's Primary key value, is programmatically posted to a corresponding column in the details table. This sets up the Master/Detail relationship between records being stored in the details table and a single record stored in the master table.

DATA GRID CONCEPTS

The **Data Grid** is essentially a data **display/capture** object, which is **tightly bound** to a **RecordSet** object. Dropping an ADODC control on the form and setting its properties appropriately will automatically create a RecordSet object at run time. Access to the RecordSet is through the ADODC, using standard **dot** notation as follows:

   ADODCname.RecordSet

Setting the ADODC's Properties:

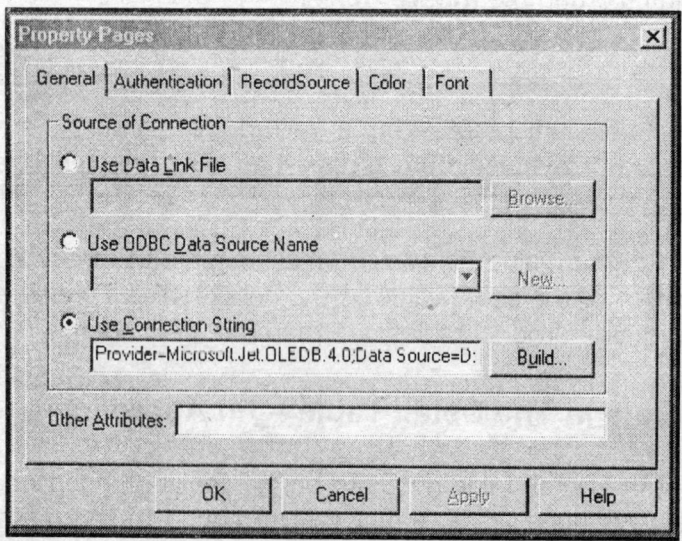

Diagram 1.4.1

CHAP 01 — CONNECTIVITY IN VB 6 USING ODBC AND ADO

Right click on the ADODC control. Select **properties** from the sticky menu that appears. Immediately the screen as shown in diagram 1.4.1 will appear.

Click on the **Build** button.

Another screen appears as shown in Diagram 1.4.2.

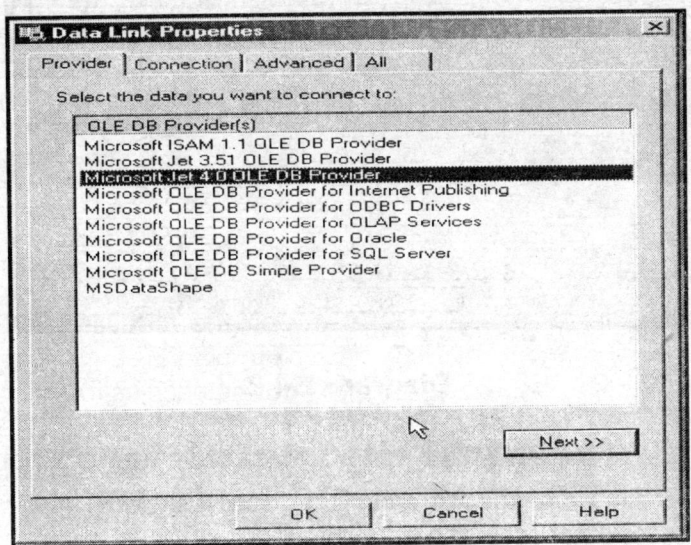

Diagram 1.4.2

From the screen that opens select the **Provider** tab, and choose the Microsoft Jet 4.0 OLE DB Provider as shown in Diagram 1.4.2. Click **Next**.

The next screen that appears allows the OLE DB data provider selected previously to be connected to the MS Access database.

Once the OLEDB provider is bound to the appropriate MS Access database the OLE DB provider will permit access to all the tables (and their data) held within the MS Access database. Refer to diagram 1.4.3.

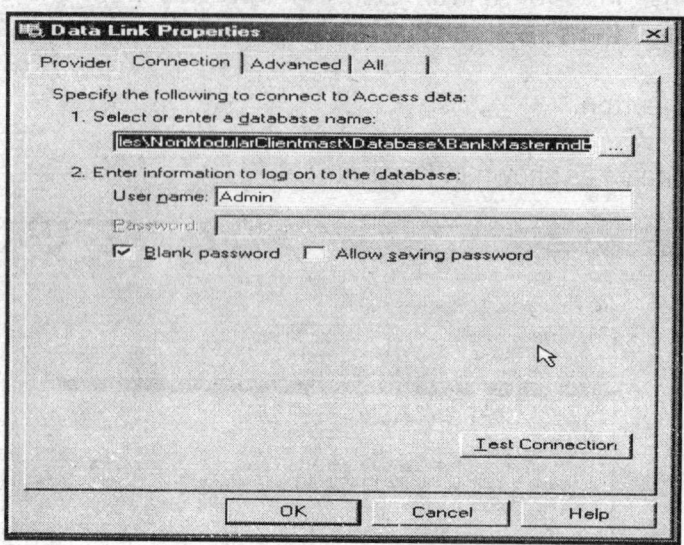

Diagram 1.4.3

On the left hand side of the **Select or enter a database name** option is a **command button** . Clicking on the command button will allow the selection of the appropriate MS Access database.

Once the MS Access database is selected and the database name is registered with the tool click on the **Test Connection** command button at the bottom of the screen. The Test connection succeeded Alert should appear as shown in Diagram 1.4.4.

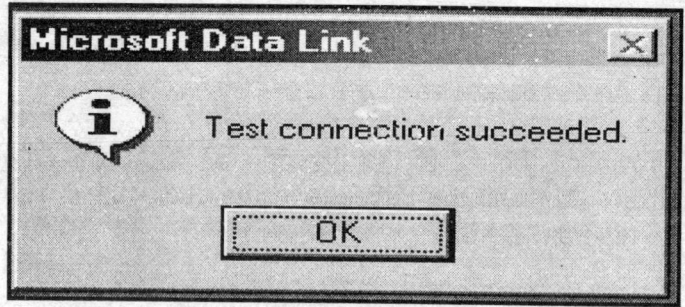

Diagram 1.4.4

Next select the **Advanced** tab as shown in diagram 1.4.5.

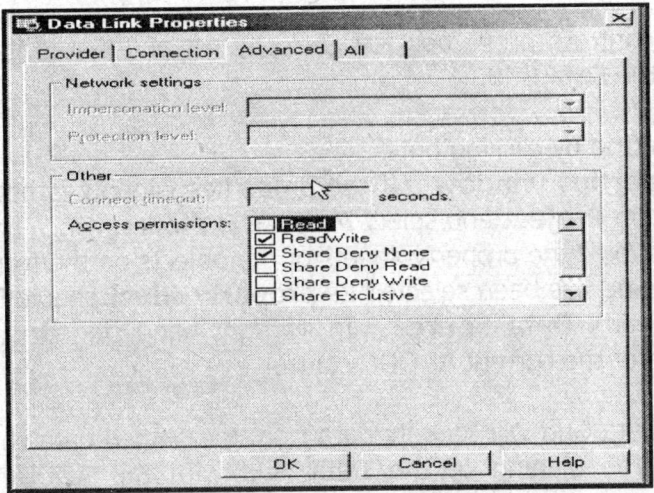

Diagram 1.4.5

In the Advanced tab set the access permissions for the MS Access database as shown in Diagram 1.4.5. Setting the **ReadWrite** and **Share Deny None** 'on' should be sufficient. These settings actually determine the type of cursor opened by the ADODC control's RecordSet.

Since Inserts, Updates and Deletes will be done through the ADODC RecordSet a **dynamic cursor** needs to be opened and hence the need to make these settings.

Click on the **OK** button. Next, click **OK** of the ADODC's **properties** window as shown in diagram 1.4.1. This **completes setting** all the appropriate properties of the ADODC control.

Binding The Data Grid To The ADODC Control

Once the ADODC control's properties are correctly set and tested its time to bind the ADODC control to the Data Grid.

- Select the Data Grid by clicking on it
- Go to the **properties window**. (If the properties window is not visible go to the textual menu item **Project** and select **Project Explorer**. Once the project explorer is visible access to all the property sheets of the objects on the form is available)
- Since the Data Grid has been selected its **property sheet** should be uppermost
- Locate the property **Data Source**. In its right hand side **drop down list box** select the name of the current ADODC control

From then on the Data Grid will seek its data from the named data source, which is the ADODC control. The binding of the Data Grid with the ADODC control is **now complete**. Since the Data Grid and the RecordSet are tightly bound any changes in the RecordSet are immediately reflected in the Data Grid. Any changes in the Data Grid are immediately reflected in the RecordSet.

The ADODC RecordSet is for all practical purposes **the controller** in the Data Grid/RecordSet relationship. Hence **all** data navigation and manipulation needs to focus on the **ADODC**<name>**.RecordSet**.

Inserting Table Data Via The Data Grid

To **Insert** data in the Data Grid, insert a new record in the **ADODC**<name>**.RecordSet** using:

   ADODC<name>**.RecordSet.AddNew**

As new record is inserted into the **ADODC<name>.RecordSet** below the Data Grid and since the Data Grid is tightly bound to the RecordSet the Data Grid will immediately display a new row in it.

The Data Grid **cursor** (a small black triangle) will be adjacent to the new row on the extreme right hand side of the Data Grid. The row is ready to accept data entry. Simply placing the form cursor on the new row and typing in new data suffices. Since the Data Grid is tightly bound to the RecordSet the data keyed into the Data Grid will be immediately (automatically) transferred to the RecordSet below.

Since a new record has been created in the RecordSet the RecordSet's focus will be on the new record. Hence whatever is keyed into the Data Grid gets transferred to the new record in the RecordSet.

The RecordSet is connected to the MS Access Database/table via the OLE DB provider, hence whatever is loaded into the RecordSet automatically gets written to the Database/table. Using the **ADODC**<name>**.RecordSet.Update** is really **not necessary**.

Viewing Table Data Via The Data Grid

When the form runs, the ADODC control connects to the MS Access database. Via its record source i.e. an SQL query 'Select * FROM Contact_Tel' all records from the ContactInfo table will be retrieved and held in its RecordSet.

Since the RecordSet is bound to the Data Grid these records will be immediately visible in the Data Grid.

Caution

Remember the Data Grid should display records that are **related** to the master record visible. Using the above technique **random records** will be visible in the Data Grid.

This specific issue will be addressed later and corrected. The Data Grid will then only display records related to the master record visible.

Updating Table Data Via The Data Grid

Updating data via the Data Grid **requires** that the data Grid be loaded with data first. A data **Update** operation is performed only on a record currently visible in the Data Grid.

Position the Data Grid's cursor on the appropriate record by clicking on the record. Use the mouse to move the form cursor the **field** in the Data Grid that needs to be updated. Simply overwrite the data visible with new data.

Since the Data Grid is tightly bound to the RecordSet below all the changes that occur in the Data Grid are correctly registered with the RecordSet below.

Since the RecordSet is connected to the Database/Table the record gets updated in the table as well.

Deleting Table Data Via The Data Grid

Deleting data via the Data Grid **requires** that the Data Grid be loaded with data first. A data **Delete** operation is performed only on a record currently visible in the Data Grid.

Position the Data Grid's cursor on the appropriate record by clicking on the record. The Data Grid's cursor will automatically navigate to the record. Since the Data Grid and ADODC RecordSet are always synchronized the RecordSet will also focus on the same record. Call the:

   ADODC<name>.**RecordSet.Delete**

The record immediately gets deleted in the RecordSet below. Since the RecordSet is connected to the Database/Table the record gets deleted in the table as well.

Next call the **DataGrid**<name>.**Refresh**. This will cause the Data Grid to get refreshed. The Data Grid refreshes itself by reading the RecordSet. Since the record has been deleted in the RecordSet it will no longer be visible in the Data Grid.

Note

 If the Data Grid is **not refreshed**, even though the record is actually deleted in the RecordSet it will **still be visible** in the Data Grid.

Diagram 1.4.6 below attempts to represent all the above concepts as a picture:

Data Grid object

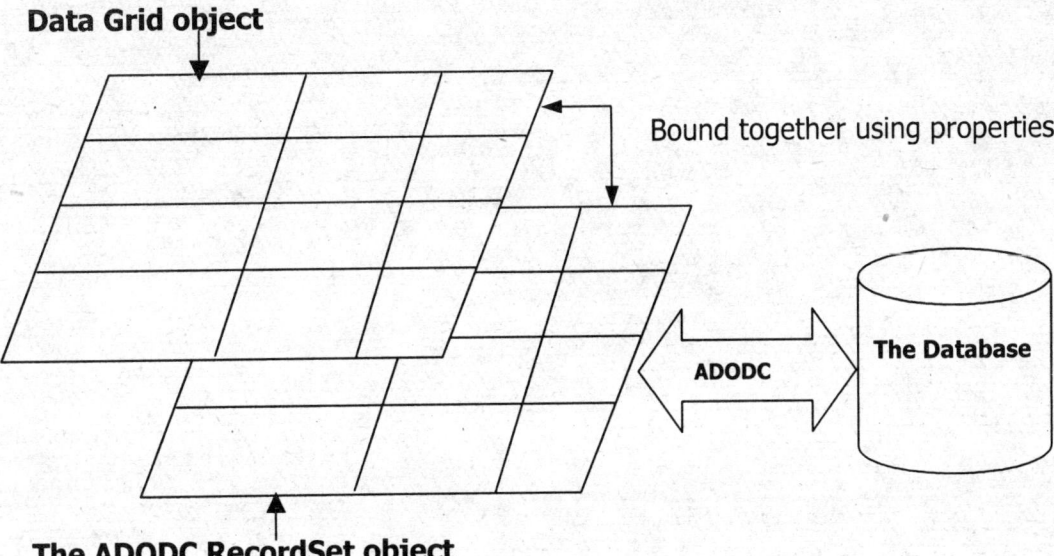

The ADODC RecordSet object

Diagram 1.4.6

 Note

The Data Grid is being used simply as a data capture/display object. All data manipulation is being done on the ADODC RecordSet below the Data Grid to which the Data Grid is very tightly bound.

Chapter 01

Self Evaluation

In This Chapter We Learned:

- **Data Storage**
  Creating And Testing A Database/Table In MS Access

- **Connecting To A Database Using ODBC**
  Middleware

- **Connecting To A Database Using ADO**
  ActiveX Data Objects
  Data Providers And Data Consumers
  Service Components
  Accessing Data Via A Visual Basic Form
  Binding ADO To A Visual Basic Form

- **Using ADO Programmatically**

- **Master Detail Concepts**
  Manipulating Data In The Detail Table - An Approach

- **Data Grid Concepts**
  Setting The ADODC's Properties
  Binding The Data Grid To The ADODC Control
  Manipulating Table Data Via The Data Grid

Chapter 02

An Application's Toolbar Logic

In This Chapter:

- **Application Modes**

- **Creating A Truth Table to Control A Toolbar**
  Toolbar Status During The No Mode
  Toolbar Status During The Insert Mode
  Toolbar Status During The View Mode
  Toolbar Status During The Update Mode
  Toolbar Status During The Delete Mode

- **The Detail Section**
  Insert Mode In Detail Section
  Update Mode In Detail Section
  Delete Mode In Detail Section
  Save Mode In Detail Section

- **Master – Detail Toolbar Buttons Interaction**

2. AN APPLICATION'S TOOLBAR LOGIC

Most commercial applications have a toolbar as a part of the application. A toolbar provides functionality similar to that provided by textual menus.

A commercial application can be divided in five modes.

- NoMode
- View Mode
- Insert Mode
- Update Mode
- Save Mode

Each mode represents an operation carried out on business data by the application.

Depending on the mode of an application, toolbar buttons on the form need to be enabled or disabled to guarantee that no cross processing of business data happens. A user has to complete the operation started and then move on to another operation.

There are two toolbars used in an application **i.e.** a toolbar on the **Master** section and a toolbar on the **Detail** section of data entry forms.

Generally, the Master section toolbar contains the following buttons

Data Manipulation Buttons

Name	Functionality
Insert	Inserts a new record in the master table
Update	Modifies the existing record in the master table
Delete	Deletes a master record
View	Displays records in master and corresponding details record
Save	Saves new or modified record of the master table
Print	Prints the current information displayed on the U.I.
Exit	Closes the application

Data Navigation Buttons

Name	Functionality
First	Displays first record in the master table
Prior	Displays previous record in the master table
Next	Displays next record in the master table
Last	Displays last record in the master table

Similarly, the Detail section toolbar generally contains the following buttons

Data Manipulation Buttons

Name	Functionality
InsertDetl	Inserts a new record in the detail table
UpdateDetl	Modifies the existing record in the detail table
DeleteDetl	Deletes a detail record
SaveDetl	Saves new or modified record in the detail table

Data Navigation Buttons

Name	Functionality
FirstDetl	Displays first record in the detail table corresponding to a master record
PriorDetl	Displays previous record in the detail table corresponding to a master record
NextDetl	Displays next record in the detail table corresponding to a master record
LastDetl	Displays last record in the detail table corresponding to a master record

GENERATING A TRUTH TABLE TO CONTROL A TOOLBAR

Toolbars are used in place of standard command buttons. Each button on the toolbar allows a specific table operation using the data entry form as a via media, to be carried out. When a user clicks on a button on the toolbar, it indicates that a user has decided to carry out that operation.

Note: The toolbar of a data entry form should restrict a user from performing **more than one operation at a time**.

If a user chooses to insert a record in the master section of the data entry form by clicking on the **Insert** button of the Master toolbar, all other data manipulation and data navigation operations need to be disabled except **Save** and **Exit**.

Cross processing should be strictly disallowed. This guarantees that a user has to **complete** an operation started and then move on to another operation.

To implement the prevention of Cross processing, the functionality of the toolbar buttons are given in tables 2.1.1 to 2.15.2. This has to be implemented via the form's codebase.

Toolbar Status During The No Mode

A data entry form always opens in '**No Mode**'. Table 2.1.1 and table 2.1.2 shows the status of toolbar buttons in '**No Mode**'.

Enabled	Disabled
Insert	Update
View	Delete
Exit	Print
	First
	Prior
	Next
	Last
	Save

Table 2.1.1

Enabled	Disabled
	InsertDetl
	UpdateDetl
	DeleteDetl
	FirstDetl
	PriorDetl
	NextDetl
	LastDetl
	SaveDetl

Table 2.1.1

Opening the data entry form in **No Mode** allows the user to determine what operation is to be carried out. This conforms naturally to the application being **User friendly**.

Diagram 2.1.1: Master section toolbar in 'No Mode'

Diagram 2.1.2: Detail section toolbar in 'No Mode'

Toolbar Status During The Insert Mode

Once a form runs, a user can either choose to **Insert** a record or **View** records.

Insert and View operations are held at one level. This is because each operation runs completely independent of the other.

Update and Delete operations must run as child processes to the View operation. The concept being if data needs to be updated or deleted, it needs to be viewed first.

CHAP 02 — AN APPLICATION'S TOOLBAR LOGIC

Table 2.2 shows the status of the Master section toolbar buttons when a user clicks on the **Insert** button.

Enabled	Disabled
Save	Insert
Exit	Update
	Delete
	View
	Print
	First
	Prior
	Next
	Last

Table 2.2

Diagram 2.2: Master section toolbar in Insert mode of Master section

Toolbar Status During The View Mode

Table 2.3.1 shows the status of the Master section toolbar buttons when the **View** button is clicked and **no records** exists in the Master table. This is the scenario when the application is run for the very first time.

Enable	Disable
Save	Insert
Exit	Update
	Delete
	View
	Print
	First
	Prior
	Next
	Last

Table 2.3.1

Diagram 2.3.1: Master section toolbar in View mode

Note

If the View button is clicked and there are no records to view, a dialog box informs the user that there are no records to view. It also prompts a confirmation to insert a record.

If a user clicks **Yes**, a data insert operation is called and the toolbar is set to **Save** mode, as shown in diagram 2.3.1.

If a user clicks **No**, the functionality of a data entry form is terminated.

Table 2.3.2 shows the status of Master section toolbar buttons when the **View** button is clicked and at **least one record** exists in the Master.

Enabled	Disabled
Insert	View
Update	Save
Delete	
Print	
First	
Prior	
Next	
Last	
Exit	

Table 2.4.2

Diagram 2.3.2: Master section toolbar in View mode

CHAP 02 — AN APPLICATION'S TOOLBAR LOGIC

Toolbar Status During The Update Mode

Table 2.4.1 shows the status of Master table toolbar buttons when a user clicks on the **Update** button in the Master section.

Enabled	Disabled
Save	Insert
Exit	Update
	Delete
	Print
	First
	Prior
	Next
	Last

Table 2.4.1

Diagram 2.5.1: Master section toolbar in Update mode of Master section

> **Note**
> Clicking on the Update button is the technique used by a user to indicate that the record currently visible must be updated.

Toolbar Status During The Delete Mode

Table 2.5.1 shows the status of the Master section toolbar buttons when user clicks on the **Delete** button in the Master section and there is **only one record** present in the master table.

Enabled	Disabled
Insert	Update
View	Delete
Exit	Print
	First
	Prior
	Next
	Last
	Save

Table 2.5.1

Diagram 2.5.1: Master section toolbar in Delete mode of Master section

Table 2.5.2 shows the status of Master section toolbar buttons when a user clicks on the **Delete** button in the Master section and **more than one record** exists in master table.

Enabled	Disabled
Insert	View
Update	Save
Delete	
Print	
First	
Prior	
Next	
Last	
Exit	

Table 2.5.2

Diagram 2.5.2: Master section toolbar in Delete mode of Master section

AN APPLICATION'S TOOLBAR LOGIC

Whenever a user inserts or updates a record, to permanently store the changes made to the data, the user is expected to **Save** the data. This can be done by clicking on the '**Save**' button of the toolbar.

Table 2.6 shows the status of Master section toolbar button when user clicks on the **Save** button in the Master section.

Enabled	Disabled
Insert	View
Update	Save
Delete	
Print	
First	
Prior	
Next	
Last	
Exit	

Table 2.6

Diagram 2.6: Master Section toolbar in Save mode of Master section

Note

If the user attempts to save an invalid information during an Insert or Update operation, the Master Section toolbar should retain the mode, prior the Save button was clicked.

THE DETAIL SECTION

When a master record is present, a user can perform Insert, Update and Delete and View operations in the detail section for the corresponding Master record.

In order to perform any data manipulation operation on the detail section, a user needs to click on the **Update** button in the Master section. Also, at least one record bound to the current master record should exist in the Details table. If no details record exists, only an insert operation is permitted on the detail section.

The tables from 2.7 to 2.10 show the status of toolbar buttons when a user selects an option from the detail section toolbar. The Detail section toolbar provides insert, update, delete and save operations for the detail section along with data navigation buttons i.e. first, prior, next and last.

Insert Mode in Details section

When the data entry form Master section is in Insert or Update mode, a user can **Insert** a record in the detail section of the form, which will be bound to the current Master record visible.

Tables 2.7 shows the status of toolbar buttons when user clicks on **Insert** button in the Details section to insert a new detail record.

Detail section toolbar

Enabled	Disabled
SaveDetl	InsertDetl
	UpdateDetl
	DeleteDetl
	FirstDetl
	PriorDetl
	NextDetl
	LastDetl

Table 2.7

CHAP 02 — AN APPLICATION'S TOOLBAR LOGIC

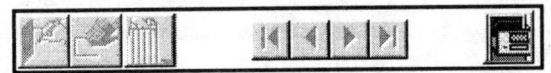

Diagram 2.7: Detail section toolbar in Insert mode of Detail section

Update Mode in details section

When the data entry form Master section is in Insert or Update mode, while viewing records in the details section retrieved to match the master record displayed, a user can modify detail record data.

Tables 2.8 shows the status of toolbar buttons when a user clicks on **Update** button in the Details section to modify details record data.

Detail section toolbar

Enabled	Disabled
SaveDetl	InsertDetl
	UpdateDetl
	DeleteDetl
	FirstDetl
	PriorDetl
	NextDetl
	LastDetl

Table 2.8

Diagram 2.8: Detail section toolbar in Update mode of Detail section

Delete Mode in details section

The Delete operation performed on the Details section has to consider two situations:
- The Details section contains only one Detail record for a Master record
- The Details section contains more than one Detail record for a Master record

Tables 2.9.1 shows the status of Details section toolbar buttons when user clicks on **Delete** button in the detail section and **only one record exists** in the detail section for a particular master section record.

PRACTICAL VB 6 PROJECTS

Detail section toolbar

Enabled	Disabled
InsertDetl	UpdateDetl
	DeleteDetl
	FirstDetl
	PriorDetl
	NextDetl
	LastDetl
	SaveDetl

Table 2.9.1

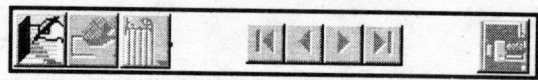

Diagram 2.9.1: Details section toolbar in Delete mode when only one Details record exist for a Master section record

Tables 2.9.2 shows the status of toolbar buttons when user clicks on **Delete** button in the Detail section and **only one record** exists in the detail section for a particular master section record.

Detail section toolbar

Enabled	Disabled
InsertDetl	FirstDetl
UpdateDetl	PriorDetl
DeleteDetl	NextDetl
	LastDetl
	SaveDetl

Table 2.9.2

Diagram 2.9.2: Detail section toolbar in Delete mode when only one Details record exist for a Master section record.

Tables 2.9.3 shows the status of toolbar buttons when user clicks on **Delete** button in the Detail section and **more than one record** exists in the detail section for a particular master section record.

CHAP 02 — AN APPLICATION'S TOOLBAR LOGIC

Detail section toolbar

Enabled	Disabled
InsertDetl	SaveDetl
UpdateDetl	
DeleteDetl	
FirstDetl	
PriorDetl	
NextDetl	
LastDetl	

Table 2.9.3

Diagram 2.9.3: Detail section toolbar in Delete mode when more than one Details record exist for a Master section record.

Save Mode In Detail Section

Whenever a user inserts or updates a record in the detail section, to permanently store the changes made to the data, the user is expected to **Save** the data. This can be done by clicking on the **Save** button of the toolbar on the detail section.

Table 2.10 shows the status of toolbar button when user clicks on the **Save** button in the Detail section to save data that is valid as per application requirements.

Detail section toolbar

Enabled	Disabled
InsertDetl	SaveDetl
UpdateDetl	
DeleteDetl	
FirstDetl	
PriorDetl	
NextDetl	
LastDetl	

Table 2.10

Diagram 2.10: Detail section toolbar in Save mode of Detail Section

MASTER-DETAIL TOOLBAR BUTTON INTERACTION

Some of the buttons on the Details Section toolbar interact with the buttons on the Master section.

This special relationship is described here.

During the data Insert operation in the Master section of the Data Entry form. Table 2.11 shows the status of Detail section toolbar.

Enabled	Disabled
InsertDetl	UpdateDetl
	DeleteDetl
	FirstDetl
	PriorDetl
	NextDetl
	LastDetl
	SaveDetl

Table 2.11

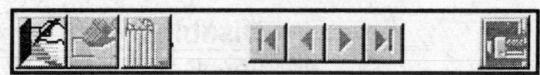

Diagram 2.11

When a user clicks on the Update button in the Master section and **more than one record** exists in the Master section, one of the following two situation occur in the Details section:
- The Details section contains **no** Details record for a Master record
- The Details section contains **only one** Details record for a Master record
- The Details section contains **more than one** Details record for a Master record

Table 2.12.1 shows the status of detail section toolbar buttons, when **Update** button in the Master section is clicked but **no Detail record exists** for the corresponding master record displayed in the Data Entry form.

Enabled	Disabled
InsertDetl	UpdateDetl
	DeleteDetl
	FirstDetl
	PriorDetl
	NextDetl
	LastDetl
	SaveDetl

Table 2.12.1

Diagram 2.12.1

Table 2.12.2 shows the status of detail section toolbar buttons, when **Update** button in the Master section is clicked and **only one Detail record exists** for the corresponding master record displayed in the Data Entry form.

Enabled	Disabled
InsertDetl	SaveDetl
UpdateDetl	FirstDetl
DeleteDetl	PriorDetl
	NextDetl
	LastDetl

Table 2.12.2

Diagram 2.12.2

Table 2.12.3 shows the status of detail section toolbar buttons, when **Update** button in the Master section is clicked and **more one Detail record exists** for the corresponding master record displayed in the Data Entry form.

Enabled	Disabled
InsertDetl	SaveDetl
UpdateDetl	
DeleteDetl	
FirstDetl	
PriorDetl	
NextDetl	
LastDetl	

Table 2.12.3

Diagram 2.12.3

During a data Delete operation in the Master section of the data entry form, one of the following two situations occurs:
- The Master section contains only one Master record
- The Master section contains more than one Master record

When a user clicks on the Delete button in the Master section and **only one record** exists in the Master section exists, the status for the Detail section toolbar buttons is a shown in tables 2.13.1 and 2.13.2.

When a user clicks on the Delete button in the Master section and **more than one record** exists in the Master section, one of the following two situation occur in the Details section:
- The Details section contains **no** Details record for a Master record
- The Details section contains **atleast one** Details record for a Master record

Table 2.13.1 shows the status of detail section toolbar buttons, when **Delete** button in the Master section is clicked but **no Detail record exists** for the corresponding master record displayed in the Data Entry form.

Enabled	Disabled
InsertDetl	SaveDetl
	UpdateDetl
	DeleteDetl
	FirstDetl
	PriorDetl
	NextDetl
	LastDetl

Table 2.13.1

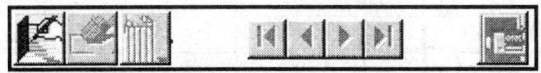

Diagram 2.13.1

Table 2.13.2 shows the status of detail section toolbar buttons, when **Delete** button in the Master section is clicked and **at least one Detail record exists** for the corresponding master record displayed in the Data Entry form.

Enabled	Disabled
InsertDetl	SaveDetl
UpdateDetl	
DeleteDetl	
FirstDetl	
PriorDetl	
NextDetl	
LastDetl	

Table 2.13.2

Diagram 2.13.2

MASTER FORM COMMAND BUTTON'S TRUTH TABLE

Status For Operation	Condition	Mstr Inst	Mstr Updt	Mstr Del	Mstr View	Mstr Prnt	Mstr Frst	Mstr Prev	Mstr Next	Mstr Last	Mstr Save	Mstr Exit
No Mode- On click of Show Form		E	D	D	E	D	D	D	D	D	D	E
Insert Mode- On click of Inst (Mstr)		D	D	D	D	D	D	D	D	D	E	E
View Mode- On click of View	At least one record exist in Mstr Rs	E	E	E	D	E	E	E	E	E	D	E
	No records in Mstr Rs	E	D	D	E	D	D	D	D	D	D	E
Update Mode- On click of Updt (Mstr)	More than one record in Dtls Rs	D	D	D	D	D	D	D	D	D	E	E
	At least one record in Dtls Rs											
	No records in Dtls Rs											
Delete Mode- On click of Del (Mstr) Cascade Del	At least 2 rows in Mstr Rs	E	E	E	D	E	E	E	E	E	D	E
	Only one record in the Mstr Rs	E	D	D	E	D	D	D	D	D	D	E
Save Mode- On click of Save (Mstr)	Valid Data In Mstr Flds	E	E	E	D	E	E	E	E	E	D	E
	Invalid Data In Mstr Flds — More than one record in Dtls Rs	D	D	D	D	D	D	D	D	D	E	E
	Invalid Data In Mstr Flds — At least one record in Dtls Rs											
	Invalid Data In Mstr Flds — No records in Dtls Rs											

Table 2.14.1: Status for the Master form's command buttons

Status For Operation	Condition		Mstr Inst	Mstr Updt	Mstr Del	Mstr View	Mstr Prnt	Mstr Frst	Mstr Prev	Mstr Next	Mstr Last	Mstr Save	Mstr Exit
Insert Mode- On click of Inst (Dtls)			D	D	D	D	D	D	D	D	D	E	E
Update Mode- On click of Updt (Dtls)			D	D	D	D	D	D	D	D	D	E	E
Delete Mode- On click of Del (Dtls)	More than one record in Dtls Rs		D	D	D	D	D	D	D	D	D	E	E
	Only one row in the Dtls Rs												
	No records in Dtls												
Save Mode- On click of Save (Dtls)	Valid Data In Dtls Flds	More than one record in Dtls Rs	D	D	D	D	D	D	D	D	D	E	E
		At least one record in Dtls Rs											
		No records in Dtls Rs											
	Invalid Data In Dtls Flds												

Table 2.14.2: Status for the Master form's command buttons

DETAILS SECTION COMMAND BUTTON'S TRUTH TABLE

Status For Operation	Condition		Dtls Inst	Dtls Updt	Dtls Del	Dtls View	Dtls Prnt	Dtls Frst	Dtls Prev	Dtls Next	Dtls Last	Dtls Save
No Mode- On click of Show Form			D	D	D	D	D	D	D	D	D	D
Insert Mode- On click of Inst (Mstr)			E	D	D	D	D	D	D	D	D	E
View Mode- On click of View	At least one record exist in Mstr Rs		D	D	D	D	D	D	D	D	D	D
	No records in Mstr Rs											
Update Mode- On click of Updt (Mstr)	More than one record in Dtls Rs		E	E	E	D	D	D	D	D	D	E
	At least one record in Dtls Rs		E	E	E	E	E	E	E	D	D	E
	No records in Dtls Rs		E	D	D	D	D	D	D	D	D	E
Delete Mode- On click of Del (Mstr) Cascade Del	At least 2 rows in Mstr Rs		D	D	D	D	D	D	D	D	D	D
	Only one record in the Mstr Rs											
Save Mode- On click of Save (Mstr)	Valid Data In Mstr Flds											
	Invalid Data In Mstr Flds	More than one record in Dtls Rs	E	E	E	D	D	D	D	D	D	E
		At least one record in Dtls Rs	E	E	E	E	E	E	E	D	D	E
		No records in Dtls Rs	E	D	D	D	D	D	D	D	D	E

Table 2.15.1: Status for the Details Section's command buttons

CHAP 02 AN APPLICATION'S TOOLBAR LOGIC

Status For Operation	Condition		Dtls Inst	Dtls Updt	Dtls Del	Dtls View	Dtls Prnt	Dtls Frst	Dtls Prev	Dtls Next	Dtls Last	Dtls Save
Insert Mode- On click of Inst (Dtls)			D	D	D	D	D	D	D	E	E	D
Update Mode- On click of Updt (Dtls)			D	D	D	D	D	D	D	E	E	D
Delete Mode- On click of Del (Dtls)	More than one record in Dtls Rs		E	E	E	D	D	D	D	D	D	E
	Only one row in the Dtls Rs		E	E	E	E	E	E	E	D	D	E
	No records in Dtls		E	D	D	D	D	D	D	D	D	E
Save Mode- On click of Save (Dtls)	Valid Data In Dtls Flds	More than one record in Dtls Rs	E	E	E	D	D	D	D	D	D	E
		At least one record in Dtls Rs	E	E	E	E	E	E	E	D	D	E
		No records in Dtls Rs	E	D	D	D	D	D	D	D	D	E
	Invalid Data In Dtls Flds		D	D	D	D	D	D	D	E	E	D

Table 2.15.2: Status for the Details Section's objects, when a Detail button is clicked

Chapter 02

Self Evaluation

In This Chapter We Learned:

- **Application Modes**

- **Creating A Truth Table to Control A Toolbar**
  Toolbar Status During The No Mode
  Toolbar Status During The Insert Mode
  Toolbar Status During The View Mode
  Toolbar Status During The Update Mode
  Toolbar Status During The Delete Mode

- **The Detail Section**
  Insert Mode In Detail Section
  Update Mode In Detail Section
  Delete Mode In Detail Section
  Save Mode In Detail Section

- **Master – Detail Toolbar Buttons Interaction**

Chapter 03

A Personal Information Manager: The Plan

In This Chapter:

- **What is a Personal Information Manager**
  Its Working And Requirements

- **Data Segregation And Relationships Within The Project**

- **Database Designing For The Project**
  Table Definitions
  Table Data Validation Rules
  Micro Help For Table Fields
  Test Data For The Application

3. A PERSONAL INFORMATION MANAGER: A PLAN

PROJECT SCOPE

Today's commercial world is built around a complex schedule of meetings, appointments, deals, and so on. This requires people to both **develop** and **maintain** a network of contacts within a community. Maintaining this network is made easy with modern communication tools and techniques such as Telephones, Mobiles, SMS, and Email.

Capturing contact information while creating a business network is done through the practice of exchanging **Business Cards** or **Visiting Cards**. This eventually results in a piling up of visiting cards. Physically retrieving specific data from within this pile of visiting cards under pressure is generally a frustrating process.

If the data contained in the visiting cards is transferred to a **P**ersonal **I**nformation **M**anager (PIM) both data maintenance and retrieval problems will be resolved.

If a telephone number is retrieved from the PIM, and the computer is connected to a telephone line via a modem, the PIM can dial the individual automatically. If a connection to the Internet is available then an SMS can be sent to a Mobile phone via a number of web sites providing such services. Email can be dispatched to anyone via any one of the many Email clients available today.

This PIM offers the facility of keying in information into the PIM while speaking on the telephone. The next time the **same** telephone number is dialed, at the press of a button, what was keyed in the last time is displayed. This allows continuity to be maintained in with any business or personal contact without relying on memory alone. This section of the PIM allows complete editing of the information keyed in, such as deletion, updation, insertion and viewing effortlessly and on demand.

Once an individual's visiting card data is keyed in, this data can be grouped under different heads such as friends, business, medical, insurance and so on. This is to make data retrieval swift. Simply select the appropriate head and from under the head retrieve the data required.

Just in case one has forgotten the head under which the data was stored a global search facility has been provided which will scan the entire database and retrieve all data that matches the search criteria.

Once the data desired has been retrieved a telephone number can be automatically dialed, Email can be dispatched using this PIM as the prime interface.

A **P**ersonal **I**nformation **M**anager was chosen as the start project because it will help explore several interesting features of Visual Basic 6.0. The use of a **tabbed notebook** as a data capture object in preference to the standard data entry form is one such feature.

A tabbed notebook is a Visual Basic object that permits a **large number** of data capture objects such as Text Boxes, Check Boxes, Radio buttons, command buttons and so on to be grouped together and placed on a form contained in a single screen. This is in preference to creating a very large form with either horizontal or vertical scroll bars (or both), which is very clumsy when doing data entry.

Several other simple but interesting programming techniques have been used. Each such technique should be studied and understood so that the reader can successfully implement it in any other project.

Another reason why a PIM was chosen to start off this book on VB projects is that a PIM can be simply plugged into any number of other projects as a useful add on.

The PIM's system design and documentation follows.

ENTITY RELATIONSHIP DIAGRAM FOR THE P. I. M.

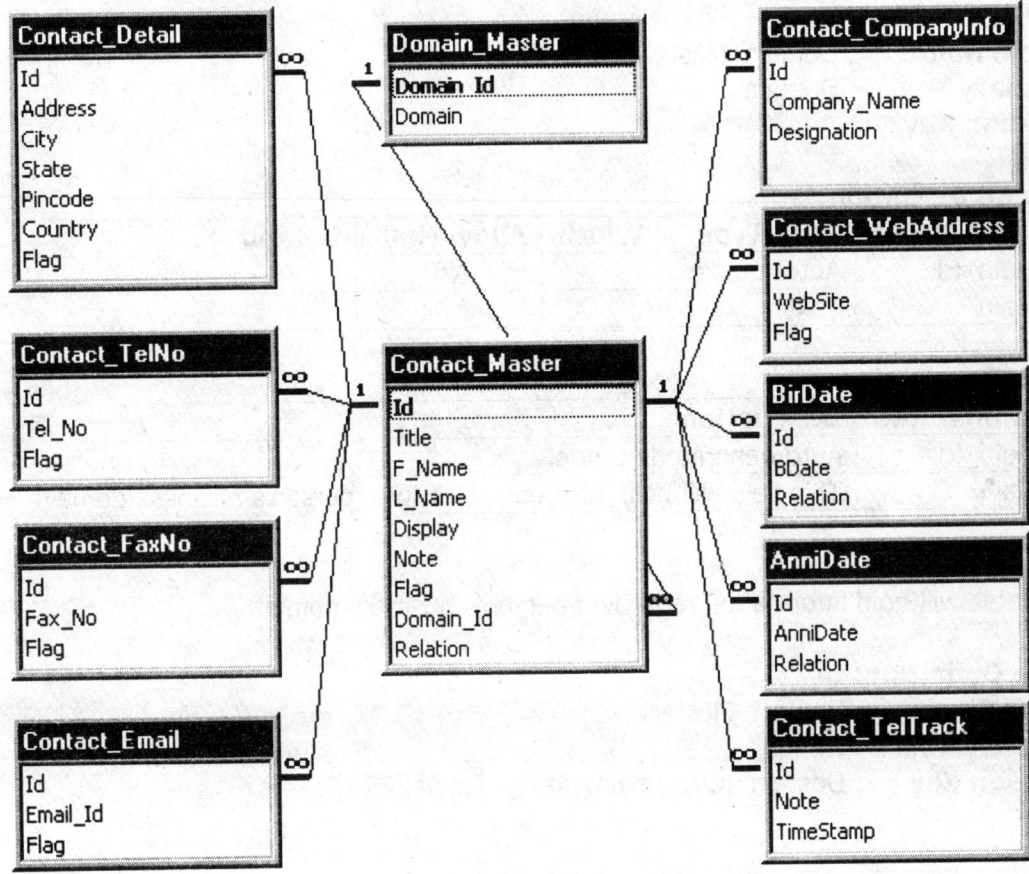

Diagram 3.1

The above diagram, attempts to give a visual representation of the Entity relationship between various tables required under the project. The symbols '**1**' and '**oo**' indicate a one-to-many relationship.

TABLE DEFINITIONS – P.I.M

Table Definition:
 Table Name : Domain_Master
 Primary Key : Domain_Id
 Foreign Key :

Column Definition:

Column Name	Data Type	Width	Allow Null	Default
Domain_Id	AutoNumber		No	
Domain	Text	75	No	

Table Description:

Column Name	Description
Domain_Id	Auto generated number
Domain	This field will hold information about a person's business domain

Explanation:
This table will hold information regarding person's business domain.

Table Definition:
 Table Name : Contact_Master
 Primary Key : Id
 Foreign Key : Domain_Id [Domain_Master:Domain_Id]

Column Definition:

Column Name	Data Type	Width	Allow Null	Default
Id	AutoNumber		No	
Title	Text	10	No	
F_Name	Text	50	No	
L_Name	Text	50	No	
Note	Memo		Yes	
Flag	Yes/No			
Domain_Id	Number			
Relation	Text	1	No	O (- for official)

Table Description:

Column Name	Description
Id	Auto generated number
Title	Key in a person's title (i.e. Mr., Ms., Dr.)
F_Name	A persons first name
L_Name	A persons last name
Note	Special note about the person
Flag	Field will hold a value indicating whether record is to be saved permanently
Domain_Id	A Domain Id, which is the Foreign key of the Domain_Master table
Relation	Field will hold a character indicating the relation with the person (**O** indicates office, **P** indicates personal and **B** indicates both contact types)

Explanation:

This table captures a person's unique Id, name and notes. Each contact is identified by the unique id. The Relation field indicates whether the user has a personal or an official relationship with the person (**O** indicates office, **P** indicates personal and **B** indicates both contact types).

Table Definition:

Table Name   : Contact_Detail
Primary Key   :
Foreign Key   : Id [Contact_Master:Id]

Column Definition:

Column Name	Data Type	Width	Allow Null	Default
Id	Number		No	
Address	Text	255	Yes	
City	Text	35	Yes	
State	Text	50	Yes	
Pincode	Text	10	Yes	
Country	Text	50	Yes	
Flag	Text	2	No	

Table Description:

Column Name	Description
Id	ID should be present in Contact_Master table
Address	Person's address
City	Person's city name
State	Person's state name
Pincode	Person's pincode
Country	Person's country name
Flag	Flag stating either office or residence

Explanation:
This table captures a person's contact information. A flag is set to indicate whether the telephone number is a residence or an office number.

Table Definition:
Table Name : Contact_TelNo
Primary Key :
Foreign Key : Id

Column Definition:

Column Name	Data Type	Width	Allow Null	Default
Id	Number		No	
Tel_No	Text	25	Yes	
Flag	Text	2	Yes	

Table Description:

Column Name	Description
Id	Should be present in Contact_Master table
Tel_No	Person's telephone number
Flag	Flag stating either office, residence or mobile number

Explanation:
This table captures information regarding a person's telephone. A flag is set which indicates whether it is a personal or official or mobile number (**R** indicates residential, **O** indicates office & **M** indicates mobile number)

Table Definition:
Table Name : Contact_FaxNo
Primary Key :
Foreign Key : Id

Column Definition:

Column Name	Data Type	Width	Allow Null	Default
Id	Number		No	
Fax_No	Text	25	Yes	
Flag	Text	2	Yes	

Table Description:

Column Name	Description
Id	Should be present in Contact_Master table
Fax_No	Person's fax number.
Flag	Flag stating either office or residence

Explanation:
This table will hold information regarding person's fax numbers and flag indicating user's personal or official fax number (**R** indicates residential & **O** indicates office)

Table Definition:
Table Name : Contact_Email
Primary Key :
Foreign Key : Id

Column Definition:

Column Name	Data Type	Width	Allow Null	Default
Id	Number		No	
Email_Id	Text	50	Yes	
Flag	Text	2	Yes	

Table Description:

Column Name	Description
Id	Should be present in Contact_Master table
Email_Id	Person's email id
Flag	Flag stating either office or residence

Explanation:
This table will hold information about a person's Email-Ids. A flag is set that indicates whether it is a personal or an office email id (**O** indicates office & **R** indicates residence).

Table Definition:
Table Name : Contact_CompanyInfo
Primary Key :
Foreign Key : ID

Column Definition:

Column Name	Data Type	Width	Allow Null	Default
Id	Number		No	
Company_Name	Text	75	No	
Designation	Text	25	Yes	

Table Description:

Column Name	Description
Id	Must exist in the Contact_Master table
Company_Name	The company name
Designation	Contact person's designation

Explanation:
This table captures information regarding a person's company name and designation.

Table Definition:
Table Name : Contact_WebAddress
Primary Key :
Foreign Key : Id

Column Definition:

Column Name	Data Type	Width	Allow Null	Default
Id	Number		No	
WebSite	Text	255	Yes	
Flag	Text	2	Yes	

Table Description:

Column Name	Description
Id	Should be present in Contact_Master table
WebSite	Person's website address.
Flag	Flag stating either office, personal website

Explanation:
This table will hold information about a person's web site address. A flag is set that indicates whether it is a personal or an official web site (**O** indicates official, **R** indicates personal)

Table Definition:
Table Name : BirDate
Primary Key :
Foreign Key : Id

Column Definition:

Column Name	Data Type	Width	Allow Null	Default
Id	Number		No	
Bdate	Date/Time		Yes	
Relation	Text	20	Yes	

Table Description:

Column Name	Description
Id	Should be present in Contact_Master table
BDate	Relative's date of birth
Relation	Relation with the client

Explanation:
This table holds the birth date of people placed into the PIM.

Table Definition:
Table Name : AnniDate
Primary Key :
Foreign Key : Id

Column Definition:

Column Name	Data Type	Width	Allow Null	Default
Id	Number		No	
AnniDate	Date/Time		Yes	
Relation	Text	20	Yes	

Table Description:

Column Name	Description
Id	Should be present in Contact_Master table
AnniDate	Event's anniversary date
Relation	Relation with the client

Explanation:
This table holds the anniversary dates of people placed into the PIM.

TABLE DATA VALIDATION RULES

Table Name: Domain_Master

Column Name	Description
Domain_Id	Domain_Id will be Unique (System generated)
Domain	Cannot be left empty

Table Name: Contact_Master

Column Name	Description
Id	Id will be Unique (System generated)
Title	Cannot be left empty
F_Name	Cannot be left empty
L_Name	Cannot be left empty
Note	
Flag	
Domain_Id	Domain_Id will be posted from Domain_Master
Relation	

Table Name: Contact_CompanyInfo

Column Name	Description
Id	Id will be posted from Contact_Master table
Company_Name	
Designation	

Table Name: Contact_Detail

Column Name	Description
Id	Id will be posted from master table
Address	
City	
State	
Pincode	
County	
Flag	

Table Name: Contact_TelNo

Column Name	Description
Id	Id will be posted from master table
Tel_No	
Flag	

Table Name: Contact_FaxNo

Column Name	Description
Id	Id will be posted from master table
Fax_No	
Flag	

Table Name: Contact_Email

Column Name	Description
Id	Id will be posted from master table
Email_Id	Should have "@" and "." Character in it
Flag	

Table Name: Contact_WebAddress

Column Name	Description
Id	Id will be posted from master table
WebSite	
Flag	

Table Name: AnniDate

Column Name	Description
Id	Id will be posted from master table
AnniDate	
Relation	

Table Name: BirDate

Column Name	Description
Id	Id will be posted from master table
BDate	
Relation	

MICRO HELP FOR TABLE FIELDS

Table Name: Domain_Master

Column Name	Description
Domain_Id	Auto generated number (System generated)
Domain	Select a person's title

Table Name: Contact_Master

Column Name	Description
Id	Auto generated number (System generated)
Title	Select a person's title
F_Name	Enter a person's first name
L_Name	Enter a person's last name
Note	Enter a note
Flag	Automatically sets flag (**T** or **F**)
Domain_Id	Automatically posted from Domain_Master
Relation	

Table Name: Contact_CompanyInfo

Column Name	Description
Id	Automatically posted from Contact_Master.id
Company_Name	Enter a person's company name
Designation	Enter a person's designation

Table Name: Contact_Detail

Column Name	Description
Id	Automatically posted from Contact_Master
Address	Enter a person's address
City	Enter a person's city
State	Enter a person's state
Pincode	Enter a person's pincode
County	Enter a person's country
Flag	Automatically posted (**O** for office and **R** for home)

Table Name: Contact_TelNo

Column Name	Description
Id	Automatically posted from Contact_Master.id
Tel_No	Enter a person's telephone number
Flag	Automatically posted (**O** for office, **R** for home and **M** for mobile)

Table Name: Contact_FaxNo

Column Name	Description
Id	Automatically posted from Contact_Master.id
Fax_No	Enter a person's fax number
Flag	Automatically posted (**O** for office and **R** for home)

Table Name: Contact_Email

Column Name	Description
Id	Automatically posted from Contact_Master.id
Email_Id	Enter a person's email address
Flag	Automatically posted (**O** for office and **R** for home)

Table Name: Contact_WebAddress

Column Name	Description
Id	Automatically posted from Contact_Master.id
WebSite	Enter a person's web address
Flag	Automatically posted (**O** for office and **R** for home)

Table Name: BirDate

Column Name	Description
Id	Automatically posted from Contact_Master.id
BDate	Select date of birth
Relation	Enter the relationship

Table Name: AnniDate

Column Name	Description
Id	Automatically posted from Contact_Master.id
AnniDate	Select date of anniversary
Relation	Enter the relationship

TEST DATA FOR THE P. I. M.

Table Name: Domain_Master

Domain_Id	Domain
1	General
2	IT
3	HR
4	Marketing
5	Finance
6	Advertisement
7	Training
8	Accounts
9	Designer
10	Artist
11	Advocate

Table Name: Contact_Master

Id	Title	F_Name	L_Name	Note	Flag	Domain_Id	Relation
1	Mr.	Devendra	Nemade		No	1	O
2	Mr.	Tarun	Choudhari	SSI Limited, Licensee: Choudhari Infotech	No	7	O
3	Mr.	Rajiv	Thakur	M. Com., L.L.B.	No	11	O
4	Mr.	M.	Rajgopal		No	7	O
5	Dr. (Mrs)	Purnima S.	Sangle	An Autonomous Institute under Department of Education, Ministry of HRD, Govt. of India	No	2	O
6	Mr.	Vikram	Vasudev		No	4	P
7	Prof.	R.	Ramaswamy		No	1	P

Id	Title	F_Name	L_Name	Note	Flag	Domain_Id	Relation
8	Mr.	Sunil G.	Karve	Member of Senate: University of MumbaiVice Chairmen & Trustee: Mumbai Education Trust, Bandra. Tel:6246428 Fax:6514056 Trustee: Rang Sharda Pratishtan, Bandra.	No	1	B
9	Mr.	Vijay	Page	MMS, JBIMS	No	1	O
10	Mr.	Pravin	Kale	MMS '69	No	1	O
11	Mr.	Dilip P.	Tikle		No	1	O
12	Mr.	Sunil	Rai		No	1	O
13	Dr.	Shamim J.	Barsrai	B.D. S. (Bom)	No	1	O
14	Mr.	Abhijeet	Singh		No	1	O
15	Mr.	Vinay	Aidasani		No	1	O
16	Mr.	Shefali	Adhikari		No	1	O
17	Mr.	Debasish	Rath	Country Licensee: Baibhav Associates	No	1	O
18	Mr.	Subhash	Menon		No	1	O
19	Mr.	Dhananjay	Bendre	Working as Dy. Manager for Business Alliance Progarmme.	No	1	O
20	Mr.	Mateen	Ramali		No	1	O
21	Mr.	Shrawan	Sharma		No	1	O
22	Mr.	Sathyamurthy	K		No	1	O
23	Mr.	H	Sundaresan		No	1	O
24	Mr.	A.	Deolekar	Company deals in software solutions, Manpower placements andcorporate training.	No	1	O

Id	Title	F_Name	L_Name	Note	Flag	Domain_Id	Relation
25	Mr.	R	Barve	Deal with Software Sub-contracting and body shopping.	No	1	O
26	Mr.	Jyotindar	Chaddha	Sub Editor and reporter of Express Computer / IT People. Workfor Business Publication Division.	No	1	O
27	Mr.	Brian	Pareira	Working for Network Magazine, The Indian Edition.	No	1	O
28	Mr.	Hitesh	Sanghavi	Working in Business Publications Division.	No	1	O

Table Name: Contact_CompanyInfo

Id	Company_Name	Designation
1	Andromeda Marketing Pvt. Ltd.	Asst. Territory Manager
2	SSI Education	Center Director
3		
4	Asoka Mehta Institue of Management And Research	Director
5	National Institute Of Industrial Engineering\(NITIE)	Asst. Professor(IT Group)
6	Yashwantrao Chavan Pratishthans Academy of Info. Tech.	CEO(Mktg & Placement)
7	National Institute Of Industrial Engineering(NITIE)	
8	Sunil Karve & Co.	
9	METs Asian Management Development Centre	Director
10	METs Asian Management Development Centre	Prof. & Student Advisor
11	METs Institute of Information Technology	Executive Director
12	BHARATIYA VIDYA BHAVANs SP Jain Inst. of Mgmt. & Rsrch.	Associate Prof.-Info. Mgm
13	Rainbow Information Technology Prvt. Ltd.	
14	Seep Guard Waterproofing	

Id	Company_Name	Designation
15	Atharva Institute of Information Technology	Director
16	Vision Multimedia	C.E.O.
17	Asoka Metha Inst. of Mgmt. & Research	Course Co-ordinator
19	Oracle Software India Ltd.	Dy. Mamager
20	Amgee Computers Pvt.Ltd.	Marketing Manager
21	Datum Technologys	C.E.O.
22	Datum Technologys	Director - Technical
23	Datum Technologys	V.P. Marketing
24	Krijal Software Ltd.	President
25	MBA Resources	Director
26	Indian Express Group	Sub-Editor / Reporter
27	Indian Express Newspapers Ltd.	
28	Indian Express Group	Consulting Editor

Table Name: Contact_Detail

Id	Address	City	State	Pincode	Country	Flag
1	121, Creative Industrial Premises, Sunder Nagar, Kalina, Santacruz (East)	Mumbai	Maharasthra	400 098	INDIA	O
2	201, Anand Commercial Centre, Next to Asha Parekh Hospital, S.V. Road, Santacruz (West)	Mumbai	Maharasthra	400 054	INDIA	O
3	Triveni Building, Gen. Arunkumar Vaidya Marg, PanchpakhadimThane (West)	Mumbai	Maharasthra	400 602	INDIA	R
4	2nd Floor, Apna Bazar, Plot No. 2, Sector 17, Vashi	Navi Mumbai	Maharasthra	400 703	INDIA	O
5	Vihar Lake	Mumbai	Maharashtra	400 087	INDIA	O
6	Y. B. Chavan Centre, Gen. Jagannathrao Bhosale Marg,	Mumbai	Maharashtra	400 021	INDIA	O

Id	Address	City	State	Pincode	Country	Flag
8	27, Indian Mercantile Insurance House, Ranade Road, Dadar	Mumbai	Maharashtra	400 028	INDIA	O
9	Gen. Arun Kumar Vaidya Chowk, Bandra Reclamation, Bandra(West)	Mumbai	Maharashtra	400 050	INDIA	O
10	Gen. Arun Kumar Vaidya Chowk, Bandra Reclamation, Bandra(West)	Mumbai	Maharashtra	400 050	INDIA	O
11	Gen. Arun Kumar Vaidya Chowk, Bandra Reclamation, Bandra(West)	Mumbai	Maharashtra	400 050	INDAI	O
12	Munshi Nagar, Dadabhai Road, Andheri(West)	Mumbai	Maharashtra	400 058	INDIA	O
13	New Sterling Apartments, 2nd Hasnabad Lane, Santacruz(West)	Mumbai	Maharashtra	400 054	INDIA	O
14	I-83A, 3rd Floor, Lajpat Nagar-II	New Delhi	Delhi	110 024	INDIA	O
15	51, Poddar Estate, Poddar Road, Malad(East)	Mumbai	Maharashtra	400 097	INDIA	O
16	Survey No. 263, Plot No. 8-12, Malad-Marve Road, Charkop Naka,Malvani, Malad(West)	Mumbai	Maharashtra	400 095	INDIA	O
17	95 A, Behind Seddem Shetty Complex, Parklane	Secunderabad	Andhra Pradesh		INDIA	O
18	2nd Floor, Apna Bazar, Plot No. 2, Sector 17, Vashi	Navi Mumbai	Maharashtra	400 703	INDIA	O
19	1020 Maker Chambers V221 Nariman Point	Mumbai	Maharashtra	400021	India	O
20	13-B Laxmi Industrial Estate,New Link Road,Andheri(W)	Mumbai	Maharashtra	400058	India	O

Id	Address	City	State	Pincode	Country	Flag
21	123/107, 2nd Floor, 2nd Main Road,27th Cross, 7th Block,Jayanagar	Bangalore	Karnataka	560082	India	O
22	123/107 2nd Floor, 2nd Main Road,27th Cross, 7th Block,Jayanagar	Bangalore	Karnataka	560082	India	O
23	123/107, 2nd Floor, 2nd Main Road,27th Cross, 7th BlockJayanagar	Bangalore	Karnataka	560082	India	O
24	A-212, Solaris-1, Opp. L & T Gate No.6Saki Vihar Road,Powai	Mumbai	Maharashtra	400072	India	O
25	21 Silver Beach,Shivaji Park	Mumbai	Maharashtra	400028	India	O
26	D-2 Mathuradas Mill Compound,Ideal Indl. Estate,Senapati Bapat Marg,Lower PArel	Mumbai	Maharashtra	400013	India	O
27	1st Floor, Express Towers,Nariman Point,	Mumbai	Maharashtra	400021	India	O
28	D-2 Mathuradas Mill Compound,Ideal Indl. Estate,Senapati Bapat Marg,Lower Parel	Mumbai	Maharashtra	400013	India	O

Table Name: Contact_TelNo

Id	Tel_No	Flag
2	6492009	O
2	6492029	O
2	6492031	O
3	5623474	R
4	5262993	R
4	7694587	O
4	7694508	O
4	9820017859	M
5	8573471(ext)204	O
5	8573507	R

Id	Tel_No	Flag
6	2128770	O
6	2143617	O
6	2143619	O
7	8673371	O
7	8675811	R
8	4427360	O
9	6553899	O
9	6501229	O
9	6557414	R
10	6453899	O
10	6501229	O
11	6452884	O
11	6403614	O
11	6453900	O
12	6242401(ext)42	O
12	6237454	O
13	6343420	O
14	011-63113298	O
14	011-6331575	O
14	011-6849105	O
14	011-6817538	O
15	022-8823228	O
16	022-8085577	O
16	022-8645100	O
16	022-8645101	O
16	9821038114	M
17	+91-40-6325315	O
17	+91-40-6325317	O
17	+91-40-6543423	O
18	7894768	O
18	7894887	O
19	91-22-2831650	O
19	91-22-2832701	O
19	91-22-2834851	O

Id	Tel_No	Flag
20	6312391	O
20	6312392	O
20	6312501	O
21	91-080-7540003	O
21	91-080-7659698	O
21	91-080-7659699	O
22	91-080-7543171	O
22	91-080-7659698	O
23	91-080-7540003	O
23	91-080-7659698	O
23	91-080-7659699	O
24	022-8373547	O
24	022-8373548	O
24	8750442	R
24	8756662	R
25	4439413	O
26	4465002	O
27	2391020	O
28	4465002	O

Table Name: Contact_FaxNo

Id	Fax_No	Flag
1	6604584	O
4	7292990	O
6	91-022-2816976	O
6	91-022-2814564	O
8	4345618	O
10	6403899	O
11	6403615	O
12	+91-22-6207042	O
14	011-6301555	O
15	022-8032113	O
16	022-8083577	O
18	7692990	O
19	91-22-2873005	O

Id	Fax_No	Flag
20	6301967	O
21	91-080-6503172	O
22	91-080-6503172	O
23	91-080-6503172	O
24	022-8568928	O
25	4469200	O
26	022-4972007	O
27	022-2301007	O
28	022-4971097	O

Table Name: Contact_Email

Id	Email_Id	Flag
1	hetal@androindia.com	O
4	stelag@vsnl.com	O
5	purimas@rediffmail.com	R
6	pait@vsnl.com	O
8	suni@hotmail.com	O
9	diramdc@im.eth.net	O
10	diramdc@im.eth.net	O
11	metmumbai@bom2.vsnl.net.in	O
12	sunil@spjimr.ernet.in	O
14	jeet@rainbow.com	O
16	atharvacl@vsnl.com	O
17	drathvm@visionmulti.com	O
18	amimrs@bom3.vsnl.net.in	O
19	bendre@in.oracle.com	O
20	jadish@giasbm01.vsnl.net.in	O
21	ss@datumtac.com	O
22	mut@datumtac.com	O
22	kumar@hotmail.com	O
23	s_dare@datumtsc.com	O
24	kri@bom3.vsnl.net.in	O
25	rt_barve@hotmail.com	O
26	ec_net@bom4.vsnl.net.in	O
27	bri@rediffmail.com	O
27	network_mag@india.com	O

Table Name: WebAddress

Id	WebSite	Flag
9	www.met.edu	O
12	www.spjimrborg	O
14	www.rainbow.com	O
21	www.datumtec.com	O
23	www.datumtec.com	O
24	www.datumtsc.com	O

Table Name: BirDate

Id	BDate	Relation

Table Name: AnniDate

Id	BDate	Relation

Chapter 03

Self Evaluation

In This Chapter We Learned:

- **What is a Personal Information Manager**
  Its Working And Requirements

- **Data Segregation And Relationships Within The Project**

- **Database Designing For The Project**
  Table Definitions
  Table Data Validation Rules
  Micro Help For Table Fields
  Test Data For The Application

Chapter 04

A Personal Information Manager: The Working

In This Chapter:

- **Behaviour Of The Personal Information Manager**
  Its Working Through Visual Basic 6

- **Built-In Components And References Required While Designing**

- **Project Source Codes**
  frmCardBook.frm
  frmDial.frm
  frmEmail.frm
  frmSearch.frm
  Module1.bas

4. A PERSONAL INFORMATION MANAGER: THE WORKING

When the application starts, the screen shown in diagram 4.1 is displayed. This screen accepts personal information of a contact.

The Personal tab captures/displays the following:

- Personal information such as title, first name, last name, business contact or a friend
- Professional information such as, company name, designation and work domain of the contact

The **Personal** tab provides a **Notes** section via which additional information about a contact can be captured.

The diagram 4.1 displays the Personal tab of the application.

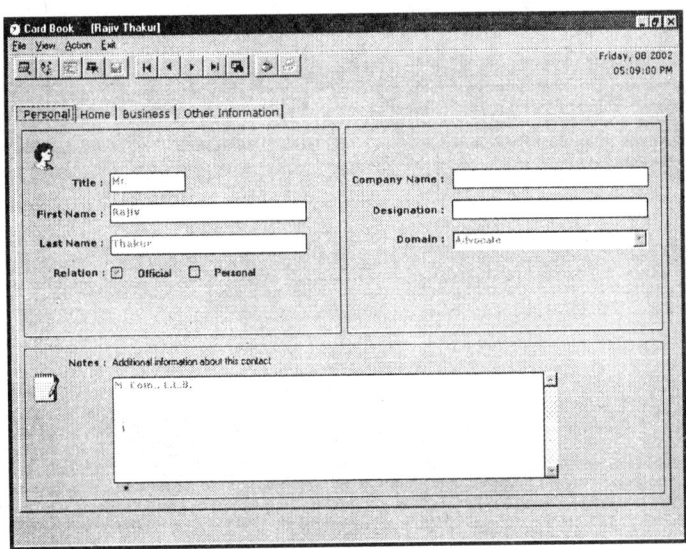

Diagram 4.1: Data entry screen of the Personal tab

The **Home** tab shown in the diagram 4.2 captures/displays the residence address consisting of street, city, state, pincode and country of a contact.

Along with the residence address, the **Home** tab also captures the telephone, fax, mobile numbers and the Email address of a contact.

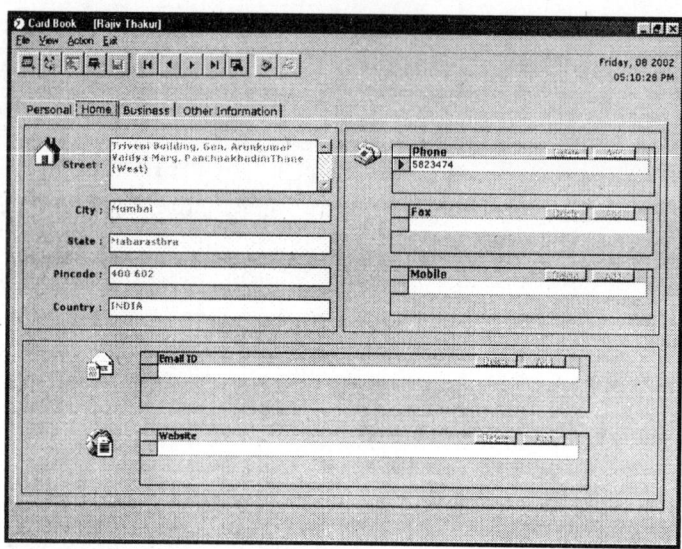

Diagram 4.2: Data entry screen of the Home tab

The **Business** tab shown in the diagram 4.2 captures/displays the office address consisting of street, city, state, pincode and country details.

Along with the office address, the **Business** tab also captures the office Email, website, telephone and fax numbers of a contact.

CHAP 04 A PERSONAL INFORMATION MANAGER: THE WORKING

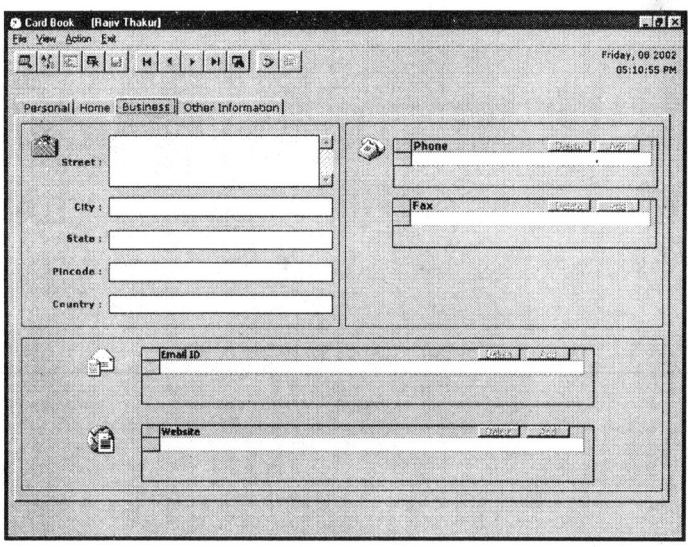

Diagram 4.3: Data entry screen of the Business tab

The **Other information** tab captures/displays additional information such as birthdays and anniversaries of a contact and contact's relatives.

The **Other Information** tab is shown in diagram 4.3 above.

When a user clicks on the **Birth Date** or **Anniversary Date** section of the tab, a calendar is displayed as shown in diagram 4.5. The user chooses a date from the calendar displayed to mark a birthday or an anniversary.

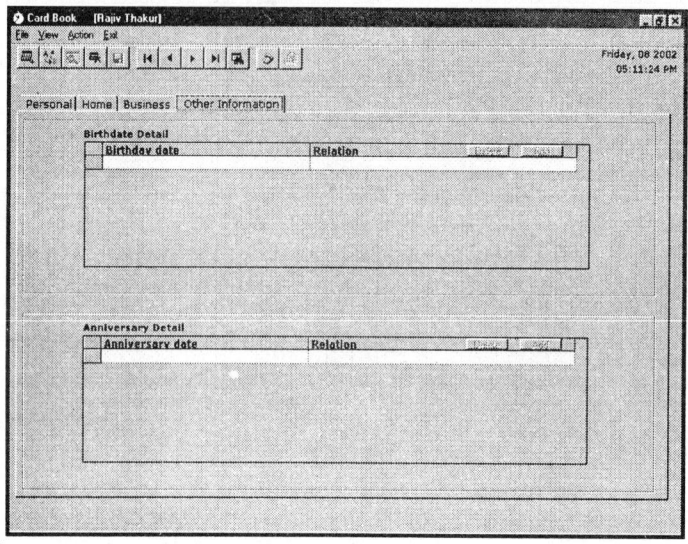

Diagram 4.4: Data entry screen of the Other Information tab

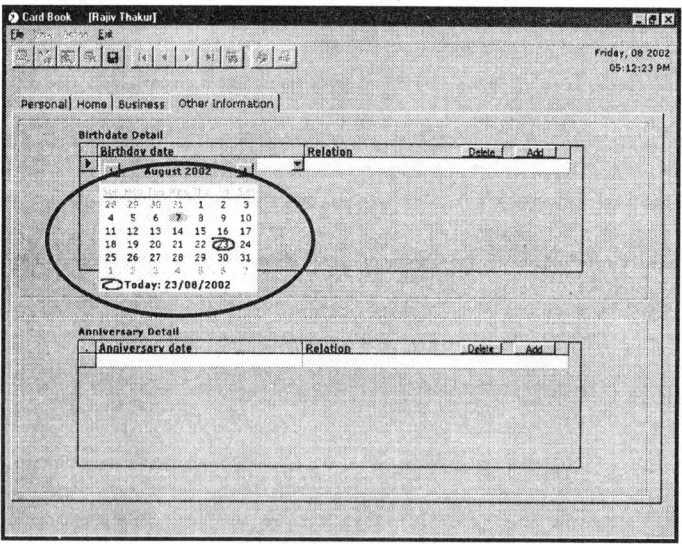

Diagram 4.5: Data entry screen displaying the calendar control for the birthday/anniversary field

The **P.I.M** provides the facility of dialing a contact's telephone numbers while viewing contact information. The user needs to click on the **Dial** button of the toolbar or select **Action → Dial** from the menu bar.

The application provides access to all contact numbers of a current contact.

The screen shown in diagram 4.6 is displayed through which a user can select a number to dial of the current contact.

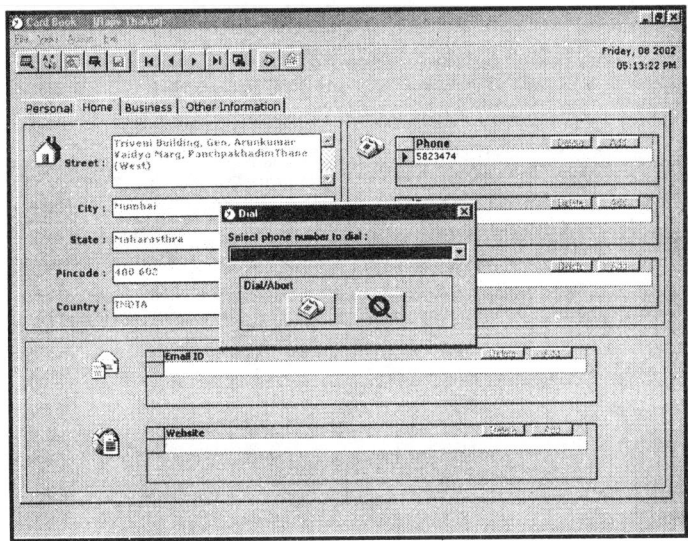

Diagram 4.6: Dialog box for Dialing

Along with the dialing out facility, the **P.I.M** also provides an Email facility. The user can Email a current contact while viewing contact information. The user needs to click on the **Email** button of a toolbar or select **Action → Email** from the menu bar.

The application provides access to all Email addresses of a current contact. As the user selects an Email address, an instance of MS Outlook Express is opened in order to compose an Email with the Email id automatically assigned as the address.

The screen shown in diagram 4.7 is displayed through which a user can select an Email address to write an Email to the current contact.

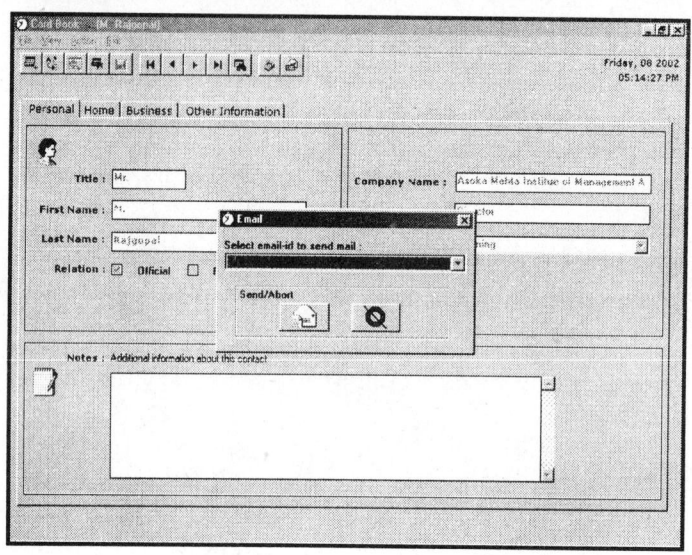

Diagram 4.7: Dialog box for Mailing

ADDITIONAL COMPONENTS AND REFERENCES

Along with the normal ActiveX control like the Labels, Textboxes, List boxes, Command button, etc the Personal Information Manager requires some additional components. These components are:

- Microsoft ADO Data Control 6.0 (OLEDB) (C:\Windows\System\MSADODC.ocx)
- Microsoft Data Grid Control 6.0 (OLEDB) (C:\Windows\System\MSDATGRD.ocx)
- Microsoft MAPI Control 6.0 (C:\Windows\System\MSMAPI32.ocx)
- Microsoft Tabbed Dialog Box Control 6.0 (C:\Windows\System\TABCTL32.ocx)
- Microsoft Windows Common Controls 6.0 (C:\Windows\System\mscomctl.ocx)
- Microsoft Windows Common Controls-2 6.0 (C:\Windows\System\MSCOMCT2.ocx)

In additions to these the following References are required:

- Microsoft ActiveX Data Object 2.0 Library (C:\Program Files\Common Files\SYSTEM\msado20.tlb)
- Microsoft DAO 3.51 Object Library (C:\Program Files\Common Files\Microsoft Shared\DAO\Dao2535.tlb)

PROJECT CODE FOR FrmCardbook.frm

```vb
Option Explicit
'Creating object variables for later use
Dim mFname As String
Dim mLname As String
Dim mSqlString As String
Dim mSavFlg As String
Dim mTitle As String
Dim mNote As String
Dim mBdate As String
Dim mADate As String
Dim mTCheck As String
Dim mBRel As String
Dim mARel As String
Dim mResStreet As String
Dim mResCity As String
Dim mResState As String
Dim mResPin As String
Dim mResCountry As String
Dim mOffStreet As String
Dim mOffCity As String
Dim mOffState As String
Dim mOffPin As String
Dim mOffCountry As String
Dim mMode As String
Dim mTempCheck As String
Dim mUnLoadState As String
Dim mSearch As String
Dim mCompName As String
Dim mDesig As String
Dim mRelation As String
Dim mTrace As Integer
Dim mDomain_Id As Integer
Dim mMidPoint As Integer
Dim mTrap As Integer
```

```
Dim mEndPoint As Integer
Dim mBeginPoint As Integer
Dim mTrack As Integer
Dim mMsgResponse As Integer
Dim mCount As Integer
Public mContactId As Integer
Public imgX As ListImage
Public btnX As Button
Public mDomain As String
```

As the form loads in memcry, images are placed on toolbar buttons at runtime and an interval setting is done for the timer control. On the **Form_Load** event, a connection to the database is established by **ConnetDB()**.

The form opens in **nomode**. A user can then choose to view the records or insert records.

```
'*****************************************************************
'************** FUNCTIONALITY OF THE FORM LOAD EVENT BEGINS **********
Public Sub Form_Load()
    frmCardBook.Icon = LoadPicture(App.Path & "\icon\Card.ico")
'Calling Loadtbr subroutine to add buttons to the toolbar
    Loadtbr
'Calling LoadImg subroutine to load toolbar images at runtime
    LoadImg
'Setting the timer1 interval to 100
    Timer1.Interval = 100
'Calling ConnectDB subroutine to connect to the database
    ConnetDB
'Calling NoMode subroutine that bring up the d/e form in nomode
    NoMode
'Setting the form caption
    frmCardBook.Caption = "Card Book"
End Sub

Public Sub Form_Unload(Cancel As Integer)
    If mUnLoadState <> "T" Then
        AppExit
    End If
End Sub
'*********** FUNCTIONALITY OF THE FORM LOAD EVENT ENDS ***************
'*****************************************************************
```

CHAP 04   A PERSONAL INFORMATION MANAGER: THE WORKING

The following section handles the menubar options. As a user selects an option from the menubar, different subroutines get called to perform the operation.

```
'****************************************************************
'*************** HANDLING CLICK EVENTS OF MENU BEGINS ***************
Public Sub mnuAdd_Click()
'Calling InsRec subroutine to insert a new record
    InsRec
End Sub

Public Sub mnuModify_Click()
'Calling ModiRec subroutine to modify a record
    ModiRec
End Sub

Public Sub mnuDelete_Click()
'Calling DelRec subroutine to delete a record
    DelRec
End Sub

Public Sub mnuSave_Click()
'Check if variable mMode holds "A" (This means that user is in Add New data Mode)
    If mMode = "A" Then
        'Calling AddSaveMode subroutine to save the record
        AddSaveMode
    End If
'Check if variable mMode holds "M" (This means that user is in Modify Mode)
    If mMode = "M" Then
        'Calling UpdtSaveMode subroutine to save the record
        UpdtSaveMode
    End If
End Sub
```

```vb
Public Sub mnuViewRec_Click()
'Calling ViewRec subroutine to view a record
    ViewRec
End Sub

Public Sub mnuSearch_Click()
'Calling SrchRec subroutine to search for a record
    SrchRec
End Sub

Public Sub mnuFirst_Click()
'Calling the MoveFirst subroutine to move to the first record
    MoveFirst
End Sub

Public Sub mnuPrior_Click()
'Calling the MovePrior subroutine to move to the previous record
    MovePrior
End Sub

Public Sub mnuNext_Click()
'Calling the MoveNext subroutine to move to the next record
    MoveNext
End Sub

Public Sub mnuLast_Click()
'Calling the MoveLast subroutine to move to the last record
    MoveLast
End Sub

Public Sub mnuCall_Click()
'Displaying the frmDial form
    frmDial.Show
'Setting the frmCardBook enabled property to flase
    frmCardBook.Enabled = False
End Sub

Public Sub mnuEmail_Click()
    frmEmail.Show
    frmCardBook.Enabled = False
End Sub
```

```
Public Sub mnuExit_Click()
'Calling the AppExit subroutine to Exit from the application
    AppExit
End Sub
'******************** HANDLING CLICK EVENTS OF MENU ENDS ************
'****************************************************************
```

The **Cardbook_ButtonClick()** subroutine handles the toolbar operations. This subroutine accepts a button object as a parameter. Depending on the value passed to the subroutine, a call is made to the subroutine to perform the operation.

```
'****************************************************************
'********** HANDLING THE CLICK EVENT OF TOOLBAR BEGINS ***************
Public Sub tbrCardbook_ButtonClick(ByVal Button As MSComctlLib.Button)
'Evaluating a Key property to decide on action
    Select Case Button.Key
    Case Is = "Add"
        InsRec
    Case Is = "Modify"
        ModiRec
    Case Is = "View"
        ViewRec
    Case Is = "Delete"
        DelRec
    Case Is = "Save"
        If mMode = "A" Then
            AddSaveMode
        End If
        If mMode = "M" Then
            UpdtSaveMode
        End If
    Case Is = "First"
        MoveFirst
    Case Is = "Prior"
        MovePrior
    Case Is = "Next"
        MoveNext
    Case Is = "Last"
        MoveLast
```

```vb
        Case Is = "Search"
'Calling SrchRec subroutine to search for a record
            SrchRec
        Case Is = "Dial"
            frmDial.Show
            frmCardBook.Enabled = False
        Case Is = "Email"
            frmEmail.Show
            frmCardBook.Enabled = False
    End Select
End Sub
'*************** HANDLING CLICK EVENT OF TOOLBAR ENDS ****************
'*******************************************************************
```

The application keeps record of all the contact information of a person. Data grid controls are used to capture the contact information such as telephone, mobile, fax numbers and e-mail address of a person.

Following code handles the insert and delete operation performed, as a user clicks on the buttons placed on the data grid.

```
'*******************************************************************
'************ SUBROUTINE TO MANUPLATE DATA IN DATA GRID BEGINS *******
```

The **cmdHEmail_Click()** subroutine adds a blank record to the recordset and makes the data grid updateable for inserting a record.

```vb
Public Sub cmdHEmail_Click()
'Checking whether AdodcResEmail recordset contains records
    If AdodcResEmail.Recordset.RecordCount > 0 Then
    'Checking if the first column of the grid is empty
        If Trim(dgdHEmail.Columns(0).Text) = "" Then
        'Prompting the user
            MsgBox "Fields cannot be left blank", vbInformation
        Else
        'Adding a blank record to the Contact_Email table recordset
            AdodcResEmail.Recordset.AddNew
        'Enabling the Data Grid's Update property
            dgdHEmail.AllowUpdate = True
```

```
        'Assigning value of mContactId to the first column of the
        recordset
            AdodcResEmail.Recordset(0) = mContactId
        'Assigning value 'R' to the last field to indicate that it is a
        personal email address
            AdodcResEmail.Recordset(2) = "R"
        End If
    Else
        AdodcResEmail.Recordset.AddNew
        dgdHEmail.AllowUpdate = True
        AdodcResEmail.Recordset(0) = mContactId
        AdodcResEmail.Recordset(2) = "R"
    End If
End Sub
```

The **cmdHEmailDel_Click()** subroutine deletes the selected record from the recordset.

```
Public Sub cmdHEmailDel_Click()
    If AdodcResEmail.Recordset.RecordCount = 0 Then
        MsgBox "No record available", vbInformation
    Else
    'Enabling the Data Grid's delete property
        dgdHEmail.AllowDelete = True
    'Prompt the user about the current action and obtain a confirmation
        mMsgResponse = MsgBox("The current personal email-id" + vbCrLf _
                            + "is about to be deleted.... proceed ?", _
                            vbYesNo + vbCritical + vbDefaultButton2, "Delete
                            Warning")
    'Checking if the user has selected cancel
        If mMsgResponse = 7 Then
            Exit Sub
        Else
        'Deleting the current record from the recordset
            AdodcResEmail.Recordset.Delete
        'Refreshing the datagrid
            dgdHEmail.Refresh
        End If
    End If
End Sub
```

PRACTICAL VB 6 PROJECTS

The **cmdHFax_Click()** subroutine adds a blank record to the recordset and makes the data grid updateable.

```
Public Sub cmdHFax_Click()
    If AdodcResFax.Recordset.RecordCount > 0 Then
        If Trim(dgdHFax.Columns(0).Text) = "" Then
            MsgBox "Field cannot be left blank", vbInformation
        Else
            AdodcResFax.Recordset.AddNew
            dgdHFax.AllowUpdate = True
    'Assigning value of the mContactId to the first column of the
    recordset
            AdodcResFax.Recordset(0) = mContactId
    'Assigning value 'R' to the last field to indicate that it is a
    personal fax number
            AdodcResFax.Recordset(2) = "R"
        End If
    Else
        AdodcResFax.Recordset.AddNew
        dgdHFax.AllowUpdate = True
        AdodcResFax.Recordset.Fields(0) = mContactId
        AdodcResFax.Recordset.Fields("Flag") = "R"
    End If
End Sub
```

The **cmdHFaxDel_Click()** subroutine deletes the selected record from the recordset.

```
Public Sub cmdHFaxDel_Click()
    If AdodcResFax.Recordset.RecordCount = 0 Then
        MsgBox "No record available", vbInformation
    Else
        dgdHFax.AllowDelete = True
        mMsgResponse = MsgBox("The current residence fax number" + vbCrLf _
                        + "is about to be deleted.... proceed ?", _
                        vbYesNo + vbCritical + vbDefaultButton2, _
                        "Delete Warning")
        If mMsgResponse = 7 Then
            Exit Sub
        Else
            AdodcResFax.Recordset.Delete
            dgdHFax.Refresh
        End If
```

End If
End Sub

The **cmdHMob_Click()** subroutine adds a blank record to the recordset and makes the data grid updateable.

```
Public Sub cmdHMob_Click()
    If AdodcResMob.Recordset.RecordCount > 0 Then
        If Trim(dgdHMob.Columns(0).Text) = "" Then
            MsgBox "Fields cannot be left blank", vbInformation
        Else
            AdodcResMob.Recordset.AddNew
            dgdHMob.AllowUpdate = True
            AdodcResMob.Recordset(0) = mContactId
            'Assigning value 'M' to the last field to indicate that it is a
            mobile number
            AdodcResMob.Recordset(2) = "M"
        End If
    Else
        AdodcResMob.Recordset.AddNew
        dgdHMob.AllowUpdate = True
        AdodcResMob.Recordset(0) = mContactId
        AdodcResMob.Recordset(2) = "M"
    End If
End Sub
```

The **cmdHMobDel_Click()** subroutine deletes the selected record from the recordset.

```
Public Sub cmdHMobDel_Click()
    If AdodcResMob.Recordset.RecordCount = 0 Then
        MsgBox "No record available", vbInformation
    Else
        dgdHMob.AllowDelete = True
        mMsgResponse = MsgBox("The current mobile number" + vbCrLf _
                        + "is about to be deleted.... proceed ?", _
                        vbYesNo + vbCritical + vbDefaultButton2, _
                        "Delete Warning")
        If mMsgResponse = 7 Then
            Exit Sub
        Else
            AdodcResMob.Recordset.Delete
```

PRACTICAL VB 6 PROJECTS

```vb
            dgdHMob.Refresh
        End If
    End If
End Sub
```

The **cmdHPhone_Click()** subroutine adds a blank record to the recordset and makes the data grid updateable.

```vb
Public Sub cmdHPhone_Click()
    If AdodcResTel.Recordset.RecordCount > 0 Then
        If Trim(dgdHPhone.Columns(0).Text) = "" Then
            MsgBox "Field cannot be left blank", vbInformation
        Else
            AdodcResTel.Recordset.AddNew
            dgdHPhone.AllowUpdate = True
            AdodcResTel.Recordset(0) = mContactId
            'Assigning the vaue 'R' to the last field to indicate that it is
            'personal phone number
            AdodcResTel.Recordset("Flag") = "R"
        End If
    Else
        AdodcResTel.Recordset.AddNew
        dgdHPhone.AllowUpdate = True
        AdodcResTel.Recordset(0) = mContactId
        AdodcResTel.Recordset("Flag") = "R"
    End If
End Sub
```

The **cmdHPhoneDel_Click()** subroutine deletes the selected record from the recordset.

```vb
Public Sub cmdHPhoneDel_Click()
'Checking whether the AdodcResTel recordset contains any records
    If AdodcResTel.Recordset.RecordCount = 0 Then
        'Prompting the user
        MsgBox "No record available", vbInformation
    Else
        'Enabling the Data Grid's Delete property
        dgdHPhone.AllowDelete = True
```

```vb
    'Promting the user about the current action and obtaining
    'confirmation
        mMsgResponse = MsgBox("The current residence telephone number" + vbCrLf _
                        + "is about to be deleted.... proceed ?", _
                        vbYesNo + vbCritical + vbDefaultButton2, "Delete _
                        Warning")
        If mMsgResponse = 7 Then
            Exit Sub
        Else
        'Deleting the current record from the recordset
            AdodcResTel.Recordset.Delete
            dgdHPhone.Refresh
        End If
    End If
End Sub
```

The **cmdHWeb_Click()** subroutine adds a blank record to the recordset and makes the data grid updateable.

```vb
Public Sub cmdHWeb_Click()
    If AdodcResWeb.Recordset.RecordCount > 0 Then
        If Trim(dgdHWeb.Columns(0).Text) = "" Then
            MsgBox "Fields cannot be left blank", vbInformation
        Else
            AdodcResWeb.Recordset.AddNew
            dgdHWeb.AllowUpdate = True
            AdodcResWeb.Recordset(0) = mContactId
        'Assigning value 'R' to the last field to indicate that it is a
        'personal Web site
            AdodcResWeb.Recordset(2) = "R"
        End If
    Else
        AdodcResWeb.Recordset.AddNew
        dgdHWeb.AllowUpdate = True
        AdodcResWeb.Recordset(0) = mContactId
        AdodcResWeb.Recordset(2) = "R"
    End If
End Sub
```

The **cmdHWebDel_Click()** subroutine deletes the selected record from the recordset.

```
Public Sub cmdHWebDel_Click()
    If AdodcResWeb.Recordset.RecordCount = 0 Then
        MsgBox "No record available", vbInformation
    Else
        dgdHWeb.AllowDelete = True
        mMsgResponse = MsgBox("The current personal website address" + vbCrLf _
                        + "is about to be deleted.... proceed ?", _
                        vbYesNo + vbCritical + vbDefaultButton2, _
                        "Delete Warning")
        If mMsgResponse = 7 Then
            Exit Sub
        Else
        'Deleting the current record from the recordset
            AdodcResWeb.Recordset.Delete
            dgdHWeb.Refresh
        End If
    End If
End Sub
```

The **cmdOEmail_Click()** subroutine adds a blank record to the recordset and makes the data grid updateable.

```
Public Sub cmdOEmail_Click()
    If AdodcOffMail.Recordset.RecordCount > 0 Then
        If Trim(dgdOEmail.Columns(0).Text) = "" Then
            MsgBox "Fields cannot be left blank", vbInformation
        Else
            AdodcOffMail.Recordset.AddNew
            dgdOEmail.AllowUpdate = True
            AdodcOffMail.Recordset(0) = mContactId
        'Assigning value 'O' to the last field to indicate that
        'it is a office Email-ID
            AdodcOffMail.Recordset(2) = "O"
        End If
```

```
        Else
            AdodcOffMail.Recordset.AddNew
            dgdOEmail.AllowUpdate = True
            AdodcOffMail.Recordset(0) = mContactId
            AdodcOffMail.Recordset(2) = "O"
        End If
End Sub
```

The **cmdOEmailDel_Click()** subroutine deletes the selected record from the recordset.

```
Public Sub cmdOEmailDel_Click()
    If AdodcOffMail.Recordset.RecordCount = 0 Then
        MsgBox "No record available", vbInformation
    Else
        dgdOEmail.AllowDelete = True
        mMsgResponse = MsgBox("The current official email-id" + vbCrLf _
                        + "is about to be deleted.... proceed ?", _
                        vbYesNo + vbCritical + vbDefaultButton2, _
                        "Delete Warning")
        If mMsgResponse = 7 Then
            Exit Sub
        Else
        'Deleting the current record from the recorset
            AdodcOffMail.Recordset.Delete
            dgdOEmail.Refresh
        End If
    End If
End Sub
```

The **cmdOFax_Click()** subroutine adds a blank record to the recordset and makes the data grid updateable.

```
Public Sub cmdOFax_Click()
    If AdodcOffFax.Recordset.RecordCount > 0 Then
        If Trim(dgdOFax.Columns(0).Text) = "" Then
            MsgBox "Fields cannot be left blank", vbInformation
        Else
            AdodcOffFax.Recordset.AddNew
            dgdOFax.AllowUpdate = True
```

```
            AdodcOffFax.Recordset(0) = mContactId
            'Assigning value 'O' to the last field to indicate that
            'it is a office fax number
            AdodcOffFax.Recordset(2) = "O"
        End If
    Else
        AdodcOffFax.Recordset.AddNew
        dgdOFax.AllowUpdate = True
        AdodcOffFax.Recordset(0) = mContactId
        AdodcOffFax.Recordset(2) = "O"
    End If
End Sub
```

The **cmdOFaxDel_Click()** subroutine deletes the selected record from the recordset.

```
Public Sub cmdOFaxDel_Click()
    If AdodcOffFax.Recordset.RecordCount = 0 Then
        MsgBox "No record available", vbInformation
    Else
        dgdOFax.AllowDelete = True
        mMsgResponse = MsgBox("The current office fax number" + vbCrLf _
                        + "is about to be deleted.... proceed ?", _
                        vbYesNo + vbCritical + vbDefaultButton2, _
                        "Delete Warning")
        If mMsgResponse = 7 Then
            Exit Sub
        Else
        'Deleting the current record from the recorset
            AdodcOffFax.Recordset.Delete
            dgdOFax.Refresh
        End If
    End If
End Sub
```

The **cmdOPhone_Click()** subroutine adds a blank record to the recordset and makes the data grid updateable.

```
Public Sub cmdOPhone_Click()
    If AdodcOffTel.Recordset.RecordCount > 0 Then
        If Trim(dgdOPhone.Columns(0).Text) = "" Then
            MsgBox "Fields cannot be left blank", vbInformation
        Else
            AdodcOffTel.Recordset.AddNew
            dgdOPhone.AllowUpdate = True
            AdodcOffTel.Recordset(0) = mContactId
        'Assigning value 'O' to the last field to indicate that
        'it is a office telephone number
            AdodcOffTel.Recordset(2) = "O"
        End If
    Else
        AdodcOffTel.Recordset.AddNew
        dgdOPhone.AllowUpdate = True
        AdodcOffTel.Recordset(0) = mContactId
        AdodcOffTel.Recordset(2) = "O"
    End If
End Sub
```

The **cmdOPhoneDel_Click** subroutine deletes the selected record from the recordset.

```
Public Sub cmdOPhoneDel_Click()
    If AdodcOffTel.Recordset.RecordCount = 0 Then
        MsgBox "No record available", vbInformation
    Else
        dgdOPhone.AllowDelete = True
        mMsgResponse = MsgBox("The current office telephone number" + vbCrLf _
                            + "is about to be deleted.... proceed ?", _
                            vbYesNo + vbCritical + vbDefaultButton2, _
                            "Delete Warning")
        If mMsgResponse = 7 Then
            Exit Sub
```

```
        Else
            'Deleting the current record from the recordset
                AdodcOffTel.Recordset.Delete
                dgdOPhone.Refresh
            End If
        End If
End Sub
```

The **cmdOWeb_Click()** subroutine adds a blank record to the recordset and makes the data grid updateable.

```
Public Sub cmdOWeb_Click()
    If AdodcOffWeb.Recordset.RecordCount > 0 Then
        If Trim(dgdOWeb.Columns(0).Text) = "" Then
            MsgBox "Fields cannot be left blank", vbInformation
        Else
            AdodcOffWeb.Recordset.AddNew
            dgdOWeb.AllowUpdate = True
            AdodcOffWeb.Recordset(0) = mContactId
            'Assigning the value 0 to the last field to indicate that it
            'is a personal fax number
            AdodcOffWeb.Recordset(2) = "O"
        End If
    Else
        AdodcOffWeb.Recordset.AddNew
        dgdOWeb.AllowUpdate = True
        AdodcOffWeb.Recordset(0) = mContactId
        AdodcOffWeb.Recordset(2) = "O"
    End If
End Sub
```

The **cmdOWebDel_Click()** subroutine deletes the selected record from the recordset.

```
Public Sub cmdOWebDel_Click()
    If AdodcOffWeb.Recordset.RecordCount = 0 Then
        MsgBox "No record available", vbInformation
```

```
        Else
            dgdOWeb.AllowDelete = True
            mMsgResponse = MsgBox("The current official website address" + vbCrLf _
                            + "is about to be deleted.... proceed ?", _
                                vbYesNo + vbCritical + vbDefaultButton2, _
                                "Delete Warning")
        If mMsgResponse = 7 Then
            Exit Sub
        Else
            'Deleting the current record from the AdodcOffWeb recordset
            AdodcOffWeb.Recordset.Delete
            dgdOWeb.Refresh
        End If
    End If
End Sub
```

The **cmdOAnniAdd_Click()** subroutine adds a blank record to the recordset and makes the data grid updateable.

```
Public Sub cmdAnniAdd_Click()
    If AdodcAnni.Recordset.RecordCount > 0 Then
        If Trim(dgdAnni.Columns(0).Text) = ""
            And Trim(dgdAnni.Columns(1).Text) = "" Then
            MsgBox "Fields cannot be left blank", vbInformation
        Else
            dgdAnni.Enabled = True
            AdodcAnni.Recordset.AddNew
            dgdAnni.AllowUpdate = True
            AdodcAnni.Recordset.Fields(0) = mContactId
        End If
    Else
        dgdAnni.Enabled = True
        AdodcAnni.Recordset.AddNew
        dgdAnni.AllowUpdate = True
        AdodcAnni.Recordset.Fields(0) = mContactId
    End If
End Sub
```

The **cmdAnniDel_Click()** subroutine deletes the selected record from the recordset.

```
Public Sub cmdAnniDelete_Click()
    If AdodcAnni.Recordset.RecordCount = 0 Then
        MsgBox "No record available", vbInformation
    Else
        dgdAnni.AllowDelete = True
        mMsgResponse = MsgBox("The current anniversary information" + vbCrLf _
                    + "is about to be deleted.... proceed ?", _
                    vbYesNo + vbCritical + vbDefaultButton2, _
                    "Delete Warning")
        If mMsgResponse = 7 Then
            Exit Sub
        Else
        'Deleting the current record from AdodcAnni recordset
            AdodcAnni.Recordset.Delete
            dgdAnni.Refresh
        End If
    End If
End Sub
```

The **cmdBirthAdd_Click()** subroutine adds a blank record to the recordset and makes the data grid updateable.

```
Public Sub cmdBirthAdd_Click()
    If AdodcBirth.Recordset.RecordCount > 0 Then
        If Trim(dgdBirth.Columns(0).Text) = ""
            And Trim(dgdBirth.Columns(1).Text) = "" Then
            MsgBox "Fields cannot be left blank", vbInformation
        Else
            dgdBirth.Enabled = True
            AdodcBirth.Recordset.AddNew
            dgdBirth.AllowUpdate = True
            AdodcBirth.Recordset.Fields(0) = mContactId
        End If
```

```
    Else
        dgdBirth.Enabled = True
        AdodcBirth.Recordset.AddNew
        dgdBirth.AllowUpdate = True
        AdodcBirth.Recordset.Fields(0) = mContactId
    End If
End Sub
```

The **cmdBirthDel_Click()** subroutine deletes the selected record from the recordset.

```
Public Sub cmdBirthDel_Click()
    If AdodcBirth.Recordset.RecordCount = 0 Then
        MsgBox "No record available", vbInformation
    Else
        dgdBirth.AllowDelete = True
        mMsgResponse = MsgBox("The current birthday information" + vbCrLf _
                        + "is about to be deleted.... proceed ?", _
                        vbYesNo + vbCritical + vbDefaultButton2, _
                        "Delete Warning")
        If mMsgResponse = 7 Then
            Exit Sub
        Else
        'Deleting the current record from the AdodcBirth recordset
            AdodcBirth.Recordset.Delete
            dgdBirth.Refresh
        End If
    End If
End Sub
'**********SUBROUTINE TO MANIPULATE DATA IN DATA GRID ENDS*************
'*********************************************************************
```

PRACTICAL VB 6 PROJECTS

Along with the contact information, this application stores aditional personal information such as birth date, anniversary dates and so on. In order to simplify the job of a user, calendar controls are used from which a user can select the dates.

These calendar controls are placed on the data grids that capture the information. So as user clicks on the data grid, the calendar associated with that data grid gets displayed.

Following blocks of code handles the operation associated with these data grids by displaying or hiding the calendar controls based on the user selection (i.e. when user selectes birth date, calendar control for anniversary dates becomes invisible).

```
'*************************************************************
'*********** HANDLING EVENTS OF CALANDER CONTROL BEGINS HERE ***********
Public Sub mvwAnni_DateClick(ByVal DateClicked As Date)
'Assigning a value to dgdAnni datagrid
    dgdAnni.Text = mvwAnni.Value
    mvwAnni.Visible = False
End Sub

Public Sub mvwBirth_DateClick(ByVal DateClicked As Date)
'Assiging a value to dgdBirth datagrid
    dgdBirth.Text = mvwBirth.Value
    mvwBirth.Visible = False
End Sub

Public Sub mvwBirth_LostFocus()
'Setting the mvwBirth control's visible property to False
    mvwBirth.Visible = False
End Sub

Public Sub mvwAnni_LostFocus()
'Setting the mvwAnni control's visible property to False
    mvwAnni.Visible = False
End Sub
'************** HANDLING EVENTS OF CALANDER CONTROL ENDS **************
'*************************************************************
```

This section of code handles events associated with controls placed on the form. Calendar controls are made visible as and when required on the **click** event of a data grid. The application also loads specific images associated with different controls.

```vb
'****************************************************************
'****************** HANDLING EVENTS OF OBJECTS BEGINS ***************
Public Sub dgdAnni_ButtonClick(ByVal ColIndex As Integer)
'Setting the Visible property for the mvwAnni control to True
    mvwAnni.Visible = True
End Sub

Public Sub dgdAnni_Click()
'Setting the Visible property for the mvwAnni and mvwBirth controls
'to False
    mvwAnni.Visible = False
    mvwBirth.Visible = False
End Sub

Public Sub dgdBirth_ButtonClick(ByVal ColIndex As Integer)
'Setting the Visible property for the mvwBirth control to True
    mvwBirth.Visible = True
End Sub

Public Sub dgdBirth_Click()
'Setting the Visible property for the mvwBirth and mvwAnni controls
'to False
    mvwAnni.Visible = False
    mvwBirth.Visible = False
End Sub

Public Sub Timer1_Timer()
'Assiging a value to the txtTime and txtDay textboxes
    txtTime.Text = Format(Now, "hh:mm:ss AM/PM")
    txtDay.Text = Format(Now, "dddd, mm yyyy")
End Sub

Public Sub cboTitle_GotFocus()
'Calling PerImg that loads an image
    Call PerImg
End Sub
```

PRACTICAL VB 6 PROJECTS

```vb
Public Sub txtFname_GotFocus()
    Call PerImg
End Sub

Public Sub txtLname_GotFocus()
    Call PerImg
End Sub

Public Sub cboDispaly_GotFocus()
    Call PerImg
End Sub

Public Sub txtNote_GotFocus()
    Call NoteIng
End Sub

Public Sub txtHStreet_GotFocus()
'Calling HAddImg that loads an image
    Call HAddImg
End Sub

Public Sub txtHCity_GotFocus()
    Call HAddImg
End Sub

Public Sub txtHCountry_GotFocus()
    Call HAddImg
End Sub

Public Sub txtHPin_GotFocus()
    Call HAddImg
End Sub

Public Sub txtHState_GotFocus()
    Call HAddImg
End Sub

Public Sub dgdHFax_GotFocus()
'Calling HTelImg that loads an image
    Call HTelImg
End Sub
```

```
Public Sub dgdHMob_GotFocus()
    Call HTelImg
End Sub

Public Sub dgdHPhone_GotFocus()
    Call HTelImg
End Sub

Public Sub dgdHEmail_GotFocus()
    Call HMailImg
End Sub

Public Sub dgdHWeb_GotFocus()
'Calling HWebImg that loads an image
    Call HWebImg
End Sub

Public Sub txtOStreet_GotFocus()
'Calling OAddImg that loads an image
    Call OAddImg
End Sub

Public Sub txtOCity_GotFocus()
    Call OAddImg
End Sub

Public Sub txtOCountry_GotFocus()
    Call OAddImg
End Sub

Public Sub txtOPin_GotFocus()
    Call OAddImg
End Sub

Public Sub txtOState_GotFocus()
    Call OAddImg
End Sub
```

PRACTICAL VB 6 PROJECTS

```
Public Sub dgdOFax_GotFocus()
'Calling OTelImg that loads an image
    Call OTelImg
End Sub

Public Sub dgdOMob_GotFocus()
    Call OTelImg
End Sub

Public Sub dgdOPhone_GotFocus()
    Call OTelImg
End Sub

Public Sub dgdOEmail_GotFocus()
'Calling OMailImg that loads an image
    Call OMailImg
End Sub

Public Sub dgdOWeb_GotFocus()
    Call OWebImg
End Sub
```

The **tabMain_Click()** subroutine gets called whenever a user tries to switch from one tab to another in the application. This function prevents the user from switching between different tabs on the tab sheet prior keying in mandatory data while inserting a record.

```
Public Sub tabMain_Click(PreviousTab As Integer)
'Checking the value of the mMode variable
    If mMode = "V" Then
    'Assigning the value of the textbox txtTitle to the mTCheck variable
        mTCheck = txtTitle.Text
    Else
    'Assigning the value of cboTitle combobox to the mTCheck variable
        mTCheck = cboTitle.Text
    End If
```

```
        If mTCheck = "" Or txtFname = "" Or txtLname = "" Then
            tabMain.Tab = 0
        'Checking for an empty Title field
            If cboTitle.Text = "" Then
                'Setting the form cursor to the Title field
                cboTitle.SetFocus
            ElseIf txtFname.Text = "" Then
                txtFname.SetFocus

            ElseIf txtLname.Text = "" Then
                txtLname.SetFocus
            End If
        ElseIf chkBuss = 0 And chkPer = 0 Then
            tabMain.Tab = 0
            chkBuss.SetFocus
        Else
        'A Case statement that checks if a user is inserting
        'a new record i.e. a user is in Add mode
            Select Case PreviousTab
            Case 0
            'Checking the value of the mMode variable
                If mMode = "A" Then
                    'Checking the value of the mTempCheck variable
                    If mTempCheck = "T" Then
                        'Calling the master subroutine
                        Call master
                        'Assigning the value 'F' to the mTempCheck variable
                        mTempCheck = "F"
                    End If
                End If
            End Select
        End If
End Sub
'***************** HANDLING EVENTS OF OBJECTS ENDS ********************
'**********************************************************************

'**********************************************************************
'***************** VALIDATION FOR OBJECT BEGINS ***********************
```

PRACTICAL VB 6 PROJECTS

```
Public Sub txtLname_Validate(Cancel As Boolean)
    If txtFname <> "" And txtLname <> "" Then
    'Assiging the value of the textboxes to mFname and mLname
        mFname = txtFname
        mLname = txtLname
    End If
End Sub
'***************** VALIDATION FOR OBJECT ENDS ************************
'*********************************************************************
```

This section describes the functionality of the subroutines used in data manipulation. Calls are made to these subroutines while performing data manipulation operations such as insertion, updation and deletion of data.

```
'*********************************************************************
'*************** DATA MANIPULATION SUBROUTINES BEGINS ***************
```

The **InsRec()** subroutine inserts a new record in the database. Since a new record is to be inserted, calls are made to different subroutines to clear the form fields and display appropriate frames on the form.

```
Public Sub InsRec()
    If mRs_ContactMaster.State = 1 Then
        mRs_ContactMaster.Close
    End If
    tabMain.Tab = 0
'Assigning value to the mTempCheck variable to indicate that the
'user is entering new record
    mTempCheck = "T"
'Calling ClrPerInfo to clear the personal information tab
    Call ClrPerInfo
'Calling ClrResInfo to clear the residence
'information tab
    Call ClrResInfo
'Calling ClrOffInfo to clear the office information tab
    Call ClrOffInfo
'Calling ClrProffInfo to clear the professional information tab
```

```
    Call ClrProffInfo
'Calling ClrGrid to clear data grids
    Call ClrGrid
'Assigning a value to the mMode variable that points to the user mode
    mMode = "A"
'Assigning a value to the mSavFlg variable
'Setting the mSavFlg value to 'F', indicating that the record is not
'saved
    mSavFlg = "F"
    InsMode
'Calling DataEnterMode that enables the textbox
    DataEnterMode
'Setting the form caption when form is in ADD-NEW-MODE
    frmCardBook.Caption = "Card Book" + "        [" + "Untitled" + "]"
    fraName.Enabled = True
    fraCompInfo.Enabled = True
    fraNote.Enabled = True
    fraResAdd.Enabled = True
    fraOffAdd.Enabled = True
    cboTitle.Visible = True
    FillDomain
End Sub
```

Where a record needs to be updated the **ModiRec()** subroutine is called. Controls on the form are enabled and disbled as per the requirment by calling various subroutines.

```
Public Sub ModiRec()
'Assinging a value to mMode variable that points to the user mode
    mMode = "M"
    InsMode
    DataEnterMode
    fraName.Enabled = True
    fraCompInfo.Enabled = True
    fraNote.Enabled = True
    fraResAdd.Enabled = True
    fraOffAdd.Enabled = True
    cboTitle.Visible = True
    If mRs_ContactMaster.State = 1 Then
        mRs_ContactMaster.Close
    End If
```

```vb
    mSqlString = "SELECT * FROM Contact_Master WHERE ID = " & mContactId & ""
    mRs_ContactMaster.Open mSqlString, mCn_CardBook, adOpenKeyset, _
                adLockOptimistic
    cboTitle.Text = mRs_ContactMaster.Fields("Title")
    If Trim(txtFname) <> "" And Trim(txtLname) <> "" Then
        mFname = txtFname.Text
        mLname = txtLname.Text
    End If

'Enabling the Data Grid's Update property
    dgdOPhone.AllowUpdate = True
    dgdOFax.AllowUpdate = True
    dgdOMob.AllowUpdate = True
    dgdOEmail.AllowUpdate = True
    dgdOWeb.AllowUpdate = True
    dgdBirth.AllowUpdate = True
    dgdAnni.AllowUpdate = True
    dgdHPhone.AllowUpdate = True
    dgdHFax.AllowUpdate = True
    dgdHMob.AllowUpdate = True
    dgdHEmail.AllowUpdate = True
    dgdHWeb.AllowUpdate = True
'Enabling dgdAnni and dgdBirth Data Grids
    dgdAnni.Enabled = True
    dgdBirth.Enabled = True
    FillDomain
End Sub
```

The **DelRec()** subroutine is used to delete a record from the database. The subroutine prompts a user before deleting a record. If the user confirms the delete operation, the subroutine deletes the current record from the database.

```vb
Public Sub DelRec()
    mMsgResponse = MsgBox("The current record is about to be deleted... proceed ?", _
                    vbYesNo + vbCritical + vbDefaultButton2, _
                    "Delete Warning")
    If mMsgResponse = 7 Then
        Exit Sub
    Else
        mSqlString = "DELETE * FROM Contact_Master WHERE ID = " & _
```

```
                mContactId & ""
    If mRs_ContactMaster.State = 1 Then
        mRs_ContactMaster.Close
    End If
    mRs_ContactMaster.Open mSqlString, mCn_CardBook, adOpenKeyset, _
                        adLockOptimistic
        ViewRec
    End If
End Sub
```

A user can view all records in the database by selecting the **View** option from the menu or by clicking on the View button on the toolbar. When this is done the, **ViewRec()** subroutine gets called.

The **ViewRec()** subroutine enables and disables all toolbar buttons and the menu options as required. It populates the data in the form controls by calling **Rs2Form()** subroutine and sets properties of the data grid by calling different subroutines.

```
Public Sub ViewRec()
    tabMain.Tab = 0
'Assigning a value to mMode variable that points to the user mode
    mMode = "V"
'Calling subroutines to clear form fields
    ClrPerInfo
    ClrResInfo
    ClrCompInfo
    ClrOffInfo
    ClrProffInfo
'Calling ViewMode that enables and disables menu items &
'toolbar buttons
    ViewMode
'Calling DataViewMode that ensures that the form is readonly and
'textbox labels as bold
    DataViewMode
'Calling Rs2Form to transfer data from the recordset to form fields
    Rs2Form
'Calling ViewCompInfo to populate the Company information
    ViewCompInfo
```

```vb
'Calling ViewResAdd to populate the residence address
    ViewResAdd
'Calling ViewOffAdd to populate the office address
    ViewOffAdd
'Calling ViewResTel to populate the dgdHPhone datagrid
    ViewResTel
'Setting dgdHPhone Data Grid's update property to False
    dgdHPhone.AllowUpdate = False
'Calling ViewResFax to populate dgdHFax datagrid
    ViewResFax
'Setting dgdHFax Data Grid's update property to False
    dgdHFax.AllowUpdate = False
'Calling ViewMobileNo to populate the dgdHMob datagrid
    ViewMobileNo
'Setting dgdHMob Data Grid's update property to False
    dgdHMob.AllowUpdate = False
'Calling ViewResEmail to populate the dgdHEmail datagrid
    ViewResEmail
'Setting dgdHEmail Data Grid's update property to False
    dgdHEmail.AllowUpdate = False
'Calling ViewResWeb to populate the dgdHWeb datagrid
    ViewResWeb
'Setting dgdHWeb Data Grid's update property to False
    dgdHWeb.AllowUpdate = False
'Calling ViewOffTel to populate the dgdOPhone datagrid
    ViewOffTel
'Setting dgdOPhone Data Grid's update property to False
    dgdOPhone.AllowUpdate = False
'Calling ViewOffFax to populate the dgdOFax datagrid
    ViewOffFax
'Setting dgdOFax Data Grid's update property to False
    dgdOFax.AllowUpdate = False
'Calling ViewOffEmail to populate the dgdOEmail datagrid
    ViewOffEmail
'Setting dgdOEmail Data Grid's update property to False
    dgdOEmail.AllowUpdate = False
'Calling ViewOffWeb to populate the dgdOWeb datagrid
    ViewOffWeb
'Setting dgdOWeb Data Grid's update property to False
    dgdOWeb.AllowUpdate = False
'Calling ViewBirth to populate the birth datagrid
    ViewBirth
```

```
'Disabling dgdBirth datagrid
    dgdBirth.Enabled = False
'Calling ViewAnni to populate the anniversary datagrid
    ViewAnni
'Disabling dgdAnni datagrid
    dgdAnni.Enabled = False
End Sub
```

The **SrchRec()** subroutine gets called when a user clicks on a Search button or selects Search option from the menu. This subroutine enables appropriate menubar and toolbar options and opens up the **Search** form.

This form is used to search for a particular record in the database.

```
Public Sub SrchRec()
'Assigning value to mMode variable that points to the user mode
    mMode = "V"
'Enabling menubar options
    mnuViewRec.Enabled = True
    mnuSearch.Enabled = True
'Enabling toolbar buttons
    tbrCardbook.Buttons.Item("View").Enabled = True
    tbrCardbook.Buttons.Item("Search").Enabled = True
    frmSearch.Show
    frmCardBook.Enabled = False
End Sub
'***************** DATA MANIPULATION SUBROUTINES ENDS ****************
'*********************************************************************
```

This section describes the code blocks used for handling data navigation. This comprises of displaying the first, prior, next and last record in the database. These subroutines are called when a user selects an option from the menubar or clicks on the data navigation buttons in the toolbar.

```
'*********************************************************************
'***************** DATA NAVIGATION SUBROUTINES BEGINS ****************
```

The **MoveFirst()** subroutine handles the functionality of displaying the first record in the database.

```
Public Sub MoveFirst()
'Setting mRs_ContactMaster recordset's pointer on the First record
    mRs_ContactMaster.MoveFirst
    Call ClrPerInfo
    Call ClrResInfo
    Call ClrOffInfo
    Call ClrProffInfo
    Call ClrCompInfo
    Call PopForm
    Call ViewCompInfo
    Call ViewResAdd
    Call ViewOffAdd
    Call ViewResTel
    Call ViewResFax
    Call ViewMobileNo
    Call ViewResEmail
    Call ViewResWeb
    Call ViewOffTel
    Call ViewOffFax
    Call ViewOffEmail
    Call ViewOffWeb
    Call ViewBirth
    Call ViewAnni
End Sub
```

The **MovePrior()** subroutine gets called when a user selects **Previous** option from the menu or clicks on the 'Prior' button on the toolbar. The **MovePrior()** subroutine displays a message whenever a user tries to go beyond the first record.

```
Public Sub MovePrior()
'Setting mRs_ContactMaster recordset's pointer on the Previous record
    mRs_ContactMaster.MovePrevious
'Checking whether the recordset pointer has gone beyond the
'FIRST record
    If mRs_ContactMaster.BOF Then
        mMsgResponse = MsgBox("You are currently at the first record", vbOKOnly _
                            + vbInformation)
        mRs_ContactMaster.MoveFirst
```

```
        Else
            Call ClrPerInfo
            Call ClrResInfo
            Call ClrOffInfo
            Call ClrProffInfo
            Call ClrCompInfo
            Call PopForm
            Call ViewCompInfo
            Call ViewResAdd
            Call ViewOffAdd
            Call ViewResTel
            Call ViewResFax
            Call ViewMobileNo
            Call ViewResEmail
            Call ViewResWeb
            Call ViewOffTel
            Call ViewOffFax
            Call ViewOffEmail
            Call ViewOffWeb
            Call ViewBirth
            Call ViewAnni
        End If
End Sub
```

The **MoveNext()** subroutine displays the next record in the database. This subroutine is called when a user clicks on the **Next** button of the toolbar or selects **Next** from the menu. This subroutine displays a message whenever a user tries to go beyond the last record.

```
Public Sub MoveNext()
'Setting mRs_ContactMaster recordset's pointer on the Next record
    mRs_ContactMaster.MoveNext
'Checking whether the recordset pointer has gone beyond the LAST record
    If mRs_ContactMaster.EOF Then
        mMsgResponse = MsgBox("You are currently at the last record", vbOKOnly _
                        + vbInformation)
        mRs_ContactMaster.MoveLast
```

```
        Else
            Call ClrPerInfo
            Call ClrResInfo
            Call ClrOffInfo
            Call ClrProffInfo
            Call ClrCompInfo
            Call PopForm
            Call ViewCompInfo
            Call ViewResAdd
            Call ViewOffAdd
            Call ViewResTel
            Call ViewResFax
            Call ViewMobileNo
            Call ViewResEmail
            Call ViewResWeb
            Call ViewOffTel
            Call ViewOffFax
            Call ViewOffEmail
            Call ViewOffWeb
            Call ViewBirth
            Call ViewAnni
        End If
End Sub
```

The **MoveLast()** subroutine displays the last record in the database.

```
Public Sub MoveLast()
    mRs_ContactMaster.MoveLast
    Call ClrPerInfo
    Call ClrResInfo
    Call ClrOffInfo
    Call ClrProffInfo
    Call ClrCompInfo
    Call PopForm
    Call ViewCompInfo
    Call ViewResAdd
    Call ViewOffAdd
    Call ViewResTel
    Call ViewResFax
```

```
        Call ViewMobileNo
        Call ViewResEmail
        Call ViewResWeb
        Call ViewOffTel
        Call ViewOffFax
        Call ViewOffEmail
        Call ViewOffWeb
        Call ViewBirth
        Call ViewAnni
End Sub
'***************** DATA NAVIGATION SUBROUTINES ENDS *****************
'********************************************************************
```

Following the application subroutines used to provide different functionality in the application.

```
'********************************************************************
'***************** APPLICATION SUBROUTINES BEGINS *******************
```

The **AppExit()** subroutine checks the value of the mMode variable to determine the mode of an application (i.e. whether it is in insert, update, delete or view mode).

Depending on the mode, it prompts a user to complete the transaction started. If the user is in a view mode, the application gets terminated without prompting a user.

If the user is in an insert or update mode, the application prompts the user to save the record. If the user demands to save a record, the application performs the save operation and then terminates, otherwise the current mode is aborted and the application terminates.

```
Public Sub AppExit()
'Checking the value of mMode variable
    If mMode = "V" Then
        Unload Me
    End If
'Checking whether the mMode variable holds value 'A' or 'M'
    If mMode = "A" Or mMode = "M" Then
        'Checking the value of mSavFlg variable
        If mSavFlg = "F" Then
            If cboTitle = "" Or txtFname = "" Or txtLname = "" Then
```

```vb
        'Assigning value to the mUnLoadState variable
            mUnLoadState = "T"
            Unload Me
            Exit Sub
        Else
            If mRs_ContactMaster.State = 1 Then
                mRs_ContactMaster.Close
            End If
            mSqlString = "SELECT * FROM Contact_Master WHERE Id = " _
                        & mContactId & ""
            mRs_ContactMaster.Open mSqlString, mCn_CardBook, adOpenKeyset, _
                                    adLockOptimistic
            mCount = mRs_ContactMaster.RecordCount
            If mCount > 0 Then
            'Storing the value of an Id field in the recordset into
            'the mContactId variable
                mContactId = mRs_ContactMaster.Fields("Id")
                mRs_ContactMaster.Close
                mMsgResponse = MsgBox("Save current record....?", vbYesNo _
                                    + vbInformation + vbDefaultButton2)
                If mMsgResponse = 7 Then
                    mSqlString = "DELETE * FROM Contact_Master " & _
                                "WHERE Id = " & mContactId & " "
                    mRs_ContactMaster.Open mSqlString, mCn_CardBook, _
                                    adOpenKeyset, adLockOptimistic
                    mUnLoadState = "T"
                    Unload frmCardBook
                    Exit Sub
                Else
                    mSqlString = "UPDATE Contact_Master SET Flag = 0 _
                                WHERE Id = " & mContactId & " "
                    mRs_ContactMaster.Open mSqlString, mCn_CardBook, _
                                    adOpenKeyset, adLockOptimistic
            'Calling InsResInfo that inserts residence information
                    InsResInfo
            'Calling InsOffInfo that inserts office information
                    InsOffInfo
```

```
            'Calling UpdtGrids that updates the data grids
                UpdtGrids
                MsgBox "Current record has saved", vbInformation
            End If
        Else
            'Calling AddSaveMode to save a record
            AddSaveMode
        End If
      End If
      mUnLoadState = "T"
      Unload Me
      Exit Sub
    End If
  End If
'Assigning a value to the mUnLoadState variable
  mUnLoadState = "T"
'Unloading the current form
  Unload Me
  Exit Sub
End Sub
```

The **Loadtbr()** subroutine places appropriate images on the toolbar buttons.

```
Public Sub Loadtbr()
'Loading images into the ImageList control.
    Set imgX = ImageList1.ListImages. _
        Add(, "Add", LoadPicture(App.Path & "\icon\addnew.bmp"))
    Set imgX = ImageList1.ListImages. _
        Add(, "Modify", LoadPicture(App.Path & "\icon\modify.bmp"))
    Set imgX = ImageList1.ListImages. _
        Add(, "View", LoadPicture(App.Path & "\icon\view.bmp"))
    Set imgX = ImageList1.ListImages. _
        Add(, "Delete", LoadPicture(App.Path & "\icon\delete.bmp"))
    Set imgX = ImageList1.ListImages. _
        Add(, "Save", LoadPicture(App.Path & "\icon\save.bmp"))
    tbrCardbook.ImageList = ImageList1
    Set imgX = ImageList1.ListImages. _
        Add(, "First", LoadPicture(App.Path & "\icon\First.bmp"))
    tbrCardbook.ImageList = ImageList1
```

```vb
    Set imgX = ImageList1.ListImages. _
        Add(, "Prior", LoadPicture(App.Path & "\icon\prior.bmp"))
    tbrCardbook.ImageList = ImageList1
    Set imgX = ImageList1.ListImages. _
        Add(, "Next", LoadPicture(App.Path & "\icon\next.bmp"))
    tbrCardbook.ImageList = ImageList1
    Set imgX = ImageList1.ListImages. _
        Add(, "Last", LoadPicture(App.Path & "\icon\Last.bmp"))
    tbrCardbook.ImageList = ImageList1
    Set imgX = ImageList1.ListImages. _
        Add(, "Search", LoadPicture(App.Path & "\icon\Search.bmp"))
    tbrCardbook.ImageList = ImageList1
    Set imgX = ImageList1.ListImages. _
        Add(, "Dial", LoadPicture(App.Path & "\icon\phone.bmp"))
    tbrCardbook.ImageList = ImageList1
    Set imgX = ImageList1.ListImages. _
        Add(, "Email", LoadPicture(App.Path & "\icon\emails.bmp"))
    tbrCardbook.ImageList = ImageList1
'Adding button objects to the Buttons collection using the Add method
'After creating each button, setting both the Description and
'ToolTipText properties
    tbrCardbook.Buttons.Add , , , tbrSeparator
    Set btnX = tbrCardbook.Buttons.Add(, "Add", , tbrDefault, "Add")
    btnX.ToolTipText = "Add new record"
    btnX.Description = btnX.ToolTipText
    Set btnX = tbrCardbook.Buttons.Add(, "Modify", , tbrDefault, "Modify")
    btnX.ToolTipText = "Modify record"
    btnX.Description = btnX.ToolTipText
    Set btnX = tbrCardbook.Buttons.Add(, "View", , tbrDefault, "View")
    btnX.ToolTipText = "View record"
    btnX.Description = btnX.ToolTipText
    Set btnX = tbrCardbook.Buttons.Add(, "Delete", , tbrDefault, "Delete")
    btnX.ToolTipText = "Delete record"
    btnX.Description = btnX.ToolTipText
    Set btnX = tbrCardbook.Buttons.Add(, "Save", , tbrDefault, "Save")
    btnX.ToolTipText = "Save record"
    btnX.Description = btnX.ToolTipText
    Set btnX = tbrCardbook.Buttons.Add(, , , tbrPlaceholder)
```

```vb
    Set btnX = tbrCardbook.Buttons.Add(, "First", , tbrDefault, "First")
    btnX.ToolTipText = "First record"
    btnX.Description = btnX.ToolTipText
    Set btnX = tbrCardbook.Buttons.Add(, "Prior", , tbrDefault, "Prior")
    btnX.ToolTipText = "Previous record"
    btnX.Description = btnX.ToolTipText
    Set btnX = tbrCardbook.Buttons.Add(, "Next", , tbrDefault, "Next")
    btnX.ToolTipText = "Next record"
    btnX.Description = btnX.ToolTipText
    Set btnX = tbrCardbook.Buttons.Add(, "Last", , tbrDefault, "Last")
    btnX.ToolTipText = "Last record"
    btnX.Description = btnX.ToolTipText
    Set btnX = tbrCardbook.Buttons.Add(, "Search", , tbrDefault, "Search")
    btnX.ToolTipText = "Search record"
    btnX.Description = btnX.ToolTipText
    Set btnX = tbrCardbook.Buttons.Add(, , , tbrPlaceholder)
    Set btnX = tbrCardbook.Buttons.Add(, "Dial", , tbrDefault, "Dial")
    btnX.ToolTipText = "Dial"
    btnX.Description = btnX.ToolTipText
    Set btnX = tbrCardbook.Buttons.Add(, "Email", , tbrDefault, "Email")
    btnX.ToolTipText = "Email"
    btnX.Description = btnX.ToolTipText
End Sub
```

The **LoadImg()** subroutine loads the images used in the form.

```vb
Public Sub LoadImg()
'Loading images
    imgPersonal.Picture = LoadPicture(App.Path & "\icon\person.bmp")
    imgNote.Picture = LoadPicture(App.Path & "\icon\note.bmp")
    imgHAdd.Picture = LoadPicture(App.Path & "\icon\add.bmp")
    imgHTel.Picture = LoadPicture(App.Path & "\icon\Tel.bmp")
    imgHMail.Picture = LoadPicture(App.Path & "\icon\email.bmp")
    imgHWeb.Picture = LoadPicture(App.Path & "\icon\www.bmp")
    imgOAdd.Picture = LoadPicture(App.Path & "\icon\business.bmp")
    imgOTel.Picture = LoadPicture(App.Path & "\icon\tel.bmp")
    imgOMail.Picture = LoadPicture(App.Path & "\icon\email.bmp")
    imgOWeb.Picture = LoadPicture(App.Path & "\icon\www.bmp")
End Sub
```

The subroutines, given below, are called to load different images into the application as required. When a user selectes an option, depending on the option selected a coloured or greyed image gets loaded.

```vb
'*****************************************************************
'************** SUBROUTINE FOR SWAPPING IMAGES BEGINS ***************
Public Sub HAddImg()
'Loading images
    imgHAdd.Picture = LoadPicture(App.Path & "\icon\Addc.bmp0000")
    imgHTel.Picture = LoadPicture(App.Path & "\icon\tel.bmp")
    imgHMail.Picture = LoadPicture(App.Path & "\icon\email.bmp")
    imgHWeb.Picture = LoadPicture(App.Path & "\icon\www.bmp")
    ODefaultImg
    PerDefault
End Sub

Public Sub HTelImg()
    imgHAdd.Picture = LoadPicture(App.Path & "\icon\Add.bmp")
    imgHTel.Picture = LoadPicture(App.Path & "\icon\telc.bmp")
    imgHMail.Picture = LoadPicture(App.Path & "\icon\email.bmp")
    imgHWeb.Picture = LoadPicture(App.Path & "\icon\www.bmp")
    ODefaultImg
    PerDefault
End Sub

Public Sub HMailImg()
    imgHAdd.Picture = LoadPicture(App.Path & "\icon\Add.bmp")
    imgHTel.Picture = LoadPicture(App.Path & "\icon\tel.bmp")
    imgHMail.Picture = LoadPicture(App.Path & "\icon\emailc.bmp")
    imgHWeb.Picture = LoadPicture(App.Path & "\icon\www.bmp")
    ODefaultImg
    PerDefault
End Sub
```

```
Public Sub HWebImg()
    imgHAdd.Picture = LoadPicture(App.Path & "\icon\Add.bmp")
    imgHTel.Picture = LoadPicture(App.Path & "\icon\tel.bmp")
    imgHMail.Picture = LoadPicture(App.Path & "\icon\email.bmp")
    imgHWeb.Picture = LoadPicture(App.Path & "\icon\wwwc.bmp")
    ODefaultImg
    PerDefault
End Sub

Public Sub OAddImg()
    imgOAdd.Picture = LoadPicture(App.Path & "\icon\businessc.bmp")
    imgOTel.Picture = LoadPicture(App.Path & "\icon\tel.bmp")
    imgOMail.Picture = LoadPicture(App.Path & "\icon\email.bmp")
    imgOWeb.Picture = LoadPicture(App.Path & "\icon\www.bmp")
    HDefaultImg
    PerDefault
End Sub

Public Sub OTelImg()
    imgOAdd.Picture = LoadPicture(App.Path & "\icon\business.bmp")
    imgOTel.Picture = LoadPicture(App.Path & "\icon\telc.bmp")
    imgOMail.Picture = LoadPicture(App.Path & "\icon\email.bmp")
    imgOWeb.Picture = LoadPicture(App.Path & "\icon\www.bmp")
    HDefaultImg
    PerDefault
End Sub

Public Sub OMailImg()
    imgOAdd.Picture = LoadPicture(App.Path & "\icon\business.bmp")
    imgOTel.Picture = LoadPicture(App.Path & "\icon\tel.bmp")
    imgOMail.Picture = LoadPicture(App.Path & "\icon\emailc.bmp")
    imgOWeb.Picture = LoadPicture(App.Path & "\icon\www.bmp")
    HDefaultImg
    PerDefault
End Sub
```

```vb
Public Sub OWebImg()
    imgOAdd.Picture = LoadPicture(App.Path & "\icon\business.bmp")
    imgOTel.Picture = LoadPicture(App.Path & "\icon\tel.bmp")
    imgOMail.Picture = LoadPicture(App.Path & "\icon\email.bmp")
    imgOWeb.Picture = LoadPicture(App.Path & "\icon\wwwc.bmp")
    HDefaultImg
End Sub

Public Sub ODefaultImg()
    imgOAdd.Picture = LoadPicture(App.Path & "\icon\business.bmp")
    imgOTel.Picture = LoadPicture(App.Path & "\icon\tel.bmp")
    imgOMail.Picture = LoadPicture(App.Path & "\icon\email.bmp")
    imgOWeb.Picture = LoadPicture(App.Path & "\icon\www.bmp")
End Sub

Public Sub PerDefault()
    imgPersonal.Picture = LoadPicture(App.Path & "\icon\personc.bmp")
    imgNote.Picture = LoadPicture(App.Path & "\icon\note.bmp")
End Sub

Public Sub HDefaultImg()
    imgHAdd.Picture = LoadPicture(App.Path & "\icon\Add.bmp")
    imgHTel.Picture = LoadPicture(App.Path & "\icon\tel.bmp")
    imgHMail.Picture = LoadPicture(App.Path & "\icon\email.bmp")
    imgHWeb.Picture = LoadPicture(App.Path & "\icon\www.bmp")
End Sub

Public Sub PerImg()
    imgPersonal.Picture = LoadPicture(App.Path & "\icon\personc.bmp")
    imgNote.Picture = LoadPicture(App.Path & "\icon\note.bmp")
    ODefaultImg
    HDefaultImg
End Sub

Public Sub NoteIng()
    imgPersonal.Picture = LoadPicture(App.Path & "\icon\person.bmp")
    imgNote.Picture = LoadPicture(App.Path & "\icon\notec.bmp")
    ODefaultImg
    HDefaultImg
End Sub
```

```
'**************** SUBROUTINE FOR SWAPPING IMAGES ENDS ****************
'****************************************************************

Public Sub master()
'Calling Domain_Master to insert a new record in the Domain_Master table
    Call Domain_Master
'Moving the form field's values into memory variables
    mTitle = cboTitle
    mFname = txtFname.Text
    mLname = txtLname.Text
    mNote = txtNote.Text
    If mRs_ContactMaster.State = 1 Then
        mRs_ContactMaster.Close
    End If
    If chkBuss = 1 And chkPer = 1 Then
        mRelation = "B"
    ElseIf chkBuss = 1 And chkPer = 0 Then
        mRelation = "O"
    ElseIf chkPer = 1 And chkBuss = 0 Then
        mRelation = "P"
    End If
    mSqlString = "Select * from Contact_Master"
    mRs_ContactMaster.Open mSqlString, mCn_CardBook, adOpenKeyset, _
                           adLockOptimistic
    If mRs_ContactMaster.RecordCount > 0 Then
    'Checking if the value of the Flag field is zero and mSavFlag holds F
        If mRs_ContactMaster.Fields("Flag") = 0 And mSavFlg = "F" Then
            mRs_ContactMaster.AddNew
        'Moving the form fields values into recordset fields
            mRs_ContactMaster.Fields("Title") = cboTitle.Text
            mRs_ContactMaster.Fields("F_Name") = txtFname.Text
            mRs_ContactMaster.Fields("L_Name") = txtLname.Text
            If Trim(cboDomain.Text) = "" Then
                mRs_ContactMaster.Fields("Domain_Id") = 1
            Else
                mRs_ContactMaster.Fields("Domain_Id") = mDomain_Id
            End If
            mRs_ContactMaster.Fields("Relation") = mRelation
```

```vb
            If Trim(txtNote.Text) <> "" Then
                mRs_ContactMaster.Fields("Note") = txtNote.Text
            End If
        'Assigning a value to the Flag field in the recordset
            mRs_ContactMaster.Fields("Flag") = -1
            mRs_ContactMaster.Update
            mRs_ContactMaster.Close
        End If
    Else
        mRs_ContactMaster.AddNew
        mRs_ContactMaster.Fields("Title") = cboTitle.Text
        mRs_ContactMaster.Fields("F_Name") = txtFname.Text
        mRs_ContactMaster.Fields("L_Name") = txtLname.Text
        If Trim(cboDomain.Text) = "" Then
            mRs_ContactMaster.Fields("Domain_Id") = 1
        Else
            mRs_ContactMaster.Fields("Domain_Id") = mDomain_Id
        End If
        mRs_ContactMaster.Fields("Relation") = mRelation
        If Trim(txtNote.Text) <> "" Then
            mRs_ContactMaster.Fields("Note") = txtNote.Text
        End If
        mRs_ContactMaster.Fields("Flag") = -1
        mRs_ContactMaster.Update
        mRs_ContactMaster.Close
    End If
'Storing an SQL query into mSqlString
'The code block below retrieves the Id for the data currently saved.
    mSqlString = "SELECT id FROM Contact_Master"
    mRs_ContactMaster.Open mSqlString, mCn_CardBook, adOpenKeyset, _
                        adLockOptimistic
    mRs_ContactMaster.MoveLast
    mContactId = mRs_ContactMaster.Fields("Id")
    mRs_ContactMaster.Close
'Calling InsCompInfo to enter Company information in the database
    InsCompInfo
End Sub
```

The **InsCompInfo()** subroutine inserts a new record in the **Contact_CompanyInfo** table.

```
Public Sub InsCompInfo()
'Assigning the form field's values to variables
    mCompName = fixQuote(Trim(txtComName.Text))
    mDesig = fixQuote(Trim(txtDesig.Text))
    If mCompName <> "" Or mDesig <> "" Then
        If mRs_ContactMaster.State = 1 Then
            mRs_ContactMaster.Close
        End If
        mSqlString = "INSERT INTO Contact_CompanyInfo (Id, Company_Name, " & _
                    "Designation) VALUES (" & mContactId & ", '" & _
                    mCompName & "', '" & mDesig & "')"
        mRs_ContactMaster.Open mSqlString, mCn_CardBook, adOpenKeyset, _
                    adLockOptimistic
    End If
End Sub
```

The **UpdtCompInfo()** subroutine checks whether the record exists in the Contact_CompanyInfo table for the current contact. If the record exists, it is updated with the new values, otherwise a new record gets inserted in the table.

```
Public Sub UpdtCompInfo()
'Assigning the form field's values to variables
    mCompName = fixQuote(Trim(txtComName.Text))
    mDesig = fixQuote(Trim(txtDesig.Text))
    If mCompName <> "" Or mDesig <> "" Then
        If mRs_ContactMaster.State = 1 Then
            mRs_ContactMaster.Close
        End If
        mSqlString = "SELECT * FROM Contact_CompanyInfo WHERE Id = "
                    & mContactId & ""
        mRs_ContactMaster.Open    mSqlString,    mCn_CardBook,    adOpenKeyset,
                    adLockOptimistic
        If mRs_ContactMaster.RecordCount > 0 Then
            mRs_ContactMaster.Close
            mSqlString = "UPDATE Contact_CompanyInfo Set Company_Name = '" & _
                    mCompName & "', Designation = '" & mDesig & _
                    "' WHERE Id = " & mContactId & ""
```

```vb
                mRs_ContactMaster.Open  mSqlString,  mCn_CardBook,  adOpenKeyset, _
                                    adLockOptimistic
        Else
            mRs_ContactMaster.Close
            mSqlString = "INSERT INTO Contact_CompanyInfo" & _
                        " (Id, Company_Name, Designation) VALUES (" & _
                        mContactId & ", '" & mCompName & "', '" & mDesig & "')"
                mRs_ContactMaster.Open  mSqlString,  mCn_CardBook,  adOpenKeyset, _
                                    adLockOptimistic
        End If
        If mRs_ContactMaster.State = 1 Then
            mRs_ContactMaster.Close
        End If
    End If
End Sub
```

The **InsResInfo()** subroutine inserts a new record in the **Contact_Detail** table.

```vb
Public Sub InsResInfo()
'Assigning the form field's values to variables
    mResStreet = fixQuote(Trim(txtHStreet.Text))
    mResCity = fixQuote(Trim(txtHCity.Text))
    mResState = fixQuote(Trim(txtHState.Text))
    mResPin = Trim(txtHPin.Text)
    mResCountry = fixQuote(Trim(txtHCountry.Text))
    If mResStreet <> "" Or mResCity <> "" Or mResState <> "" Or mResPin <> "" _
    Or mResCountry <> "" Then
        mSqlString = "INSERT INTO Contact_Detail (Id, Address, City, State," & _
                    "Pincode, Country, Flag) VALUES (" & mContactId & ", '" & _
                    mResStreet & "', '" & mResCity & "', '" & mResState & "', '" & _
                    mResPin & "', '" & mResCountry & "', 'R')"
            mRs_ContactMaster.Open mSqlString, mCn_CardBook, adOpenKeyset, _
                                    adLockOptimistic
    End If
End Sub
```

CHAP 04 — A PERSONAL INFORMATION MANAGER: THE WORKING

The **UpdtResInfo()** subroutine checks whether the record exists in the **Contact_Detail** table for the current contact. If the record exists, it is updated with the new values, otherwise a new record gets inserted in the table.

```
Public Sub UpdtResInfo()
'Assigning the form field's values to variables
    mResStreet = fixQuote(Trim(txtHStreet.Text))
    mResCity = fixQuote(Trim(txtHCity.Text))
    mResState = fixQuote(Trim(txtHState.Text))
    mResPin = Trim(txtHPin.Text)
    mResCountry = fixQuote(Trim(txtHCountry.Text))
    If mResStreet <> "" Or mResCity <> "" Or mResState <> "" Or mResPin <> "" _
    Or mResCountry <> "" Then
        If mRs_ContactMaster.State = 1 Then
            mRs_ContactMaster.Close
        End If
        mSqlString = "SELECT * FROM Contact_Detail WHERE Id = " & _
                    mContactId & " AND Flag = 'R'"
        mRs_ContactMaster.Open mSqlString, mCn_CardBook, adOpenKeyset, _
                    adLockOptimistic
        If mRs_ContactMaster.RecordCount > 0 Then
            mRs_ContactMaster.Close
            mSqlString = "UPDATE Contact_Detail Set Address = '" & mResStreet & _
                    "', City = '" & mResCity & "', State = '" & mResState & _
                    "', Pincode = '" & mResPin & "', Country = '" & _
                    mResCountry & "', Flag = 'R' WHERE Id = " & _
                    mContactId & " AND Flag = 'R'"
            mRs_ContactMaster.Open mSqlString, mCn_CardBook, adOpenKeyset, _
                    adLockOptimistic
        Else
            mRs_ContactMaster.Close
            mSqlString = "INSERT INTO Contact_Detail (Id, Address, City," & _
                    "State, Pincode, Country, Flag) VALUES (" & _
                    mContactId & ", '" & mResStreet & "', '" & mResCity & _
                    "', '" & mResState & "', '" & mResPin & "', '" & _
                    mResCountry & "', 'R')"
            mRs_ContactMaster.Open mSqlString, mCn_CardBook, adOpenKeyset, _
                    adLockOptimistic
        End If
```

```vb
            If mRs_ContactMaster.State = 1 Then
                mRs_ContactMaster.Close
            End If
        End If
End Sub
```

The **UpdtMasterInfo()** subroutine updates the current record in the **Contact_Master** table.

```vb
Public Sub UpdtMasterInfo()
    Call Domain_Master
'Assigning the form field's values to variables
    mTitle = cboTitle
    mFname = Trim(txtFname.Text)
    mLname = Trim(txtLname.Text)
    mNote = Trim(txtNote.Text)
    If mRs_ContactMaster.State = 1 Then
        mRs_ContactMaster.Close
    End If
    If chkBuss = 1 And chkPer = 1 Then
        mRelation = "B"
    ElseIf chkBuss = 1 And chkPer = 0 Then
        mRelation = "O"
    ElseIf chkPer = 1 And chkBuss = 0 Then
        mRelation = "P"
    End If
    mSqlString = "SELECT * FROM Contact_Master WHERE Id = " & mContactId & ""
    mRs_ContactMaster.Open mSqlString, mCn_CardBook, adOpenKeyset, _
                        adLockOptimistic
    If mRs_ContactMaster.RecordCount > 0 Then
    'Moving the variable values into recordset fields
        mRs_ContactMaster.Fields("Title") = mTitle
        mRs_ContactMaster.Fields("F_Name") = mFname
        mRs_ContactMaster.Fields("L_Name") = mLname
        mRs_ContactMaster.Fields("Note") = mNote
        If Trim(cboDomain.Text) = "" Then
            mRs_ContactMaster.Fields("Domain_Id") = 1
        Else
            mRs_ContactMaster.Fields("Domain_Id") = mDomain_Id
        End If
```

```
            mRs_ContactMaster.Fields("Relation") = mRelation
            mRs_ContactMaster.Update
        End If
        If mRs_ContactMaster.State = 1 Then
            mRs_ContactMaster.Close
        End If
End Sub
```

The **InsOffInfo()** subroutine inserts a record in the **Contact_Detail** table.

```
Public Sub InsOffInfo()
'Assigning the form field's values to variables
    mOffStreet = fixQuote(Trim(txtOStreet.Text))
    mOffCity = fixQuote(Trim(txtOCity.Text))
    mOffState = fixQuote(Trim(txtOState.Text))
    mOffPin = Trim(txtOPin.Text)
    mOffCountry = fixQuote(Trim(txtOCountry.Text))
    If mOffStreet <> "" Or mOffCity <> "" Or mOffState <> "" Or mOffPin <> "" & _
    Or mOffCountry <> "" Then
        mSqlString = "INSERT INTO Contact_Detail (Id, Address, City, State, " & _
                    Pincode, Country, Flag) VALUES (" & mContactId & _
                    "', '" & mOffStreet & "', '" & mOffCity & "', '" & mOffState & _
                    "', '" & mOffPin & "', '" & mOffCountry & "', 'O')"
        mRs_ContactMaster.Open mSqlString, mCn_CardBook, adOpenKeyset, _
                    adLockOptimistic
    End If
End Sub
```

The **UpdtOffInfo()** subroutine checks whether the record exists in the **Contact_Detail** table for the current contact. If there exists any record, it is updated with the new values, otherwise a new record gets inserted in the table.

```
Public Sub UpdtOffInfo()
'Assigning the form field's values to variables
    mOffStreet = fixQuote(Trim(txtOStreet.Text))
    mOffCity = fixQuote(Trim(txtOCity.Text))
    mOffState = fixQuote(Trim(txtOState.Text))
    mOffPin = Trim(txtOPin.Text)
    mOffCountry = fixQuote(Trim(txtOCountry.Text))
```

```
        If mOffStreet <> "" Or mOffCity <> "" Or mOffState <> "" Or mOffPin <> "" & _
        Or mOffCountry <> "" Then
            If mRs_ContactMaster.State = 1 Then
                mRs_ContactMaster.Close
            End If
            mSqlString = "SELECT * FROM Contact_Detail WHERE Id = " & _
                        mContactId & " AND Flag = 'O'"
            mRs_ContactMaster.Open mSqlString, mCn_CardBook, adOpenKeyset, _
                            adLockOptimistic
            If mRs_ContactMaster.RecordCount > 0 Then
                mRs_ContactMaster.Close
                mSqlString = "UPDATE Contact_Detail Set Address = '" & mOffStreet & _
                            "', City = '" & mOffCity & "', State = '" & mOffState & _
                            "', Pincode = '" & mOffPin & "', Country = '" & _
                            mOffCountry & "', Flag = 'O' WHERE Id = " & _
                            mContactId & " AND Flag = 'O'"
                mRs_ContactMaster.Open mSqlString, mCn_CardBook, adOpenKeyset, _
                                adLockOptimistic
            Else
                mRs_ContactMaster.Close
                mSqlString = "INSERT INTO Contact_Detail (Id, Address, City, & _
                            "State, Pincode, Country, Flag) VALUES (" & mContactId & _
                            ", '" & mOffStreet & "', '" & mOffCity & "', '" & _
                            mOffState & "', '" & mOffPin & "', '" & _
                            mOffCountry & "', 'O')"
                mRs_ContactMaster.Open mSqlString, mCn_CardBook, adOpenKeyset, _
                                adLockOptimistic
            End If
            If mRs_ContactMaster.State = 1 Then
                mRs_ContactMaster.Close
            End If
        End If
End Sub
```

CHAP 04 A PERSONAL INFORMATION MANAGER: THE WORKING

The **Rs2Form()** subroutine transfers the recordset field values to form fields, for the current contact id. The subroutine makes a call to the **PopForm** subroutine that actually transfers the recordset data into the form fields.

```
Public Sub Rs2Form()
    If mRs_ContactMaster.State = 1 Then
        mRs_ContactMaster.Close
    End If
        mSqlString = "SELECT * FROM Contact_Master"
    'Calling PopRs to open a recordset and check for records
        PopRs
End Sub
```

The **PopForm()** subroutine transfers data from the recordset into the form fields.

```
Public Sub PopForm()
    mContactId = mRs_ContactMaster.Fields("ID")
'Checking if the Title field of mRs_ContactMaster recordset is null
    If IsNull(mRs_ContactMaster.Fields("Title")) Then
        txtTitle.Text = ""
    Else
        txtTitle.Text = mRs_ContactMaster.Fields("Title")
    End If
    If IsNull(mRs_ContactMaster.Fields("F_Name")) Then
        txtFname.Text = ""
    Else
        txtFname.Text = mRs_ContactMaster.Fields("F_Name")
    End If
    If IsNull(mRs_ContactMaster.Fields("L_Name")) Then
        txtLname.Text = ""
    Else
        txtLname.Text = mRs_ContactMaster.Fields("L_Name")
    End If
    If IsNull(mRs_ContactMaster.Fields("Note")) Then
        txtNote.Text = ""
    Else
        txtNote.Text = mRs_ContactMaster.Fields("Note")
    End If
```

PRACTICAL VB 6 PROJECTS

```vb
    If mRs_ContactMaster.Fields("Relation") = "O" Then
        chkBuss.Value = 1
    ElseIf mRs_ContactMaster.Fields("Relation") = "P" Then
        chkPer.Value = 1
    ElseIf mRs_ContactMaster.Fields("Relation") = "B" Then
            chkBuss.Value = 1
            chkPer.Value = 1
    End If
    If txtFname.Text = "" And txtLname.Text = "" Then
        frmCardBook.Caption = "Card Book"
    Else
        'Assigning value to the frmCardBook form's caption property
        frmCardBook.Caption = "Card Book" + " [" + txtFname.Text + " " _
                            + txtLname.Text + "]"
    End If
    'The variable mDomain holds the value of Domain_Id from the
    'Contact_Master recordset
        mDomain = mRs_ContactMaster.Fields("Domain_Id")
End Sub
```

The **ViewCompInfo()** subroutine gets called when a user navigates through records in the database. The **ViewCompInfo()** subroutine displays company information of the current contact.

```vb
Public Sub ViewCompInfo()
    mSqlString = "SELECT * FROM Contact_CompanyInfo WHERE ID = " & mContactId & ""
    mRs_Add.Open mSqlString, mCn_CardBook, adOpenKeyset, adLockOptimistic
    If mRs_Add.RecordCount > 0 Then
    'Checking if the Company_Name field of the mRs_Add recordset is null
        If IsNull(mRs_Add.Fields("Company_Name")) Then
            txtComName.Text = ""
        Else
            txtComName.Text = mRs_Add.Fields("Company_Name")
        End If
        If IsNull(mRs_Add.Fields("Designation")) Then
            txtDesig.Text = ""
        Else
            txtDesig.Text = mRs_Add.Fields("Designation")
        End If
    End If
```

```
    mRs_Add.Close
    mSqlString = "SELECT * FROM Domain_Master WHERE Domain_Id = " & _
                 mDomain & ""
    mRs_Add.Open mSqlString, mCn_CardBook, adOpenKeyset, adLockOptimistic
    If mRs_Add.RecordCount > 0 Then
        cboDomain.Text = mRs_Add.Fields("Domain")
    End If
    mRs_Add.Close
End Sub
```

When a user navigates through the records in the database, the **ViewResAdd()** subroutine displays residential information of the current contact.

```
Public Sub ViewResAdd()
    mSqlString = "SELECT * FROM Contact_Detail WHERE ID = " & _
                 mContactId & " AND Flag = 'R'"
    mRs_Add.Open mSqlString, mCn_CardBook, adOpenKeyset, adLockOptimistic
    If mRs_Add.RecordCount > 0 Then
        If IsNull(mRs_Add.Fields("Address")) Then
            txtHStreet.Text = ""
        Else
            txtHStreet.Text = mRs_Add.Fields("Address")
        End If
        If IsNull(mRs_Add.Fields("City")) Then
            txtHCity.Text = ""
        Else
            txtHCity.Text = mRs_Add.Fields("City")
        End If
        If IsNull(mRs_Add.Fields("State")) Then
            txtHState.Text = ""
        Else
            txtHState.Text = mRs_Add.Fields("State")
        End If
        If IsNull(mRs_Add.Fields("Pincode")) Then
            txtHPin.Text = ""
        Else
            txtHPin.Text = mRs_Add.Fields("Pincode")
        End If
        'Checking whether the Country field of the mRs_Add recordset is null
```

```
            If IsNull(mRs_Add.Fields("Country")) Then
                txtHCountry.Text = ""
            Else
                txtHCountry.Text = mRs_Add.Fields("Country")
            End If
        End If
        mRs_Add.Close
End Sub
```

The **ViewOffAdd()** subroutine displays the office address of the current contact.

```
Public Sub ViewOffAdd()
    mSqlString = "SELECT * FROM Contact_Detail WHERE ID = " & _
                 mContactId & " AND Flag = 'O'"
    mRs_Add.Open mSqlString, mCn_CardBook, adOpenKeyset, adLockOptimistic
    If mRs_Add.RecordCount > 0 Then
        If IsNull(mRs_Add.Fields("Address")) Then
            txtOStreet.Text = ""
        Else
            txtOStreet.Text = mRs_Add.Fields("Address")
        End If
        If IsNull(mRs_Add.Fields("City")) Then
            txtOCity.Text = ""
        Else
            txtOCity.Text = mRs_Add.Fields("City")
        End If
        If IsNull(mRs_Add.Fields("State")) Then
            txtOState.Text = ""
        Else
            txtOState.Text = mRs_Add.Fields("State")
        End If
        If IsNull(mRs_Add.Fields("Pincode")) Then
            txtOPin.Text = ""
        Else
            txtOPin.Text = mRs_Add.Fields("Pincode")
        End If
```

```
        If IsNull(mRs_Add.Fields("Country")) Then
            txtOCountry.Text = ""
        Else
            txtOCountry.Text = mRs_Add.Fields("Country")
        End If
    End If
    mRs_Add.Close
End Sub
```

The **ViewResTel()**, **ViewResFax()** and **ViewMobileNo()** subroutines display residential telephone, mobile, fax numbers of the current contact when navigating through records.

```
Public Sub ViewResTel()
    mSqlString = "SELECT Tel_No FROM Contact_TelNo WHERE ID = "&mContactId&""
'Passing the SQL string to the ADODC recordset
    AdodcResTel.RecordSource = mSqlString
'Refreshing the ADODC recordset
    AdodcResTel.Refresh
    If AdodcResTel.Recordset.RecordCount > 0 Then
        mnuCall.Enabled = True
        tbrCardbook.Buttons.Item("Dial").Enabled = True
    Else
        mnuCall.Enabled = False
        tbrCardbook.Buttons.Item("Dial").Enabled = False
    End If
    mSqlString = "SELECT * FROM Contact_TelNo WHERE ID = " & _
                mContactId & "AND Flag = 'R'"
    AdodcResTel.RecordSource = mSqlString
    AdodcResTel.Refresh
End Sub

Public Sub ViewResFax()
    mSqlString = "SELECT * FROM Contact_FaxNo WHERE ID = " & _
                mContactId & " AND Flag = 'R'"
    AdodcResFax.RecordSource = mSqlString
    AdodcResFax.Refresh
End Sub
```

```vb
Public Sub ViewMobileNo()
    mSqlString = "SELECT * FROM Contact_TelNo WHERE ID = " & _
                mContactId & " AND Flag = 'M'"
    AdodcResMob.RecordSource = mSqlString
    AdodcResMob.Refresh
End Sub
```

The **ViewResEmail()** subroutine displays email addresses and company information of the current contact when a user is navigating through the records in the database.

```vb
Public Sub ViewResEmail()
    mSqlString = "SELECT Email_id FROM Contact_Email WHERE ID = " & _
                mContactId & ""
    AdodcResEmail.RecordSource = mSqlString
    AdodcResEmail.Refresh
    If AdodcResEmail.Recordset.RecordCount > 0 Then
        mnuEmail.Enabled = True
        tbrCardbook.Buttons.Item("Email").Enabled = True
    Else
        mnuEmail.Enabled = False
        tbrCardbook.Buttons.Item("Email").Enabled = False
    End If
    mSqlString = "SELECT * FROM Contact_Email WHERE ID = " & _
                mContactId & " AND Flag = 'R'"
    AdodcResEmail.RecordSource = mSqlString
    AdodcResEmail.Refresh
End Sub

Public Sub ViewResWeb()
    mSqlString = "SELECT * FROM Contact_WebAddress WHERE ID = " & _
                mContactId & "    AND Flag = 'R' "
    AdodcResWeb.RecordSource = mSqlString
    AdodcResWeb.Refresh
End Sub
```

The **ViewOffTel()** and **ViewOffFax()** subroutines display office telephone and fax numbers of the current contact when a user navigates through the records in the database.

```
Public Sub ViewOffTel()
    mSqlString = "SELECT * FROM Contact_TelNo WHERE ID = " & _
                mContactId & "   AND Flag = 'O' "
    AdodcOffTel.RecordSource = mSqlString
    AdodcOffTel.Refresh
End Sub

Public Sub ViewOffFax()
    mSqlString = "SELECT * FROM Contact_FaxNo WHERE ID = " & _
                mContactId & " AND Flag = 'O'"
    AdodcOffFax.RecordSource = mSqlString
    AdodcOffFax.Refresh
End Sub
```

The **ViewOffEmail()** and **ViewOffWeb()** subroutines transfer office email address and company email address respectively in the form fields while the user is viewing records in the database.

```
Public Sub ViewOffEmail()
    mSqlString = "SELECT * FROM Contact_Email WHERE ID = " & _
                mContactId & " AND Flag = 'O'"
    AdodcOffMail.RecordSource = mSqlString
    AdodcOffMail.Refresh
End Sub

Public Sub ViewOffWeb()
    mSqlString = "SELECT * FROM Contact_WebAddress WHERE ID = " & _
                mContactId & " AND Flag = 'O'"
    AdodcOffWeb.RecordSource = mSqlString
    AdodcOffWeb.Refresh
End Sub
```

The **ViewBirth()** and **ViewAnni()** subroutines display the birthdays and anniversary days of the current contact when a user navigates through dat in the database.

```
Public Sub ViewBirth()
    mSqlString = "SELECT * FROM BirDate WHERE ID = " & mContactId & ""
    AdodcBirth.RecordSource = mSqlString
    AdodcBirth.Refresh
End Sub

Public Sub ViewAnni()
    mSqlString = "SELECT * FROM AnniDate WHERE ID = " & mContactId & ""
    AdodcAnni.RecordSource = mSqlString
    AdodcAnni.Refresh
End Sub
```

The **ClrGrid()** subroutine clears all the data grids used in the form. It is accomplished by firing a query that returns no rows from the database/table.

```
Public Sub ClrGrid()
    mSqlString = "SELECT * FROM Contact_TelNo WHERE ID = 0"
    AdodcResTel.RecordSource = mSqlString
    AdodcResTel.Refresh
    mSqlString = "SELECT * FROM Contact_FaxNo WHERE ID = 0"
    AdodcResFax.RecordSource = mSqlString
    AdodcResFax.Refresh
    mSqlString = "SELECT * FROM Contact_TelNo WHERE ID = 0"
    AdodcResMob.RecordSource = mSqlString
    AdodcResMob.Refresh
    mSqlString = "SELECT * FROM Contact_Email WHERE ID = 0"
    AdodcResEmail.RecordSource = mSqlString
    AdodcResEmail.Refresh
    mSqlString = "SELECT * FROM Contact_WebAddress WHERE ID = 0"
    AdodcResWeb.RecordSource = mSqlString
    AdodcResWeb.Refresh
    mSqlString = "SELECT * FROM Contact_TelNo WHERE ID = 0"
    AdodcOffTel.RecordSource = mSqlString
    AdodcOffTel.Refresh
    mSqlString = "SELECT * FROM Contact_FaxNo WHERE ID = 0"
    AdodcOffFax.RecordSource = mSqlString
    AdodcOffFax.Refresh
```

```
    mSqlString = "SELECT * FROM Contact_Email WHERE ID = 0"
    AdodcOffMail.RecordSource = mSqlString
    AdodcOffMail.Refresh
    mSqlString = "SELECT * FROM Contact_WebAddress WHERE ID = 0"
    AdodcOffWeb.RecordSource = mSqlString
    AdodcOffWeb.Refresh
    mSqlString = "SELECT * FROM BirDate WHERE ID = 0"
    AdodcBirth.RecordSource = mSqlString
    AdodcBirth.Refresh
    mSqlString = "SELECT * FROM AnniDate WHERE ID = 0"
    AdodcAnni.RecordSource = mSqlString
    AdodcAnni.Refresh
End Sub
```

The **AddSaveMode()** subroutine gets called when a user is in **add mode** and clicks the **save** button or selects the **save option** from the menu. The subroutine saves a record in the **Contact_Master** table.

```
Public Sub AddSaveMode()
'Checking for empty form fields
    If cboTitle = "" And txtFname.Text = "" And txtLname.Text = "" Then
        MsgBox "Following fields cannot be left empty" & vbCrLf & "Title, First Name, _
                Last Name", vbInformation
    ElseIf chkBuss = 0 And chkPer = 0 Then
        MsgBox "Select relation type", vbInformation
    Else
    'Checking the values of mMode and mTempCheck
        If mMode = "A" And mTempCheck = "T" Then
        'Calling master subroutine
            Call master
            mSqlString = "UPDATE Contact_Master SET Flag = 0 WHERE Id = " & _
                        mContactId & ""
            mRs_ContactMaster.Open mSqlString, mCn_CardBook, adOpenKeyset, _
                        adLockOptimistic
        'Assigning a value to the mSavFlg variable
            mSavFlg = "T"
        End If
```

```vb
        If mMode = "A" And mTempCheck = "F" Then
            mSqlString = "UPDATE Contact_Master SET Flag = 0 WHERE Id = " & _
                    mContactId & ""
            mRs_ContactMaster.Open mSqlString, mCn_CardBook, adOpenKeyset, _
                        adLockOptimistic
            mSavFlg = "T"
        'Calling InsResInfo to load residence information in the database
            InsResInfo
        'Calling insOffInfo to load office information in the database
            InsOffInfo
        'Calling InsCompInfo to load Company information in the database
            InsCompInfo
        'Calling UpdtGrids to load grid data in the database
            UpdtGrids
        End If
        MsgBox "Current record has saved", vbInformation
        Call mnuViewRec_Click
    End If
End Sub
```

The **UpdtSaveMode()** subroutine gets called when a user is in the update mode and clicks the **save button** in the toolbar or selects the save option in the menu to save an updated record.

```vb
Public Sub UpdtSaveMode()
    If cboTitle = "" And txtFname.Text = "" And txtLname.Text = "" Then
        MsgBox "Following fields cannot be left empty" & vbCrLf & _
                "Title, First Name, Last Name", vbInformation
    Else
    'Checking the value of mMode variable
        If mMode = "M" Then
            If mRs_ContactMaster.State = 1 Then
                mRs_ContactMaster.Close
            End If
        'Calling UpdtMasterInfo to update personal information
        'in the database
            UpdtMasterInfo
```

```
        'Calling UpdtCompInfo to update company information
        'in the database
            UpdtCompInfo
        'Calling UpdtResInfo to update residence information
        'in the database
            UpdtResInfo
        'Calling UpdtOffInfo to update office information in the database
            UpdtOffInfo
        'Calling UpdtGrids to enter grid data in database
            UpdtGrids
            MsgBox "Current record has saved", vbInformation
        End If
    End If
    Call mnuViewRec_Click
End Sub
```

The **UpdtGrids()** subroutine updates all recordsets with new values entered into each data grid.

```
Public Sub UpdtGrids()
    If AdodcResTel.Recordset.RecordCount <> 0 Then
    'Moving the data grid's values into the recordset
        AdodcResTel.Recordset.Fields(1) = dgdHPhone.Text
        AdodcResTel.Recordset.Update
    End If
    If AdodcResFax.Recordset.RecordCount <> 0 Then
        AdodcResFax.Recordset.Fields(1) = dgdHFax.Text
        AdodcResFax.Recordset.Update
    End If
    If AdodcResMob.Recordset.RecordCount <> 0 Then
        AdodcResMob.Recordset.Fields(1) = dgdHMob.Text
        AdodcResMob.Recordset.Update
    End If
    If AdodcResEmail.Recordset.RecordCount <> 0 Then
        AdodcResEmail.Recordset.Fields(1) = dgdHEmail.Text
        AdodcResEmail.Recordset.Update
    End If
```

```
        If AdodcResWeb.Recordset.RecordCount <> 0 Then
            AdodcResWeb.Recordset.Fields(1) = dgdHWeb.Text
            AdodcResWeb.Recordset.Update
        End If
        If AdodcOffTel.Recordset.RecordCount <> 0 Then
            AdodcOffTel.Recordset.Fields(1) = dgdOPhone.Text
            AdodcOffTel.Recordset.Update
        End If
        If AdodcOffFax.Recordset.RecordCount <> 0 Then
            AdodcOffFax.Recordset.Fields(1) = dgdOFax.Text
            AdodcOffFax.Recordset.Update
        End If
        If AdodcOffMail.Recordset.RecordCount <> 0 Then
            AdodcOffMail.Recordset.Fields(1) = dgdOEmail.Text
            AdodcOffMail.Recordset.Update
        End If
        If AdodcOffWeb.Recordset.RecordCount <> 0 Then
            AdodcOffWeb.Recordset.Fields(1) = dgdOWeb.Text
            AdodcOffWeb.Recordset.Update
        End If
        If AdodcBirth.Recordset.RecordCount <> 0 Then
            AdodcBirth.Recordset.Fields(2) = dgdBirth.Text
            AdodcBirth.Recordset.Update
        End If
        If AdodcAnni.Recordset.RecordCount <> 0 Then
            AdodcAnni.Recordset.Fields(2) = dgdAnni.Text
            AdodcAnni.Recordset.Update
        End If
End Sub
```

The **PopRs()** subroutine opens a recordset and checks whether the recordset holds any records. If a recordset holds more than 0 records, the subroutine enables appropriate form controls.

```vb
Public Sub PopRs()
    mRs_ContactMaster.Open mSqlString, mCn_CardBook, adOpenKeyset, _
                    adLockOptimistic
    mCount = mRs_ContactMaster.RecordCount
    If mCount > 0 Then
    'Calling EnbNav which enables navigational buttons
        EnblNav
        tabMain.TabEnabled(0) = True
        tabMain.TabEnabled(1) = True
        tabMain.TabEnabled(2) = True
        tabMain.TabEnabled(3) = True
        cboTitle.Visible = False
        txtTitle.Visible = True
    'Calling PopForm to populate form fields
        PopForm
    Else
        frmCardBook.Caption = "Card Book"
    'Calling DisNav which disables navigational buttons
        DisNav
        tabMain.TabEnabled(0) = False
        tabMain.TabEnabled(1) = False
        tabMain.TabEnabled(2) = False
        tabMain.TabEnabled(3) = False
        mnuDelete.Enabled = False
        mnuModify.Enabled = False
        tbrCardbook.Buttons.Item("Delete").Enabled = False
        tbrCardbook.Buttons.Item("Modify").Enabled = False
    End If
End Sub
```

The **FillDomain()** is used to populate the cboDomain combo box with domain names retrieved from the Domain_Master table.

```vb
Public Sub FillDomain()
    If mRs_Domain.State = 1 Then
        mRs_Domain.Close
    End If
    mSqlString = "SELECT DISTINCT Domain FROM Domain_Master"
    mRs_Domain.Open mSqlString, mCn_CardBook, adOpenKeyset, adLockOptimistic
    mCount = mRs_Domain.RecordCount
```

```vb
        If mCount = 0 Then
            Exit Sub
        Else
            mRs_Domain.MoveFirst
            For mTrace = 0 To mCount - 1
                'Adding an item in the drop down listbox
                cboDomain.AddItem mRs_Domain.Fields("Domain"), mTrace
                mRs_Domain.MoveNext
            Next
        End If
        cboDomain.Refresh
        mRs_Domain.Close
End Sub
```

The **Domain_Master()** subroutine inserts a new record in the Domain_Master table. If the user does not select any domain from the domain names provided, the user is allowed to type in a new domain name. This added entry is then inserted as a new record in the Domain_Master table.

```vb
Public Sub Domain_Master()
    If Trim(cboDomain.Text) <> "" Then
        mDomain = cboDomain.Text
        mSqlString = "SELECT Domain FROM Domain_Master Where Domain = '" & _
                    mDomain & "'"
        mRs_Domain.Open mSqlString, mCn_CardBook, adOpenKeyset, _
                    adLockOptimistic
        mCount = mRs_Domain.RecordCount
        If mCount = 0 Then
            mRs_Domain.Close
            mSqlString = "INSERT INTO Domain_Master (Domain) VALUES ('" & _
                        mDomain & "')"
            mRs_Domain.Open mSqlString, mCn_CardBook, adOpenKeyset, _
                        adLockOptimistic
        End If
        If mRs_Domain.State = 1 Then
            mRs_Domain.Close
        End If
        mSqlString = "SELECT * FROM Domain_Master Where Domain = '" & _
                    mDomain & "'"
```

```
        mRs_Domain.Open mSqlString, mCn_CardBook, adOpenKeyset, _
                adLockOptimistic
        mDomain_Id = mRs_Domain.Fields("Domain_Id")
        mRs_Domain.Close
    End If
End Sub
'***************** APPLICATION SUBROUTINES ENDS ***********************
'*********************************************************************
```

This section clears all the controls on the form. Each subroutine is used to clear the form fields associated with a particular tab.

```
'*********************************************************************
'*************** SUBROUTINE TO CLEAR FORM FIELD BEGINS ***************
Public Sub ClrPerInfo()
    txtTitle.Text = ""
    txtFname.Text = ""
    txtLname.Text = ""
    txtNote.Text = ""
    chkBuss.Value = 0
    chkPer.Value = 0
End Sub

Public Sub ClrResInfo()
    txtHStreet.Text = ""
    txtHCity.Text = ""
    txtHState.Text = ""
    txtHPin.Text = ""
    txtHCountry.Text = ""
End Sub

Public Sub ClrCompInfo()
    txtComName.Text = ""
    txtDesig.Text = ""
    cboDomain.Clear
End Sub
```

```vb
Public Sub ClrOffInfo()
    txtOStreet.Text = ""
    txtOCity.Text = ""
    txtOState.Text = ""
    txtOPin.Text = ""
    txtOCountry.Text = ""
End Sub

Public Sub ClrProffInfo()
    txtComName.Text = ""
    txtDesig.Text = ""
End Sub
'****************** SUBROUTINE TO CLEAR FORM FEILD ENDS **************
'*********************************************************************
'*********************************************************************
'**SUBROUTINEs FOR ENABLING & DISABLING MENU ITEMS & TOOLBAR BUTTONS***
'********************BASED TRUTH TABLE BEGINS ************************
```

The **NoMode()** subroutine is called to determine the state of the form's menubar and toolbar options so as to allow **Insert** and **View** operations only.

This subroutine is called when the form loads for the first time.

```vb
Public Sub NoMode()
'Disabling the frames on the form
    fraName.Enabled = False
    fraCompInfo.Enabled = False
    fraNote.Enabled = False
    fraResAdd.Enabled = False
    fraOffAdd.Enabled = False
'Enabling and disabling the menu options
    mnuAdd.Enabled = True
    mnuModify.Enabled = False
    mnuDelete.Enabled = False
    mnuSave.Enabled = False
    mnuExit.Enabled = True
    mnuView.Enabled = True
    mnuViewRec.Enabled = True
    mnuFirst.Enabled = False
    mnuNext.Enabled = False
    mnuPrior.Enabled = False
```

```
    mnuLast.Enabled = False
    mnuSearch.Enabled = True
    mnuAction.Enabled = False
'Enabling and disabling the toolbar buttons
    tbrCardbook.Buttons.Item("Add").Enabled = True
    tbrCardbook.Buttons.Item("Modify").Enabled = False
    tbrCardbook.Buttons.Item("View").Enabled = True
    tbrCardbook.Buttons.Item("Delete").Enabled = False
    tbrCardbook.Buttons.Item("Save").Enabled = False
    tbrCardbook.Buttons.Item("First").Enabled = False
    tbrCardbook.Buttons.Item("Prior").Enabled = False
    tbrCardbook.Buttons.Item("Next").Enabled = False
    tbrCardbook.Buttons.Item("Last").Enabled = False
    tbrCardbook.Buttons.Item("Search").Enabled = True
    tbrCardbook.Buttons.Item("Dial").Enabled = False
    tbrCardbook.Buttons.Item("Email").Enabled = False
'Setting the tabEnabled property to False
    tabMain.TabEnabled(0) = False
    tabMain.TabEnabled(1) = False
    tabMain.TabEnabled(2) = False
    tabMain.TabEnabled(3) = False
End Sub
```

The **InsMode()** subroutine is called to determine the state of form's menubar and toolbar options to allow **only a save operation**.

This subroutine is called when a record is either inserted or updated.

```
Public Sub InsMode()
'Enabling and disabling the menu options
    nuAdd.Enabled = False
    mnuModify.Enabled = False
    mnuDelete.Enabled = False
    mnuSave.Enabled = True
    mnuExit.Enabled = True
    mnuView.Enabled = False
    mnuAction.Enabled = False
'Enabling and disabling the toolbar buttons
    tbrCardbook.Buttons.Item("Add").Enabled = False
    tbrCardbook.Buttons.Item("Modify").Enabled = False
```

PRACTICAL VB 6 PROJECTS CHAP 04

```vb
    tbrCardbook.Buttons.Item("View").Enabled = False
    tbrCardbook.Buttons.Item("Delete").Enabled = False
    tbrCardbook.Buttons.Item("Save").Enabled = True
    tbrCardbook.Buttons.Item("First").Enabled = False
    tbrCardbook.Buttons.Item("Prior").Enabled = False
    tbrCardbook.Buttons.Item("Next").Enabled = False
    tbrCardbook.Buttons.Item("Last").Enabled = False
    tbrCardbook.Buttons.Item("Search").Enabled = False
    tbrCardbook.Buttons.Item("Dial").Enabled = False
    tbrCardbook.Buttons.Item("Email").Enabled = False
'Calling GrdBtnEnbl to enable the buttons on the grid
    GrdBtnEnbl
    tabMain.TabEnabled(0) = True
    tabMain.TabEnabled(1) = True
    tabMain.TabEnabled(2) = True
    tabMain.TabEnabled(3) = True
End Sub
```

The **ViewMode()** subroutine is called to determine the state of form's menubar and toolbar options so as to allow data manipulation and navigation operations.

A call is made to this subroutine when a user wishes to view records in the database.

```vb
Public Sub ViewMode()
'Enabling and disabling menu options
    mnuAdd.Enabled = True
    mnuModify.Enabled = True
    mnuDelete.Enabled = True
    mnuSave.Enabled = False
    mnuExit.Enabled = True
    mnuView.Enabled = True
    mnuSearch.Enabled = False
    mnuViewRec.Enabled = False
    mnuFirst.Enabled = True
    mnuPrior.Enabled = True
    mnuNext.Enabled = True
    mnuLast.Enabled = True
    mnuAction.Enabled = True
```

```
'Enabling and disabling the toolbar buttons
    tbrCardbook.Buttons.Item("Add").Enabled = True
    tbrCardbook.Buttons.Item("Modify").Enabled = True
    tbrCardbook.Buttons.Item("View").Enabled = False
    tbrCardbook.Buttons.Item("Delete").Enabled = True
    tbrCardbook.Buttons.Item("Save").Enabled = False
    tbrCardbook.Buttons.Item("First").Enabled = True
    tbrCardbook.Buttons.Item("Prior").Enabled = True
    tbrCardbook.Buttons.Item("Next").Enabled = True
    tbrCardbook.Buttons.Item("Last").Enabled = True
    tbrCardbook.Buttons.Item("Search").Enabled = False
    tbrCardbook.Buttons.Item("Dial").Enabled = True
    tbrCardbook.Buttons.Item("Email").Enabled = True
'Calling GrdBtnDsbl that disables the buttons on the grid
    GrdBtnDsbl
End Sub
```

The **GrdBtnDsbl()** subroutine disables all the command buttons placed on the data grid.

```
Public Sub GrdBtnDsbl()
'Disabling the buttons on the data grid
    cmdHPhone.Enabled = False
    cmdHPhoneDel.Enabled = False
    cmdHFax.Enabled = False
    cmdHFaxDel.Enabled = False
    cmdHMob.Enabled = False
    cmdHMobDel.Enabled = False
    cmdHEmail.Enabled = False
    cmdHEmailDel.Enabled = False
    cmdHWeb.Enabled = False
    cmdHWebDel.Enabled = False
    cmdOPhone.Enabled = False
    cmdOPhoneDel.Enabled = False
    cmdOFax.Enabled = False
    cmdOFaxDel.Enabled = False
    cmdOMob.Enabled = False
    cmdOMobDel.Enabled = False
    cmdOEmail.Enabled = False
    cmdOEmailDel.Enabled = False
```

```vb
        cmdOWeb.Enabled = False
        cmdOWebDel.Enabled = False
        cmdAnniAdd.Enabled = False
        cmdAnniDelete.Enabled = False
        cmdBirthAdd.Enabled = False
        cmdBirthDel.Enabled = False
End Sub
```

The **GrdBtnEnbl()** enables all the command buttons placed on the data grid.

```vb
Public Sub GrdBtnEnbl()
'Enabling the buttons on the data grid
    cmdHPhone.Enabled = True
    cmdHPhoneDel.Enabled = True
    cmdHFax.Enabled = True
    cmdHFaxDel.Enabled = True
    cmdHMob.Enabled = True
    cmdHMobDel.Enabled = True
    cmdHEmail.Enabled = True
    cmdHEmailDel.Enabled = True
    cmdHWeb.Enabled = True
    cmdHWebDel.Enabled = True
    cmdOPhone.Enabled = True
    cmdOPhoneDel.Enabled = True
    cmdOFax.Enabled = True
    cmdOFaxDel.Enabled = True
    cmdOMob.Enabled = True
    cmdOMobDel.Enabled = True
    cmdOEmail.Enabled = True
    cmdOEmailDel.Enabled = True
    cmdOWeb.Enabled = True
    cmdOWebDel.Enabled = True
    cmdBirthAdd.Enabled = True
    cmdBirthDel.Enabled = True
    cmdAnniAdd.Enabled = True
    cmdAnniDelete.Enabled = True
End Sub
```

The **DataEnterMode()** subroutine enables all the data capture objects on the form. This subroutine is called when a record is inserted or updated.

```
Public Sub DataEnterMode()
'Enabling form fields
    cboTitle.Enabled = True
    txtTitle.Enabled = True
    txtFname.Enabled = True
    txtLname.Enabled = True
    chkBuss.Enabled = True
    chkPer.Enabled = True
    cboDomain.Enabled = True
    txtComName.Enabled = True
    txtDesig.Enabled = True
    txtNote.Enabled = True
    txtHStreet.Enabled = True
    txtHCity.Enabled = True
    txtHState.Enabled = True
    txtHPin.Enabled = True
    txtHCountry.Enabled = True
    txtOStreet.Enabled = True
    txtOCity.Enabled = True
    txtOState.Enabled = True
    txtOPin.Enabled = True
    txtOCountry.Enabled = True
'Setting the FontBold property of the textboxes to False
    txtTitle.FontBold = False
    txtFname.FontBold = False
    txtLname.FontBold = False
    txtComName.FontBold = False
    txtDesig.FontBold = False
    txtNote.FontBold = False
    txtHStreet.FontBold = False
    txtHCity.FontBold = False
    txtHState.FontBold = False
    txtHPin.FontBold = False
    txtHCountry.FontBold = False
    txtOStreet.FontBold = False
    txtOCity.FontBold = False
    txtOState.FontBold = False
```

```
        txtOPin.FontBold = False
        txtOCountry.FontBold = False
        cboDomain.FontBold = False
'Setting a value for the check box
        chkBuss.Value = 1
End Sub
```

The **DataViewMode()** subroutine disables all the data capture objects on the form. This subroutine is called when a user is viewing data.

```
Public Sub DataViewMode()
'Disabling form fields
        cboTitle.Enabled = False
        txtTitle.Enabled = False
        txtFname.Enabled = False
        txtLname.Enabled = False
        chkBuss.Enabled = False
        chkPer.Enabled = False
        txtNote.Enabled = False
        txtComName.Enabled = False
        txtDesig.Enabled = False
        cboDomain.Enabled = False
        txtHStreet.Enabled = False
        txtHCity.Enabled = False
        txtHState.Enabled = False
        txtHPin.Enabled = False
        txtHCountry.Enabled = False
        txtOStreet.Enabled = False
        txtOCity.Enabled = False
        txtOState.Enabled = False
        txtOPin.Enabled = False
        txtOCountry.Enabled = False
'Setting the FontBold property of the textboxes to True
        txtTitle.FontBold = True
        txtFname.FontBold = True
        txtLname.FontBold = True
        txtNote.FontBold = True
        txtComName.FontBold = True
        txtDesig.FontBold = True
        txtHStreet.FontBold = True
```

```
    txtHCity.FontBold = True
    txtHState.FontBold = True
    txtHPin.FontBold = True
    txtHCountry.FontBold = True
    txtOStreet.FontBold = True
    txtOCity.FontBold = True
    txtOState.FontBold = True
    txtOPin.FontBold = True
    txtOCountry.FontBold = True
    cboDomain.FontBold = True
'Setting datagrid properties
    dgdOPhone.AllowUpdate = False
    dgdOFax.AllowUpdate = False
    dgdOMob.AllowUpdate = False
    dgdOEmail.AllowUpdate = False
    dgdOWeb.AllowUpdate = False
    dgdHPhone.AllowUpdate = False
    dgdHFax.AllowUpdate = False
    dgdHMob.AllowUpdate = False
    dgdHEmail.AllowUpdate = False
    dgdHWeb.AllowUpdate = False
    dgdAnni.Enabled = True
    dgdBirth.Enabled = True
    dgdBirth.AllowUpdate = True
    dgdAnni.AllowUpdate = True
End Sub
```

The **DisNav()** subroutine disables all data navigation buttons on the toolbar and menubar options.

```
Public Sub DisNav()
'Enabling and disabling menu options
    mnuViewRec.Enabled = True
    mnuSearch.Enabled = True
    mnuFirst.Enabled = False
    mnuPrior.Enabled = False
    mnuNext.Enabled = False
    mnuLast.Enabled = False
```

```
'Enabling and disabling toolbar buttons
    tbrCardbook.Buttons.Item("View").Enabled = True
    tbrCardbook.Buttons.Item("First").Enabled = False
    tbrCardbook.Buttons.Item("Prior").Enabled = False
    tbrCardbook.Buttons.Item("Next").Enabled = False
    tbrCardbook.Buttons.Item("Last").Enabled = False
    tbrCardbook.Buttons.Item("Search").Enabled = True
End Sub
```

The **EnblNav()** subroutine enables all data navigation buttons on the toolbar and menubar options.

```
Public Sub EnblNav()
'Enabling menu options
    mnuSearch.Enabled = True
    mnuFirst.Enabled = True
    mnuPrior.Enabled = True
    mnuNext.Enabled = True
    mnuLast.Enabled = True
'Enabling toolbar buttons
    tbrCardbook.Buttons.Item("First").Enabled = True
    tbrCardbook.Buttons.Item("Prior").Enabled = True
    tbrCardbook.Buttons.Item("Next").Enabled = True
    tbrCardbook.Buttons.Item("Last").Enabled = True
    tbrCardbook.Buttons.Item("Search").Enabled = True
End Sub
'**SUBROUTINE FOR ENABLING & DISABLING MENU ITEMS & TOOLBAR BUTTONS ***
'******************** BASED TRUTH TABLE ENDS ************************
'********************************************************************
```

PROJECT CODE FOR FrmDial.frm

```vb
Option Explicit
'Creating object variables for later use
Dim mSqlString As String
Dim mName As String
Dim mType As String
Dim mTelNo As String
Dim mDisplay As String
Dim mDialDisp As String
Dim FlsFlg As String

Dim mMsgResponse As Integer
Dim mCheck As Integer
Dim mCount As Integer
Dim mMidPoint As Integer
Dim mEndPoint As Integer
Dim mBeginPoint As Integer
Public mContactId As Integer
Dim Success As Integer

Dim lonTAPIStatus  As Long

'*************************************************************
'*********** FUNCTIONALITY OF THE FORM LOAD EVENT BEGINS ************
Public Sub Form_Load()
'Setting the form's height and width attributes
    frmDial.Width = 4605
    frmDial.Height = 2490
'Setting an icon for UI objects using the LoadPicture function
    frmDial.Icon = LoadPicture(App.Path & "\icon\Card.ico")
    cmdAbort.Picture = LoadPicture(App.Path & "\icon\buttoncancel.bmp")
    cmdDial.Picture = LoadPicture(App.Path & "\icon\buttontelc.bmp")
    cmdCallPrior.Picture = LoadPicture(App.Path & "\icon\prior.bmp")
    cmdCallNext.Picture = LoadPicture(App.Path & "\icon\next.bmp")
    cmdCallFirst.Picture = LoadPicture(App.Path & "\icon\first.bmp")
    cmdCallLast.Picture = LoadPicture(App.Path & "\icon\last.bmp")
```

```vb
'Assigning the value of mContactId of the frmCardBook form to the
 variable mContactId
    mContactId = frmCardBook.mContactId
'Concatenating the first name and last name and storing it in the
 variable mName
    mName = Trim(frmCardBook.txtFname) + " " + Trim(frmCardBook.txtLname)
'Calling a subroutine FillComb to populate the cboNumber combobox
    Call FillComb
'Setting the Timer interval property
    Timer1.Interval = GetCaretBlinkTime()
    Timer1.Enabled = False
End Sub

Public Sub Form_GotFocus()
    Timer1.Enabled = False
End Sub

Public Sub Form_LostFocus()
    Timer1.Enabled = True
End Sub

Public Sub Form_Resize()
'Setting the Top and Left attributes of the form to ensure that the
 search form will always be centered even if the form window is resized
 by the user
    frmDial.Top = (Screen.Height - frmDial.Height) \ 2
    frmDial.Left = (Screen.Width - frmDial.Width) \ 2
End Sub

'*********** FUNCTIONALITY FOR THE FORM LOAD EVENT ENDS ************
'******************************************************************
```

```
'*****************************************************************
'*********** FUNCTIONALITY OF THE COMMAND BUTTONS BEGINS **********
Public Sub cmdCallFirst_Click()
'Setting the mRs_TelTrack recordset pointer to the First record
    mRs_TelTrack.MoveFirst
'Calling a view subroutine that displays time and notes
    Call view
End Sub

Public Sub cmdCallLast_Click()
'Setting the mRs_TelTrack recordset pointer to the Last record
    mRs_TelTrack.MoveLast
    Call view
End Sub

Public Sub cmdCallNext_Click()
'Setting the mRs_TelTrack recordset pointer to the Next record
    mRs_TelTrack.MoveNext
'Checking whether the recordset pointer has moved beyond the LAST record in the recordset
    If mRs_TelTrack.EOF Then
        mMsgResponse = MsgBox("You are currently at the last record", vbOKOnly _
                            + vbInformation)
            mRs_TelTrack.MoveLast
    End If
    Call view
End Sub

Public Sub cmdCallPrior_Click()
'Setting the mRs_TelTrack recordset pointer to the Previous record
    mRs_TelTrack.MovePrevious
'Checking whether the recordset pointer has moved beyond the FIRST record in the recordset
    If mRs_TelTrack.BOF Then
        mMsgResponse = MsgBox("You are currently at the first record", vbOKOnly _
                            + vbInformation)
            mRs_TelTrack.MoveFirst
    End If
    Call view
End Sub
```

```vb
Public Sub cmdCancel_Click()
'Unloading the form frmDial
    Unload frmDial
'Enabling the form frmCardBook
    frmCardBook.Enabled = True
End Sub

Public Sub cmdChange_Click()
'Calling the Form_Load handler
    Form_Load
'Setting the fraLoad's frame visible property to True
    fraLoad.Visible = True
End Sub

Public Sub cmdNew_Click()
    Timer1.Enabled = False
    cmdNew.Enabled = False
    cmdNewSave.Enabled = True
'Checking whether fraPrevious and fraNew frames are visible
    If fraPrevious.Visible = True And fraNew.Visible = True Then
        Exit Sub
    Else
        If fraPrevious.Visible = False Then
'Setting attributes for the frmDial form and fraNew frame
            frmDial.Height = 4700
            fraNew.Visible = True
            fraNew.Top = 2085
        Else
            frmDial.Height = 6540
            fraNew.Visible = True
            fraNew.Top = 3950
        End If
    End If
End Sub

Public Sub cmdNewAbort_Click()
'Calling the cmdAbort_Click handler
    cmdAbort_Click
End Sub
```

```vb
Public Sub cmdNewSave_Click()
'Checking whether the mRs_TelTrack recordset is open
    If mRs_TelTrack.State = 1 Then
    'Closing the mRs_TelTrack recordset
        mRs_TelTrack.Close
    End If
'Storing an SQL query into the variable mSqlString
    mSqlString = "SELECT * FROM Contact_TelTrack WHERE ID = " & _
                mContactId & ""
'Opening the mRs_TelTrack recordset
    mRs_TelTrack.Open mSqlString, mCn_CardBook, adOpenKeyset, adLockOptimistic
'Adding a blank record to the mRs_TelTrack recordset
    mRs_TelTrack.AddNew
'Inserting values into the Id and Note fields of the mRs_TelTrack recordset
    mRs_TelTrack.Fields("Id") = mContactId
    mRs_TelTrack.Fields("Note") = txtCurrent.Text
'Updating the Contact_TelTrack table in the database
    mRs_TelTrack.Update
    cmdNewSave.Enabled = False
    cmdNew.Enabled = True
    txtCurrent.Text = ""
End Sub

Public Sub cmdPrevious_Click()
    Timer1.Enabled = False
    If fraPrevious.Visible = True And fraNew.Visible = True Then
        Exit Sub
    Else
        If fraNew.Visible = False Then
            frmDial.Height = 4350
            fraPrevious.Visible = True
            fraPrevious.Top = 2085
        Else
            frmDial.Height = 6540
            fraPrevious.Visible = True
            fraPrevious.Top = 4250
        End If
    End If
```

```
    If mRs_TelTrack.State = 1 Then
        mRs_TelTrack.Close
    End If
    mSqlString = "SELECT * FROM Contact_TelTrack WHERE ID = " & mContactId & ""
    mRs_TelTrack.Open mSqlString, mCn_CardBook, adOpenKeyset, adLockOptimistic
    If mRs_TelTrack.RecordCount > 0 Then
        cmdCallPrior.Enabled = True
        cmdCallNext.Enabled = True
        cmdCallFirst.Enabled = True
        cmdCallLast.Enabled = True
    Else
        cmdCallPrior.Enabled = False
        cmdCallNext.Enabled = False
        cmdCallFirst.Enabled = False
        cmdCallLast.Enabled = False
    End If
    Call view
End Sub

Public Sub cmdDial_Click()
'Checking whether any item in the combobox is selected
    If cboNumber = "" Then
        MsgBox "Select phone number", vbInformation
    Else
    'Calling the extract subroutine that displays name and telephone
        number
        Call extract
        mMsgResponse = MsgBox("Dial " & mDisplay & " number " & mTelNo & _
                    vbCrLf & " of " & mName, vbYesNo + vbInformation _
                    + vbDefaultButton2, "Confirmation")
    'Checking whether the user wishes to cancel the operation
        If mMsgResponse = 7 Then
            Exit Sub
        Else
        'Assigning a value to the mDialDisp variable
            mDialDisp = "to " + mName
            Timer1.Enabled = True
        'Initiating the TAPI session using tapiRequestMakeCall Function
            lonTAPIStatus = tapiRequestMakeCall(mTelNo, "CardBook", mDialDisp, "")
```

```vb
    'Checking whether the phone line is busy using the TAPI status
        If lonTAPIStatus = -10 Then
            MsgBox "In Use"
        End If
    'Checking whether the phone line is available using the TAPI
        status
        If lonTAPIStatus = 0 Then
            fraStatus.Visible = True
            fraLoad.Visible = False
            If mRs_TelTrack.State = 1 Then
                mRs_TelTrack.Close
            End If
            lblTo.Caption = frmCardBook.txtTitle.Text + " " + mName
            lblTelno.Caption = mTelNo
            mSqlString = "SELECT * FROM Contact_TelTrack WHERE Id = " & _
                    mContactId & " "
            mRs_TelTrack.Open mSqlString, mCn_CardBook, adOpenKeyset, _
                    adLockOptimistic
            If mRs_TelTrack.RecordCount > 0 Then
                cmdPrevious.Enabled = True
            Else
                cmdPrevious.Enabled = False
            End If
        End If
     End If
   End If
End Sub

Public Sub cmdAbort_Click()
    Unload frmDial
    frmCardBook.Enabled = True
End Sub

Public Sub fraOptions_Click()
    Timer1.Enabled = False
End Sub
```

```vb
Public Sub fraStatus_Click()
    Timer1.Enabled = False
End Sub


Public Sub Timer1_Timer()
'Assigning the value returned by FlashWindow() to the variable Success
    Success = FlashWindow(frmDial.hWnd, 1)
End Sub
'*************** FUNCTIONALITY OF THE COMMAND BUTTONS ENDS ********
'***************************************************************


'***************************************************************
'**************** APPLICATION SUBROUTINES BEGINS ****************
Public Sub FillComb()
    If mRs_Util.State = 1 Then
        mRs_Util.Close
    End If
    cboNumber.Clear
    mSqlString = "SELECT * FROM Contact_TelNo WHERE Id = " & _
                mContactId & " ORDER BY Flag"
    mRs_Util.Open mSqlString, mCn_CardBook, adOpenKeyset, adLockOptimistic
    mCount = mRs_Util.RecordCount
    If mCount = 0 Then
        Exit Sub
    Else
        mRs_Util.MoveFirst
    'Using a For loop to navigate through all the records in the
    'recordset
        For mCheck = 0 To mCount - 1
            mTelNo = mRs_Util.Fields("Tel_No")
        'Checking if Flag in the recordset holds 'R'
            If mRs_Util.Fields("Flag") = "R" Then
                mType = "Residence"
            ElseIf mRs_Util.Fields("Flag") = "M" Then
                mType = "Mobile"
            Else
                mType = "Office"
            End If
            mDisplay = mType + "   " + mTelNo
```

```vb
        'Adding an item in the cboNumber combobox
            cboNumber.AddItem mDisplay, mCheck

            mRs_Util.MoveNext
        Next
    End If
'Refreshing the combobox
    cboNumber.Refresh
    mRs_Util.Close
End Sub

Public Sub extract()
'Checking for SPACE to find the start position of the first occurrence
    of a digit in the combobox
    mMidPoint = InStr(cboNumber, " ")
'Locating the END of Firstname
    mEndPoint = mMidPoint - 1
'Locating the START of Lastname
    mBeginPoint = mMidPoint + 3
'Assigning a value to the variable mDisplay
    mDisplay = Left(cboNumber, mEndPoint)
'Assigning a value to the variable mTelNo
    mTelNo = Mid(cboNumber, mBeginPoint)
End Sub

Public Sub view()
'Assigning a value to the txtprevious textbox
    txtprevious.Text = "Date :-" + CStr(mRs_TelTrack.Fields("TimeStamp")) & vbCrLf & _
                        vbCrLf & mRs_TelTrack.Fields("Note")
End Sub
'***************** APPLICATION SUBROUTINES ENDS ******************
'****************************************************************
```

Subroutines Within frmDial.frm

The **FillComb** subroutine is used to fill a combo box with the telephone numbers of a contact. When the **frmDial** form loads in memory, a call is made to **FillComb** subroutine to display a contacts residence and office telephone numbers.

The subroutine fires an SQL query to retrieve records belonging to the current contact person.

Records returned by the query are added to the combo box. The value in the **Flag** field in the table **Contact_TelNo** indicates whether the telephone number is a residential, office or a mobile number.

```vb
Public Sub FillComb()
'Checking whether the mRs_Util recordset is open
    If mRs_Util.State = 1 Then
    'Closing the mRs_Util recordset
        mRs_Util.Close
    End If
'Clearing the cboNumber combobox
    cboNumber.Clear
'Storing an SQL query into mSqlString
    mSqlString = "SELECT * FROM Contact_TelNo WHERE Id = " & _
            mContactId & " ORDER BY Flag"
'Opening the mRs_Util recordset
    mRs_Util.Open mSqlString, mCn_CardBook, adOpenKeyset, adLockOptimistic
'Storing the record count of the mRs_Util recordset into mCount
    mCount = mRs_Util.RecordCount
'Checking whether the record count is zero
    If mCount = 0 Then
        Exit Sub
    Else
    'Setting the mRs_Util recordset pointer on the First record
        mRs_Util.MoveFirst
    'Using For loop to navigate through all the records in the recordset
        For mCheck = 0 To mCount - 1
        'Storing the value of the 'TelNo' field into mTelNo
            mTelNo = mRs_Util.Fields("Tel_No")
```

```
        'Checking if Flag holds the value 'R'
            If mRs_Util.Fields("Flag") = "R" Then
                'Assigning value to the variable mType
                    mType = "Residence"
                'Checking if Flag holds the value 'M'
                ElseIf mRs_Util.Fields("Flag") = "M" Then
                    'Assigning value to the variable mType
                        mType = "Mobile"
                Else
                    'Assigning value to the variable mType
                        mType = "Office"
                End If
            'Assigning value to the variable mDisplay
                mDisplay = mType + "   " + mTelNo
            'Adding an item in the combobox
                cboNumber.AddItem mDisplay, mCheck
            'Setting the mRs_Util recordset pointer on the Next record
                mRs_Util.MoveNext
        Next
    End If
'Refreshing the combobox
    cboNumber.Refresh
'Closing the mRs_Util recordset
    mRs_Util.Close
End Sub
```

After selecting a telephone number of a contact person from the combo box, a user is prompted to confirm the operation. A message box displays the contact persons name and number prior dialing.

The **extract()** subroutine is used to extract the name, telephone number and Flag from the combo box's contents. This subroutine is called when user clicks on the dial button after selecting a telephone number.

```
Public Sub extract()
'Checking for SPACE to find the starting position of the first
    occurrence of a digit in the combobox
    mMidPoint = InStr(cboNumber, " ")
'Locating the END of Firstname
    mEndPoint = mMidPoint - 1
```

```
'Locating the START of Lastname
    mBeginPoint = mMidPoint + 3
'Assigning value to the variable mDisplay
    mDisplay = Left(cboNumber, mEndPoint)
'Assigning value to the variable mTelNo
    mTelNo = Mid(cboNumber, mBeginPoint)
End Sub
```

The application provides a facility to store the notes regarding conversations carried out with a contact person. It always helps to make a reference to earlier conversations before dialing/making a call.

The **view** subroutine retrieves the date and notes jotted down dumping earlier conversations with the current contact person.

The **view** subroutine gets called when a user dials a telephone number and wishes to read the notes made during earlier conversations.

```
Public Sub view()
'Assigning value to the txtprevious textbox
    txtprevious.Text = "Date :-" + CStr(mRs_TelTrack.Fields("TimeStamp")) & _
                vbCrLf & vbCrLf & mRs_TelTrack.Fields("Note")
End Sub
```

PROJECT CODE FOR FrmEmail.frm

```vb
Option Explicit
'Creating object variables for later use
Dim mSqlString As String
Dim mName As String
Dim mType As String
Dim mEmailId As String
Dim mDisplay As String
Dim strMessage As String
Dim mDailDisp
Dim mMsgResponse As Integer
Dim mCheck As Integer
Dim mCount As Integer
Dim mMidPoint As Integer
Dim mEndPoint As Integer
Dim mBeginPoint As Integer
Public mContactId As Integer
Dim lonTAPIStatus    As Long
'Flag to signal logon status
Public bNewSession As Boolean


'****************************************************************
'********** FUNCTIONALITY OF THE FORM LOAD EVENT BEGINS ************
Public Sub Form_Load()
'Setting an icon for the form using LoadPicture()
    frmEmail.Icon = LoadPicture(App.Path & "\icon\Card.ico")
'Assigning the value of frmCardBook's mContactId to mContactId
    mContactId = frmCardBook.mContactId
'Assigning a value to the variable mName
    mName = Trim(frmCardBook.txtFname) + " " + Trim(frmCardBook.txtLname)
    cmdAbort.Picture = LoadPicture(App.Path & "\icon\buttoncancel.bmp")
    cmdMail.Picture = LoadPicture(App.Path & "\icon\buttonemail.bmp")
'Calling FillComb()to populate the drop down listbox
    Call FillComb
End Sub
```

```vb
Public Sub Form_Resize()
'Setting Top and Left attributes of the frmEmail form to ensure that
'the search form will always be centered even if the window is resized
'by the user
    frmEmail.Top = (Screen.Height - frmEmail.Height) \ 2
    frmEmail.Left = (Screen.Width - frmEmail.Width) \ 2
End Sub
'*********** FUNCTIONALITY FOR THE FORM LOAD EVENT ENDS ************
'******************************************************************


'******************************************************************
'*********** FUNCTIONALITY OF THE COMMAND BUTTONS BEGINS **********
Public Sub cmdMail_Click()
'Checking whether any item in the drop down listbox is selected
    If cboEmailId = "" Then
        MsgBox "Select email-id", vbInformation
    Else
    'Calling extract which displays name and emailid
        Call extract
        mMsgResponse = MsgBox("Send mail to " & mName & " at " & mEmailId, _
                        vbYesNo + vbInformation + vbDefaultButton2, _
                        "Confirmation")
    'Checking whether the user wishes to cancel the operation
        If mMsgResponse = 7 Then
            Exit Sub
        Else
        'Calling SendMail which sends an Email
            SendMail
        End If
    End If
End Sub

Public Sub cmdAbort_Click()
'Unloading the frmEmail form
    Unload frmEmail
    frmCardBook.Enabled = True
End Sub
'************ FUNCTIONALITY OF THE COMMAND BUTTONS ENDS ***********
'******************************************************************
```

```
'*****************************************************************
'***************** APPLICATION SUBROUTINES BEGINS *****************
Public Sub FillComb()
    If mRs_Util.State = 1 Then
            mRs_Util.Close
    End If
    mSqlString = "SELECT * FROM Contact_Email WHERE Id = " & _
                mContactId & " ORDER BY Flag"
    mRs_Util.Open mSqlString, mCn_CardBook, adOpenKeyset, adLockOptimistic
'Storing the record count of the mRs_Util recordset into the mCount
'variable
    mCount = mRs_Util.RecordCount
    If mCount = 0 Then
        Exit Sub
    Else
        mRs_Util.MoveFirst
    'Using a For loop to navigate through all the records in the
    'recordset
        For mCheck = 0 To mCount - 1
        'Storing the value of the Email_Id field into mEmailId
            mEmailId = mRs_Util.Fields("Email_Id")
        'Checking if Flag holds the value 'R'
            If mRs_Util.Fields("Flag") = "R" Then
                mType = "Personal"
            Else
                mType = "Official"
            End If
            mDisplay = mType + " " + mEmailId
        'Adding an item in the cboEmailId combobox
            cboEmailId.AddItem mDisplay, mCheck
            mRs_Util.MoveNext
        Next
    End If
'Refreshing the cboEmailId combobox
    cboEmailId.Refresh
'Closing the mRs_Util recordset
    mRs_Util.Close
End Sub
```

Note

 Refer to **Subroutines Within frmDial.frm** for the explanation of the **extract** subroutine.

```vb
Public Sub extract()
    mMidPoint = InStr(cboEmailId, " ")
    mEndPoint = mMidPoint - 1
    mBeginPoint = mMidPoint + 3
    mDisplay = Left(cboEmailId, mEndPoint)
    mEmailId = Mid(cboEmailId, mBeginPoint)
End Sub

Public Sub SendMail()
'Calling a LogOn subroutine
    Call LogOn
    On Error GoTo ComposeErr
    'Calling the Compose method of MAPIMessages to compose a new Email
        mapMess.Compose
    'Using its RecipType property to indicate recipient type
        mapMess.RecipType = 1
        mapMess.RecipAddress = mEmailId
        mapMess.RecipDisplayName = mName
    'Sending an Email
        mapMess.Send True
        Call LogOff
        Exit Sub
    ComposeErr:
        Debug.Print Err.Number, Err.Description
        Resume Next
End Sub

'A subroutine used to sign in through a MAPI SESSION
Public Function LogOn() As Boolean
'Checking whether the session has been started
    If mapSess.NewSession Then
        MsgBox "Session already established"
        Exit Function
    End If
```

```
    With mapSess
        'Setting DownLoadMail to False to prevent immediate download
        .DownLoadMail = False
        .SignOn
        LogOn = True
        .NewSession = True
        mapMess.SessionID = .SessionID
    End With
End Function

'A subroutine used to sign off through a MAPI SESSION
Public Sub LogOff()
    With mapSess
        'Closing the session
        .SignOff
        .NewSession = False
    End With
End Sub
'*************** APPLICATION SUBROUTINES ENDS *****************
'*************************************************************
```

Subroutines Within frmEmail.frm

The **FillComb** subroutine is used to fill a combo box with the email address of a contact. When the **frmEmail** form loads in memory, a call is made to the **FillComb** subroutine to display a contact's personal and office email addresses.

The subroutine fires an SQL query to retrieve records belonging to the current contact person.

Records returned by the query are added to the combo box. The value in the **Flag** field in the table **Contact_Email** indicates whether the email address is a personal or office email address.

```vb
Public Sub FillComb()
    If mRs_Util.State = 1 Then
        mRs_Util.Close
    End If
    mSqlString = "SELECT * FROM Contact_Email WHERE Id = " & _
                mContactId & " ORDER BY Flag"
    mRs_Util.Open mSqlString, mCn_CardBook, adOpenKeyset, adLockOptimistic
    mCount = mRs_Util.RecordCount
    If mCount = 0 Then
        Exit Sub
    Else
        mRs_Util.MoveFirst
'Using a For loop to navigate through all the records in the
'recordset
        For mCheck = 0 To mCount - 1
        'Storing the value of the Email_Id field in mEmailId
            mEmailId = mRs_Util.Fields("Email_Id")
        'Checking if Flag holds the value 'R'
            If mRs_Util.Fields("Flag") = "R" Then
                mType = "Personal"
            Else
                mType = "Official"
            End If
        'Assigning a value to the variable mDisplay
            mDisplay = mType + " " + mEmailId
        'Adding an item in the cboEmailId combobox
            cboEmailId.AddItem mDisplay, mCheck
            mRs_Util.MoveNext
        Next
    End If
    cboEmailId.Refresh
    mRs_Util.Close
End Sub
```

The application provides the functionality of sending an Email to a contact person while navigating through the contact list. This is accomplished using a MAPI control.

After selecting an Email address of a contact person from the combo box, the user is prompted to confirm the Email operation.

CHAP 04   A PERSONAL INFORMATION MANAGER: THE WORKING

A session of MS Outlook Express is opened in order to compose an Email.

The **LogOn** subroutine is used to access the internet by starting a session through the default ISP .

```
'A subroutine used to sign in through MAPI SESSION
Public Function LogOn() As Boolean
'Checking whether the session has been started
    If mapSess.NewSession Then
        MsgBox "Session already established"
        Exit Function
    End If

    With mapSess
    'Setting DownLoadMail to False to prevent immediate download
        .DownLoadMail = False
        .SignOn
        LogOn = True
        .NewSession = True
        mapMess.SessionID = .SessionID
    End With
End Function
```

The **SendMail** subroutine provides the functionality of invoking MS Outlook Express. It also transfers the Email address into the recipient's address bar within MS Outlook Express's message composer.

```
Public Sub SendMail()
'Calling the LogOn subroutine
    Call LogOn
    On Error GoTo ComposeErr
    'Calling the Compose method of MAPIMessages to compose a new Email
        mapMess.Compose
    'The RecipType property is used to indicate recipient type
        mapMess.RecipType = 1
    'Assigning recipient's email address
        mapMess.RecipAddress = mEmailId
    'Assigning the name of the recipient
        mapMess.RecipDisplayName = mName
```

```
'Sending Email
    mapMess.Send True
'Calling the LogOff subroutine
    Call LogOff
    Exit Sub
ComposeErr:
    Debug.Print Err.Number, Err.Description
    Resume Next
End Sub
```

The **LogOff** subroutine closes the internet session.

```
'A subroutine used to sign off through a MAPI SESSION
Public Sub LogOff()
    With mapSess
        .SignOff
        'Close the session.
        .NewSession = False
    End With
End Sub
```

PROJECT CODE FOR FrmSearch.frm

```vb
Option Explicit
'Creating object variables for later use
Public mSqlString As String
Public mFirstName As String
Public mLastName As String
Public mFullName As String

Public mCount As Integer
Public mCheck As Integer

'*************************************************************
'********** FUNCTIONALITY OF THE FORM LOAD EVENT BEGINS ************
Public Sub Form_Load()
'Setting an icon for the form using LoadPicture()
    frmSearch.Icon = LoadPicture(App.Path & "\icon\Card.ico")
'Setting attributes of the frmSearch form
    frmSearch.Width = 6360
    frmSearch.Height = 3405
    frmSearch.Top = 1500
    frmSearch.Left = 2505
'Calling FillComb subroutine to populate the drop down listbox
    FillComb
End Sub

Public Sub Form_Resize()
'Setting the Top and Left attributes of the frmSearch to
'ensure that the search form will always be centered even
'if the window is resized by the user
    frmSearch.Top = (Screen.Height - frmSearch.Height) \ 2
    frmSearch.Left = (Screen.Width - frmSearch.Width) \ 2
End Sub

'********** FUNCTIONALITY FOR THE FORM LOAD EVENT ENDS ************
'*************************************************************
```

```vb
'*****************************************************************
'*********** FUNCTIONALITY OF THE COMMAND BUTTONS BEGINS **********
Public Sub cmdSearch_Click()
'Calling a Search subroutine from the frmCardBook form which populates
'a recordset based on the items selected by a user in the search form
    Call frmCardBook.Search
    Unload frmSearch
    frmCardBook.Enabled = True
End Sub

Public Sub cmdCancel_Click()
    frmCardBook.Enabled = True
    Unload frmSearch
End Sub
'*********** FUNCTIONALITY OF THE COMMAND BUTTONS ENDS ************
'*****************************************************************


'*****************************************************************
'***************** APPLICATION SUBROUTINES BEGINS *****************
Public Sub FillComb()
    If mRs_Search.State = 1 Then
        mRs_Search.Close
    End If
    mSqlString = "SELECT F_Name, L_Name FROM Contact_Master"
    mRs_Search.Open mSqlString, mCn_CardBook, adOpenKeyset, adLockOptimistic
    mCount = mRs_Search.RecordCount
    If mCount = 0 Then
        Exit Sub
    Else
        mRs_Search.MoveFirst
        For mCheck = 0 To mCount - 1
            mFirstName = mRs_Search.Fields("F_Name")
            mLastName = mRs_Search.Fields("L_Name")
            mFullName = mFirstName + " " + mLastName
            cmbName.AddItem mFullName, mCheck
            mRs_Search.MoveNext
        Next
    End If
```

```
        cmbName.Refresh
        mRs_Search.Close
End Sub
'***************** APPLICATION SUBROUTINES ENDS ********************
'*******************************************************************
```

Subroutine Within frmSearch.frm

The **FillComb** subroutine is used to fill a combo box with the first name and last name of all the contacts in the **Contact_Master** table. When the **frmSearch** form loads in memory, a call is made to the **FillComb** subroutine.

The subroutine fires an SQL query to retrieve first name and last name of all the records in the table **Contact_Master**.

Records returned by the query are added to the combo box after concatenating the first name and last name.

```
Public Sub FillComb()
    If mRs_Search.State = 1 Then
        mRs_Search.Close
    End If
    mSqlString = "SELECT F_Name, L_Name FROM Contact_Master"
    mRs_Search.Open mSqlString, mCn_CardBook, adOpenKeyset, adLockOptimistic
'Storing the record count of the mRs_Search recordset into mCount
    mCount = mRs_Search.RecordCount
    If mCount = 0 Then
        Exit Sub
    Else
        mRs_Search.MoveFirst
'Using the For loop to navigate through all the records in the
'recordset
        For mCheck = 0 To mCount - 1
            mFirstName = mRs_Search.Fields("F_Name")
            mLastName = mRs_Search.Fields("L_Name")
        'Assigning a value to the mFullName variable
            mFullName = mFirstName + " " + mLastName
```

```
        'Adding an item in the drop down listbox
            cmbName.AddItem mFullName, mCheck
            mRs_Search.MoveNext
        Next
    End If
    cmbName.Refresh
    mRs_Search.Close
End Sub
```

PROJECT CODE FOR Module1

```vb
'Creating Connection and Recordset objects
Public mCn_CardBook As ADODB.Connection
Public mRs_ContactMaster As ADODB.Recordset
Public mRs_Add As ADODB.Recordset
Public mRs_Search As ADODB.Recordset
Public mRs_Util As ADODB.Recordset
Public mRs_TelTrack As ADODB.Recordset
Public mRs_Domain As ADODB.Recordset

'A TAPI Function makes a call to the Dialer control of MS Windows
'and passes the Telephone number and persons name for dialing
Declare Function tapiRequestMakeCall Lib "tapi32" _
    (ByVal lpszDestAddress As String, _
    ByVal lpszAppName As String, _
    ByVal lpszCalledParty As String, _
    ByVal lpszComment As String) As Long

'Constants which trap/give the status of the call
Global Const TAPIERR_CONNECTED = 0&
Global Const TAPIERR_DROPPED = -1&
Global Const TAPIERR_NOREQUESTRECIPIENT = -2&
Global Const TAPIERR_REQUESTQUEUEFULL = -3&
Global Const TAPIERR_INVALDESTADDRESS = -4&
Global Const TAPIERR_INVALWINDOWHANDLE = -5&
Global Const TAPIERR_INVALDEVICECLASS = -6&
Global Const TAPIERR_INVALDEVICEID = -7&
Global Const TAPIERR_DEVICECLASSUNAVAIL = -8&
Global Const TAPIERR_DEVICEIDUNAVAIL = -9&
Global Const TAPIERR_DEVICEINUSE = -10&
Global Const TAPIERR_DESTBUSY = -11&
Global Const TAPIERR_DESTNOANSWER = -12&
Global Const TAPIERR_DESTUNAVAIL = -13&
Global Const TAPIERR_UNKNOWNWINHANDLE = -14&
Global Const TAPIERR_UNKNOWNREQUESTID = -15&
Global Const TAPIERR_REQUESTFAILED = -16&
Global Const TAPIERR_REQUESTCANCELLED = -17&
Global Const TAPIERR_INVALPOINTER = -18&
```

PRACTICAL VB 6 PROJECTS — CHAP 04

```vb
'A call is made to the FlashWindow API
    #If Win32 Then
        Declare Function FlashWindow Lib "user32" (ByVal hWnd As Long, _
                                    ByVal bInvert As Long) As Long
        Declare Function GetCaretBlinkTime Lib "user32" () As Long
        Dim Success As Long
    #Else
        Declare Function FlashWindow Lib "User" (ByVal hWnd As Integer, _
                                    ByVal bInvert As Integer) As Integer
        Declare Function GetCaretBlinkTime Lib "User" () As Integer
        Dim Success As Integer
    #End If
```

The **ConnetDB** subroutine is responsible for opening up a connection with the database. It also initializes all the ADODB recordset objects that are used throughout the application.

```vb
Public Sub ConnetDB()
' Initialising mCn_CardBook ADODB connection object
    Set mCn_CardBook = New ADODB.Connection
'Indicating the OLEDb provider to use with the Access database
    mCn_CardBook.Provider = "MSDASQL.1;Persist Security Info=False;Data
                            Source=Card"
' Opening up the database connection
    mCn_CardBook.Open
' Initializing the ADODB recordset objects
    Set mRs_ContactMaster = New ADODB.Recordset
    Set mRs_Add = New ADODB.Recordset
    Set mRs_Search = New ADODB.Recordset
    Set mRs_Util = New ADODB.Recordset
    Set mRs_TelTrack = New ADODB.Recordset
    Set mRs_Domain = New ADODB.Recordset
End Sub
```

The **fixQuote** subroutine is used to replace the **single quote** (') notation with the **double quote** (") notation.

```vb
Public Function fixQuote(theVar)
    fixQuote = Replace(theVar, "'", """")
End Function
```

Chapter 04

Self Evaluation

In This Chapter We Learned:

- **Behaviour Of The Personal Information Manager**
  Its Working Through Visual Basic 6

- **Built-In Components And References Required While Designing**

- **Project Source Codes**
  frmCardBook.frm
  frmDial.frm
  frmEmail.frm
  frmSearch.frm
  Module1.bas

Chapter 05

A Commercial Banking System: The Plan

In This Chapter:

- **What is a Commercial Banking System**
  Its Working And Requirements

- **Data Segregation And Relationships Within The Project**

- **Database Designing For The Project**
  Table Definitions
  Table Data Validation Rules
  Micro Help For Table Fields
  Test Data For The Application

5. A COMMERCIAL BANKING SYSTEM: THE PLAN

PROJECT SCOPE

Today's commercial world is built around money. Every commercial transaction needs to be supported using a financial transaction. Banks facilitate financial transactions and hence are an integral part of the commercial world. Banking services has grown by leaps and bounds. Today a bank that offers its customers the widest spread of services mapped to their business (and personal) needs is the bank that is successful.

Banking is essentially a business model. Each business model has a number of master business processes that determines and shapes the business model. Each master business process will have a number of sub-processes that govern the way that the master business process flows.

Business sub-processes also capture, validate and store business data. Validated business data is stored for future reference by business managers who are responsible for running the business model.

A quick look at the master business processes of the banking business model is shown in diagram 2.1.

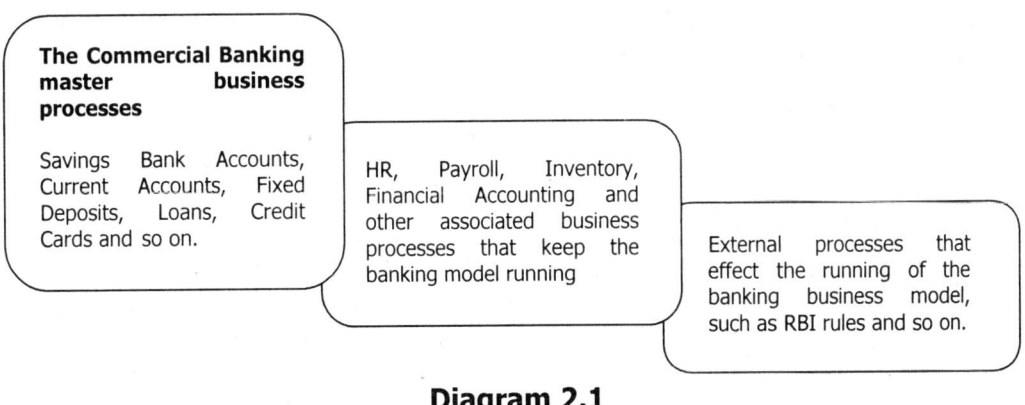

Diagram 2.1

This project is bound to two master business processes of a banking business model. **Savings** accounts and **Current** accounts. At face value; these two banking processes seem quite similar but in actual fact there are substantial differences between them.

Some of the differences are:

- The monies deposited (and held) in a savings account attract an annual interest of 4.5%

- The monies deposited into a current account attract nothing. In fact, banks normally charge a customer to setup and run a current account

- A bank normally has **R**eserve **B**ank Of **I**ndia (RBI) guidelines to follow which restricts the amount of money that can be withdrawn from a saving bank account

- There are no such limitations on the withdrawal of money from a current account

- There is always a minimum balance that has to be maintained in a savings and/or current account. However, the minimum balance to be maintained in a current account is **substantially larger** than the minimum balance that has to be maintained in a savings account

Having said all this, the way both the accounts are operated by their respective account holders is identical.

Money is deposited and money is withdrawn. There is simply a running check kept of all deposit and withdrawal transactions in each type of account. Money can be deposited by cash, cheque or bank draft (i.e. a bankers cheque). Money can be withdrawn by cash, cheque or bank draft (i.e. a bankers cheque).

The monthly statement of an account holder's transactions (i.e. deposits and withdrawals) is accepted by all government agencies such as Income Tax, Sales Tax and so on as proof that the transaction actually took place. This is the significance of running a savings or current account with a bank.

CHAP 05 — A COMMERCIAL BANKING SYSTEM: THE PLAN

Irrespective of the type of account being opened at a bank, there is a banking sub-process that captures specific information about a potential customer, prior opening a bank account on the client's behalf.

This sub-process requires:
1. An account opening form is filled up by the prospective client

2. Xerox copies of one or two documents must be submitted along with the account opening form such as:
   - The individual's Income Tax **P**ermanent **A**ccount **N**umber (PAN)
   - A copy of an individual's Passport, or driving license, or recent electricity bill as proof of residence address

3. The account application form with its support documents will be physically verified by a bank's staff member and then accepted for further processing
   - The act of physically verifying these documents is captured on the application form as a signature **i.e.** signature of the bank official who physically verified the documents

Only when this sub-process completes successfully will either a savings or current account be opened on behalf of a prospective client by the bank. This converts a prospective client to a client **i.e.** a bank account holder.

When the account is opened at a bank it is ready to capture and document deposit and withdrawal transactions.

If a reference is made to diagram 2.1 there are several other master business processes associated with a banking business model.

These are:
- Fixed deposits
- Loans
- Credit Cards
- Over Drafts

And so on. These master business processes are not being dealt with in this project.

The bulk transactions of a banking business model are the daily combination of savings and current account transactions. Hence this project is focused on defining, documenting and creating a system that will computerize a bank's savings and current account transaction requirements.

This system fits a bank's master business process that caters to the bulk of a bank's business transactions.

The system starts with the design of the savings and current account opening form. All data that has to be captured (in accordance with RBI regulations) by the savings and/or current account opening form has to be captured on screen.

The data captured has to be validated and then stored for future reference by the bank's managerial staff. The rules of validating this data has to be documented and then programmatically bound to the data capture form. Once the data captured has been validated it must be stored in a database for instant retrieval and viewing on demand.

Each data capture form allows its user to Insert (thus permanently save) data into a database. Additionally, complete data **editing** facilities such as Updation, Deletion and Viewing of data in the database is available.

Once data captured by the account opening form is inserted into the database the account is deemed to be opened and ready for transactions. Subsequently, another data entry form is used to capture and track all savings and current account deposits and withdrawals.

The report drawn from such a system is the account holder's passbook that documents every deposit and withdrawal transaction of the bank account holder.

The commercial banking system design and documentation follows.

ENTITY RELATION DIAGRAM FOR THE BANKING SYSTEM

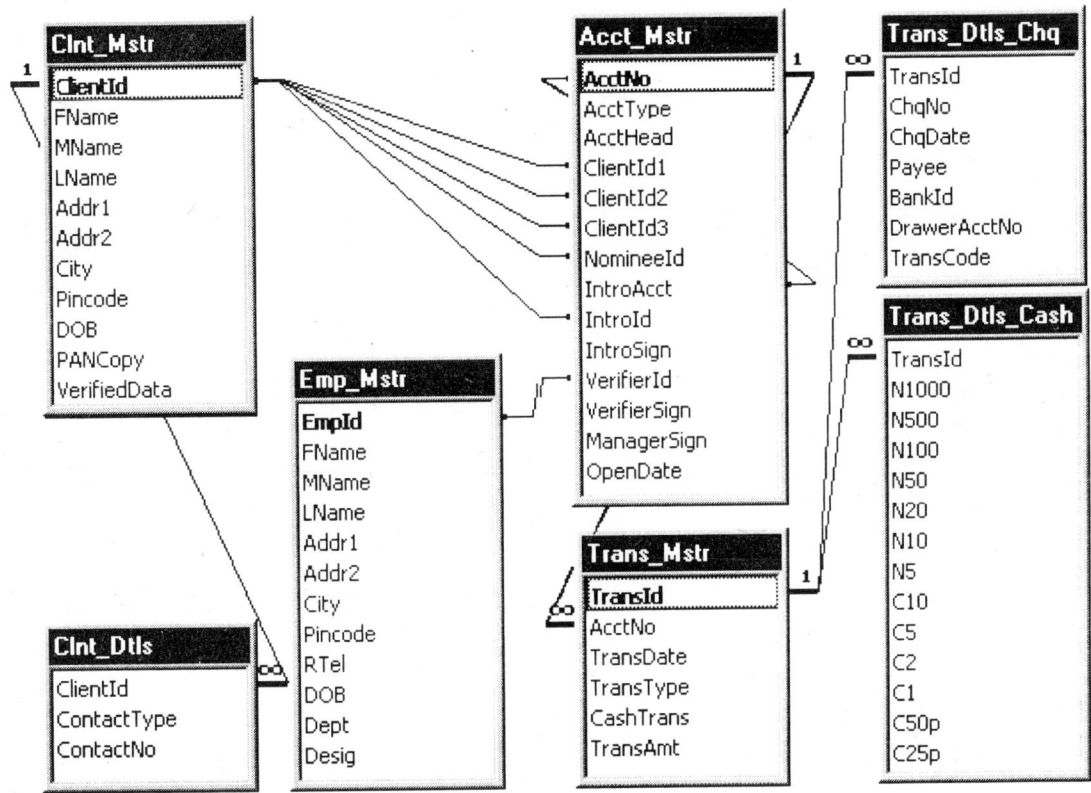

Diagram 2.2

The above diagram, attempts to give a visual representation of the Entity relationship between various tables required under the project. The symbols '**1**' and '**oo**' indicate a one-to-many relationship.

TABLE DEFINITION – BANKING SYSTEM

Table Definition:
Table Name : Emp_Mstr
Primary Key : EmpId
Foreign Key :

Column Definition:

Column Name	Data Type	Width	Allow Null	Default
EmpId	Number		No	
FName	Text	25	No	
MName	Text	25		
LName	Text	25	No	
Addr1	Text	40	No	
Addr2	Text	40	No	
City	Text	25	No	
Pincode	Text	6	No	
RTel	Text	15	No	
DOB	Date/Time		No	
Dept	Text	20	No	
Desig	Text	20	No	

Table Description:

Column Name	Description
EmpId	System generated number
FName	First name of a bank employee
MName	Middle name of a bank employee
LName	Last name of a bank employee
Addr1	Bank employee's address (House no. & name, Rd. name)
Addr2	Bank employee's address (Locality & area)
City	Bank employee's address (City name)
Pincode	Bank employee's address (Pin code)
RTel	Bank employee's residence telephone number
DOB	Bank employee's date of birth
Dept	Bank employee's department
Desig	Bank employee's official designation

Explanation:
This table captures a Bank employee's name, postal address, residence telephone number, department, date of birth and official designation at the bank.

A COMMERCIAL BANKING SYSTEM: THE PLAN

Table Definition:
- **Table Name** : Clnt_Mstr
- **Primary Key** : ClientId
- **Foreign Key** :

Column Definition:

Column Name	Data Type	Width	Allow Null	Default
ClientId	Number		No	
FName	Text	25	No	
MName	Text	25		
LName	Text	25	No	
Addr1	Text	40	No	
Addr2	Text	40	No	
City	Text	25	No	
Pincode	Text	6	No	
DOB	Date/Time		No	
PANCopy	Yes/No			
VerifiedData	Yes/No			

Table Description:

Column Name	Description
ClientId	System generated number
FName	First name of an account holder
MName	Middle name of an account holder
LName	Last name of an account holder
Addr1	Account holder's address (House no. & name, Rd. name)
Addr2	Account holder's address (Locality & area)
City	Account holder's address (City name)
Pincode	Account holder's address (Pin code)
DOB	Account holder's date of birth
PANCopy	Holds **Y** if a copy of client's PAN card has been submitted
VerifiedData	Holds **Y** if data has been verified by the bank's manager

Explanation:
This table captures a client's name and postal address along with other information required to open an account at the bank.

Table Definition:
Table Name : Clnt_Dtls
Primary Key :
Foreign Key : ClientId

Column Definition:

Column Name	Data Type	Width	Allow Null	Default
ClientId	Number		No	
ContactType	Text	1	No	
ContactNo	Text	15	No	

Table Description:

Column Name	Description
ClientId	Should be present in Clnt_Mter table
ContactType	Holds value **R** for Residence, **O** for Office, **M** for Mobile, **P** for Pager and **F** for Fax
ContactNo	Contact number of a client

Explanation:
This table captures a client's contact details. It holds residence, office, telephone, mobile, pager and fax numbers.

Table Definition:
Table Name : Acct_Mstr
Primary Key : AcctNo
Foreign Key : ClientId1, (ClientId2, Clientd3), IntroId

Column Definition:

Column Name	Data Type	Width	Allow Null	Default
AcctNo	Number		No	
AcctType	Text	2	No	
AcctHead	Memo			
ClientId1	Number		No	
ClientId2	Number			
ClientId3	Number			
Nominee	Text	50	No	
IntroAcct	Number		No	
IntroId	Number		No	

Column Name	Data Type	Width	Allow Null	Default
IntroSign	Yes/No			
VerifierId	Number		No	
VerifierSign	Yes/No			
ManagerSign	Yes/No			
OpenDate	DateTime		No	

Table Description:

Column Name	Description
AcctNo	System generated number
AcctType	Description for the account type (i.e. Savings or Current)
AcctHead	Name of the organisation in case the account is jointly operated
ClientId1	Foreign key, Client's id for the first person
ClientId2	Foreign key, Client's id for the second person
ClientId3	Foreign key, Client's id for the third person
Nominee	Name of a nominee
IntroAcct	Foreign key, Introducer's bank account number
IntroId	Foreign key, Client's id for the person acting as an introducer
IntroSign	Holds **Y** if an introducer has signed the form
VerifierId	Foreign key, Employee's id for the banking officer who has verified the application form
VerifierSign	Holds **Y** if verifier has signed the form
ManagerSign	Holds **Y** if the bank manager has signed the form
OpenDate	Date on which the account has been opened

Explanation:
This table holds account information. This includes account number, account type, information about account holder(s), nominee, introducer and so on.

Table Definition:
Table Name : Trans_Mstr
Primary Key : TransId
Foreign Key : AcctNo

Column Definition:

Column Name	Data Type	Width	Allow Null	Default
TransId	AutoNumber		No	
AcctNo	Number		No	
TransDate	DateTime		No	
TransType	Text	1	No	
CashTrans	Yes/No			
TransAmt	Number		No	

Table Description:

Column Name	Description
TransId	System generated number
AcctNo	Should be present in Acct_Mstr table
TransDate	Transaction date
TransType	Transaction type (**D** - Deposit & **W** - Withdrawal)
CashTrans	Holds **Y**, if transaction is through cash
TransAmt	The amount of a transaction

Explanation:

This table captures daily transactions carried out by all account holders.

Table Definition:

Table Name : Trans_Dtls_Chq
Primary Key :
Foreign Key : TransId

Column Definition:

Column Name	Data Type	Width	Allow Null	Default
TransId	Number		No	
ChqNo	Number		No	
Chqdate	Date/Time		No	
Payee	Text	50	No	
BankId	Number		No	
DrawerAcctNo	Number		No	
TransCode	Number		No	

Table Description:

Column Name	Description
TransId	Should be present in Trans_Mstr table
ChqNo	Cheque number
Chqdate	Cheque date
Payee	Party name to whom payment is being made
BankId	Bank MICR code
DrawerAcctNo	Account number of the drawer
TransCode	Holds transaction code (10<SB>, 11<CA>, 14<Dividend Warrant>, 19<Interest Warrant>, 28<Refund Order>)

Explanation:
This table captures client's cheque transaction.

Table Definition:
Table Name : Trans_Dtls_Cash
Primary Key :
Foreign Key : TransId

Column Definition:

Column Name	Data Type	Width	Allow Null	Default
TransId	Number		No	
N1000	Number		No	0
N500	Number		No	0
N100	Number		No	0
N50	Number		No	0
N20	Number		No	0
N10	Number		No	0
N5	Number		No	0
C10	Number		No	0
C5	Number		No	0
C2	Number		No	0
C1	Number		No	0
C50p	Number		No	0
C25p	Number		No	0

Table Description:

Column Name	Description
TransId	Should be present in Trans_Mstr table
N1000	Number of notes of Rs. 1000 transferred during the transaction
N500	Number of notes of Rs. 500 transferred during the transaction
N100	Number of notes of Rs. 100 transferred during the transaction
N50	Number of notes of Rs. 50 transferred during the transaction
N20	Number of notes of Rs. 20 transferred during the transaction
N10	Number of notes of Rs. 10 transferred during the transaction
N5	Number of notes of Rs. 5 transferred during the transaction
C10	Number of coins of Rs. 10 transferred during the transaction
C5	Number of coins of Rs. 5 transferred during the transaction
C2	Number of coins of Rs. 2 transferred during the transaction
C1	Number of coins of Re. 1 transferred during the transaction
C50p	Number of coins of 50 ps. transferred during the transaction
C25p	Number of coins of 25 ps. transferred during the transaction

Explanation:
This table captures client's cash transaction.

TABLE DATA VALIDATION RULES

Table Name: Emp_Mstr

Column Name	Description
EmpId	Emp_Id will be Unique (System generated number)
FName	Cannot be left empty and should contain only English alphabets
MName	Must contain only English alphabets
LName	Cannot be left empty and should contain only English alphabets
Addr1	Cannot be left empty
Addr2	Cannot be left empty
City	Cannot be left empty
Pincode	Contains only 6 digits
RTel	Cannot be less than 7 digits
DOB	Cannot be left empty
Dept	Cannot be left empty and should contain only English alphabets
Desig	Cannot be left empty and should contain only English alphabets

Table Name: Clnt_Mstr

Column Name	Description
ClientId	Client_Id will be Unique (System generated number)
FName	Cannot be left empty and should contain only English alphabets
MName	Must contain only English alphabets
LName	Cannot be left empty and should contain only English alphabets
Addr1	Cannot be left empty
Addr2	Cannot be left empty
City	Cannot be left empty
Pincode	Cannot be less than 6 digits
DOB	Cannot be left empty
PANCopy	
VerifiedData	

Table Name: Clnt_Dtls

Column Name	Description
ClientId	Client_Id will be posted from Clnt_Mstr table
ContactType	
ContactNo	Cannot be less than 7 digits

Table Name: Acct_Mstr

Column Name	Description
AcctNo	AcctNo will be Unique (System generated number)
AcctType	Cannot be left empty
AcctHead	
ClientId1	Client_Id will be posted from Clnt_Mstr table
ClientId2	Client_Id will be posted from Clnt_Mstr table
ClientId3	Client_Id will be posted from Clnt_Mstr table
Nominee	Client_Id will be posted from Clnt_Mstr table
IntroAcct	AcctNo will be posted from Acct_Mstr table
IntroId	Client_Id will be posted from Clnt_Mstr table
IntroSign	
VerifierId	Emp_Id will be posted from Emp_Mstr table
VerifierSign	
ManagerSign	
OpenDate	Cannot be left empty

Table Name: Trans_Mstr

Column Name	Description
TransId	TransId will be Unique (System generated number)
AcctNo	AcctNo will be posted from Acct_Mstr table
TransDate	Cannot be left empty
TransType	Cannot be left empty
CashTrans	
TransAmt	Cannot be left empty and should contain only numeric data

Table Name: Trans_Dtls_Chq

Column Name	Description
TransId	TransId will be posted from Trans_Mstr table
ChqNo	Contains only 6 digits
Chqdate	Cannot be left empty
Payee	Cannot be left empty
BankId	Contains only 9 digits
DrawerAcctNo	Contains only 6 digits
TransCode	Contains only 2 digits

Table Name: Trans_Dtls_Csh

Column Name	Description
TransId	TransId will be posted from Trans_Mstr table
N1000	Cannot be left empty and should contain only numeric data
N500	Cannot be left empty and should contain only numeric data
N100	Cannot be left empty and should contain only numeric data
N50	Cannot be left empty and should contain only numeric data
N20	Cannot be left empty and should contain only numeric data
N10	Cannot be left empty and should contain only numeric data
N5	Cannot be left empty and should contain only numeric data
C10	Cannot be left empty and should contain only numeric data
C5	Cannot be left empty and should contain only numeric data
C2	Cannot be left empty and should contain only numeric data
C1	Cannot be left empty and should contain only numeric data
C50p	Cannot be left empty and should contain only numeric data
C25p	Cannot be left empty and should contain only numeric data

MICROHELP

Table Name: Emp_Mstr

Object Name	Description
EmpId	Employee's identity number is system generated
FName	Enter the employee's first name
MName	Enter the employee's middle name
LName	Enter the employee's last name
Addr1	Enter employee's date of birth
Addr2	Enter the employee's postal address (House name and number)
City	Enter the employee's postal address (Locality)
Pincode	Enter the employee's postal address (City/Town name)
RTel	Enter the employee's postal pin code
DOB	Enter the employee's residential telephone number
Dept	Enter the employee's department name
Desig	Enter the employee's official Designation

Table Name: Clnt_Mstr

Object Name	Description
ClientId	Client's identity number is system generated
FName	Enter the client's first name
MName	Enter the client's middle name
LName	Enter the client's last name
Addr1	Enter the client's date of birth
Addr2	Enter the client's postal address (House name and number)
City	Enter the client's postal address (Locality)
Pincode	Enter the client's postal address (City/Town name)
DOB	Enter the client's postal pin code
PANCopy	Select this when the client's I.T. PAN information has been submitted
VerifiedData	Select this when the client's name and address has been verified

CHAP 05 — A COMMERCIAL BANKING SYSTEM: THE PLAN

Table Name: Clnt_Dtls

Column Name	Description
ClientId	(Automatically posted from Clnt_Mstr)
ContactType	Select the contact type for the contact number
ContactNo	Enter the contact number

Table Name: Acct_Mstr

Column Name	Description
AcctNo	Account number is system generated
AcctType	Select the account type
AcctHead	Enter the organisation's name
ClientId1	(Automatically posted from Clnt_Mstr)
ClientId2	(Automatically posted from Clnt_Mstr)
ClientId3	(Automatically posted from Clnt_Mstr)
Nominee	(Automatically posted from Clnt_Mstr)
IntroAcct	(Automatically posted from Clnt_Mstr)
IntroId	(Automatically posted from Clnt_Mstr)
IntroSign	Select if the introducer has the application form signed
VerifierId	(Automatically posted from Emp_Mstr)
VerifierSign	Select if the bank officer, who verifies the information has signed the application form
ManagerSign	Select if the bank manager has signed the application form
OpenDate	Select date on which the account is opened

Table Name: Trans_Mstr

Column Name	Description
TransId	Transaction's Id number is system generated
AcctNo	(Automatically posted from Acct_Mstr)
TransDate	Select the date on which the transaction has occured
TransType	Select this when an amount is deposited Select this if an amount is withdrawn
CashTrans	Select if the transaction is in cash
TransAmt	Enter the amount of rupees deposited (in figures)

Table Name: Trans_Dtls_Chq

Column Name	Description
TransId	(Automatically posted from Trans_Mstr)
ChqNo	Enter the cheque number
Chqdate	Enter the cheque date
Payee	Enter the payee's name
BankId	Enter the bank's sort code for the drawer's bank
DrawerAcctNo	Enter the drawer's account number
TransCode	Enter the cheque's transaction code

Table Name: Trans_Dtls_Csh

Column Name	Description
TransId	(Automatically posted from Trans_Mstr)
N1000	Enter the number of notes in the denomination of Rs. 1000
N500	Enter the number of notes in the denomination of Rs. 500
N100	Enter the number of notes in the denomination of Rs. 100
N50	Enter the number of notes in the denomination of Rs. 50
N20	Enter the number of notes in the denomination of Rs. 20
N10	Enter the number of notes in the denomination of Rs. 10
N5	Enter the number of notes in the denomination of Rs. 5
C10	Enter the number of coins in the denomination of Rs. 10
C5	Enter the number of coins in the denomination of Rs. 5
C2	Enter the number of coins in the denomination of Rs. 2
C1	Enter the number of coins in the denomination of Rs. 1
C50p	Enter the number of coins in the denomination of 50 ps.
C25p	Enter the number of coins in the denomination of 25ps.

TEST RECORDS FOR THE BANKING SYSTEM

Table Name : Emp_Mstr

EmpId	FName	MName	LName	DOB	Dept	Desig
1	Ivan	Nelson	Bayross	26/06/52	Administration	Managing Director
2	Amit		Desai	14/12/67	Loans & Financing	Head Of Dept.
3	Maya	Mahima	Joshi	05/03/75	Accounts	Head Of Dept.
4	Peter	Iyer	Joseph	29/02/60	Client Servicing	Clerk
5	Mandhar	Dilip	Dalvi	12/05/76	Marketing	Head Of Dept.
6	Sonal	Abdul	Khan	08/08/79	Administration	Admin. Executive
7	Anil	Ashutosh	Kambli	05/10/70	Administration	Office Asst.
8	Seema	P.	Apte	26/03/68	Client Servicing	Clerk
9	Vikram	Vilas	Randive	30/04/72	Accounts	Office Asst.
10	Anjali	Sameer	Pathak	10/10/72	Marketing	Marketing Manager

EmpId	Addr1	Addr2	City	Pincode	RTel
1	F-12, Diamond Palace, West Avenue,	North Avenue, Santacruz (West)	Mumbai	400056	6045953
2	Desai House, Plot No. 25, P.G. Marg	Near Malad Rly. Stat., Malad (West)	Mumbai	400078	8883779
3	Room No. 56, 3rd Floor, Swamibhavan,	J. P. Road Junction, Andheri (East)	Mumbai	400059	8377634
4	301, Thomas Palace, Opp. Indu Child Care	Yadnik Nagar, Andheri (West)	Mumbai	400058	6323560
5	456/A, Bldg. No. 4, Vahatuk Nagar,	Amboli, Andheri (West)	Mumbai	400058	6793231
6	201, Meena Towers, Nr. Sun Gas Agency,	S. V. Rd., Goregoan (West),	Mumbai	400076	8085654
7	Patel Chawl, Rm. No. 15, B. P. Lal Marg,	Mahim (West)	Mumbai	400016	4442342
8	A - 10, Neelam, L.J.Road	Mahim	Mumbai	400016	4365672
9	1/12 Bal Govindas Society, M.B.Raut Rd.	Dadar	Mumbai	400028	4327349
10	Pathak Nagar, Cadal Road	Mahim	MUMBAI	400016	4302579

Table Name : Clnt_Mstr

ClientId	FName	MName	LName	PANCopy	VerifiedData
1	Ivan	Nelson	Bayross	Yes	Yes
2	Chriselle	Ivan	Bayross	No	Yes
3	Mamta	Arvind	Muzumdar	Yes	Yes
4	Chhaya	Sudhakar	Bankar	Yes	Yes
5	Ashwini	Dilip	Joshi	Yes	Yes
6	Hansel	I.	Colaco	No	Yes
7	Anil	Arun	Dhone	No	Yes
8	Alex	Austin	Fernandes	Yes	Yes
9	Ashwini	Shankar	Apte	Yes	Yes
10	Namita	S.	Kanade	Yes	Yes

ClientId	Addr1	Addr2	City	Pincode	DOB
1	F-12, Diamond Palace, West Avenue,	North Avenue, Santacruz (West)	Mumbai	400056	25/06/52
2	F-12, Diamond Queen,	North Avenue,Samtacruz	Mumbai	400056	29/10/82
3	Magesh Prasad	Saraswati Baug, Jogeshwari(E)	Mumbai	400060	28/08/75
4	4, Sampada	Kataria Road, Mahim	Mumbai	400016	06/10/76
5	104, Vikram Apts. Bhagat Lane	Shivaji Park,Mahim	Mumbai	400016	20/11/78
6	12, Radha kunj, N.C Kelkar Road	Dadar	Mumbai	400028	01/01/82
7	A/14, Shanti Society, Mogal Lane,	Mahim	Mumbai	400016	12/10/83
8	5, Vagdevi, Senapati Bapat Rd.	Dadar	Mumbai	400016	30/09/62
9	A-10 Nutan Vaishali	Shivaji Park,Mahim	Mumbai	400016	19/04/79
10	B-10, Makarand Society	Cadal Road, Mahim	Mumbai	400016	10/06/78

Table Name : Clnt_Dtls

ClientId	ContactType	ContactNo
1	R	6405853
1	O	6134553
1	M	9820178955
1	O	6134571
2	R	60455754
2	O	6134571
3	R	8324567
3	O	6197654
4	R	4449852
4	O	8741370
5	R	4302934
5	O	2819964
6	R	4217592
7	R	4372247
8	O	6480903
9	R	4313408
9	M	9821176651
10	R	4362680
10	O	8973355
10	M	9820484648

Table Name : Acct_Mstr

AcctNo	Acct Type	AcctHead	ClientId1	ClientId2	ClientId3	NomineeId	IntroAcct	IntroId
1	SB		1	0	0	0	1	1
2	SB	Uttam Stores	2	3	0	0	1	1
3	CA	Sun's Pvt. Ltd.	4	5	6	0	2	2
4	SB		7	3	0	0	1	1
5	SB	Puru Hsg. Soc	6	8	0	3	2	2
6	SB		9	0	0	10	4	5

Table Name : Acct_Mstr (Continued)

AcctNo	IntroSign	VerifierId	VerifierSign	ManagerSign	OpenDate
1	Yes	1	Yes	Yes	01/09/01
2	Yes	1	Yes	Yes	30/10/01
3	Yes	4	Yes	Yes	16/12/01
4	Yes	8	Yes	Yes	02/02/02
5	Yes	9	Yes	Yes	15/03/02
6	Yes	7	Yes	Yes	20/12/01

Table Name : Trans_Mstr

TransId	AcctNo	TransDate	TransType	CashTrans	TransAmt
1	1	01/09/02	D	Yes	500
2	2	30/10/01	D	Yes	1500
3	3	16/12/01	D	Yes	5000
4	4	02/02/02	D	Yes	1000
5	5	15/03/02	D	Yes	2500
6	6	20/12/01	D	Yes	500
7	1	01/11/01	D	Yes	5000
8	2	30/11/01	D	Yes	500
9	3	02/01/02	W	No	500
10	3	10/01/02	W	Yes	500
11	6	20/03/02	D	No	1000
12	5	15/06/02	W	Yes	250
13	5	20/06/02	D	No	2000
14	5	29/06/02	D	Yes	1000
15	1	02/08/02	D	Yes	1000
16	1	15/08/02	W	Yes	500
17	2	05/08/02	D	Yes	1500
18	2	20/08/02	W	Yes	1000
19	3	10/08/02	D	No	3000
20	3	29/08/02	W	Yes	1000
21	5	07/08/02	D	No	5000
22	5	25/08/02	W	No	1500
23	6	09/08/02	D	Yes	2500
24	6	15/08/02	D	Yes	600
25	6	29/08/02	W	Yes	1100

Table Name : Trans_Dtls_Chq

TransId	ChqNo	ChqDate	Payee	BankId	DrawerAcctNo	TransCode
9	96523	30/12/01	Self	400019021	3	11
11	34987	18/03/02	Self	400023022	3467	10
13	2128	19/06/02	Self	400000310	65987	10
19	34998	05/08/02	Self	400001501	37459	10
21	128764	01/08/02	Self	400020009	963636	10
22	98776	23/08/02	S.S.Mehta	400006125	864234	10

Table Name : Trans_Dtls_Csh

TransId	N1000	N500	N100	N50	N20	N10	N5	C10	C5	C2	C1	C50p	C25p
1	0	0	5	0	0	0	0	0	0	0	0	0	0
2	1	0	5	0	0	0	0	0	0	0	0	0	0
3	0	0	50	0	0	0	0	0	0	0	0	0	0
4	0	0	10	0	0	0	0	0	0	0	0	0	0
5	0	4	5	0	0	0	0	0	0	0	0	0	0
6	0	0	3	4	0	0	0	0	0	0	0	0	0
7	0	6	20	0	0	0	0	0	0	0	0	0	0
8	0	0	4	2	0	0	0	0	0	0	0	0	0
10	0	0	0	10	0	0	0	0	0	0	0	0	0
12	0	0	2	1	0	0	0	0	0	0	0	0	0
14	0	0	10	0	0	0	0	0	0	0	0	0	0
15	0	0	5	10	0	0	0	0	0	0	0	0	0
16	0	0	2	6	0	0	0	0	0	0	0	0	0
17	0	2	5	0	0	0	0	0	0	0	0	0	0
18	0	0	8	4	0	0	0	0	0	0	0	0	0
20	0	0	5	10	0	0	0	0	0	0	0	0	0
23	0	1	20	0	0	0	0	0	0	0	0	0	0
24	0	1	1	0	0	0	0	0	0	0	0	0	0
25	0	0	10	0	0	10	0	0	0	0	0	0	0

Chapter 05

Self Evaluation

In This Chapter We Learned:

- **What is a Personal Information Manager**
  Its Working And Requirements

- **Data Segregation And Relationships Within The Project**

- **Database Designing For The Project**
  Table Definitions
  Table Data Validation Rules
  Micro Help For Table Fields
  Test Data For The Application

Chapter 06

A Commercial Banking System: The Working

In This Chapter:

- **Behaviour Of The Commercial Banking System**
  Its Working Through Visual Basic 6

- **Built-In Components And References Required While Designing**

- **Project Source Codes**
  frmMain.frm
  modBnkSys.bas
  frmOpenFrm.frm
  frmEmpMstr.frm
  frmClntMstr.frm
  frmSlctClnt.frm
  frmAcctMstr.frm
  frmTransMstr.frm

6. A COMMERCIAL BANKING SYSTEM: THE WORKING

When the application starts, a window as shown in diagram 6.1 is displayed. This window contains a menu bar and a toolbar. A user can start a data entry or reporting operation by selecting any one sub menu items below **Form** or **Reports**. Refer to diagrams 6.2 and 6.3.

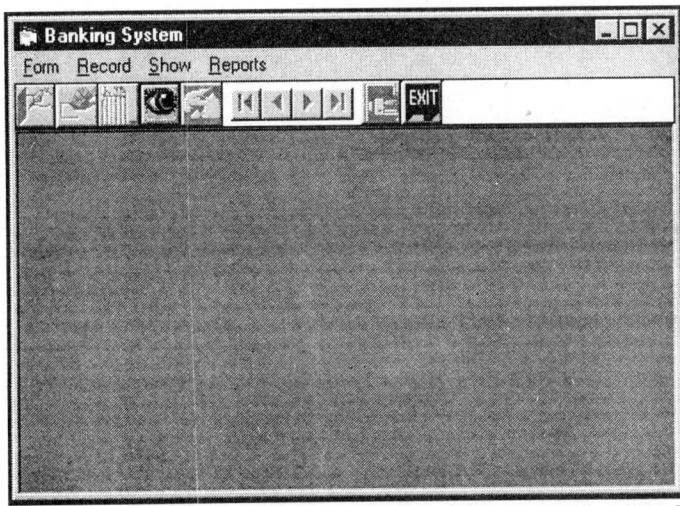

Diagram 6.1: Data entry screen when the application's MDI form loads

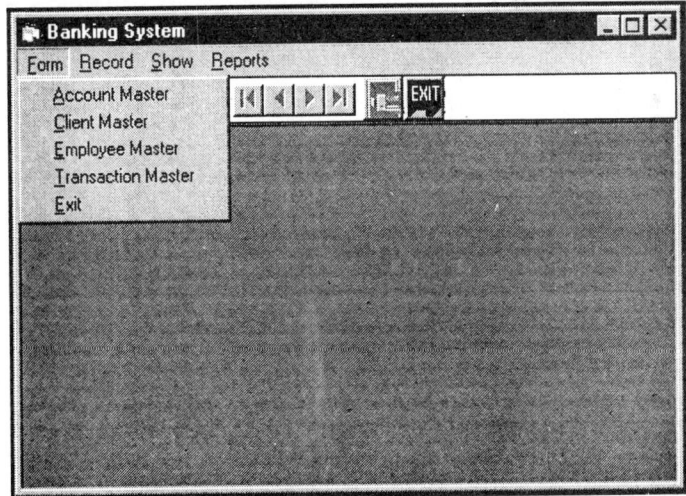

Diagram 6.2: Sub-options under the **Form** menu option

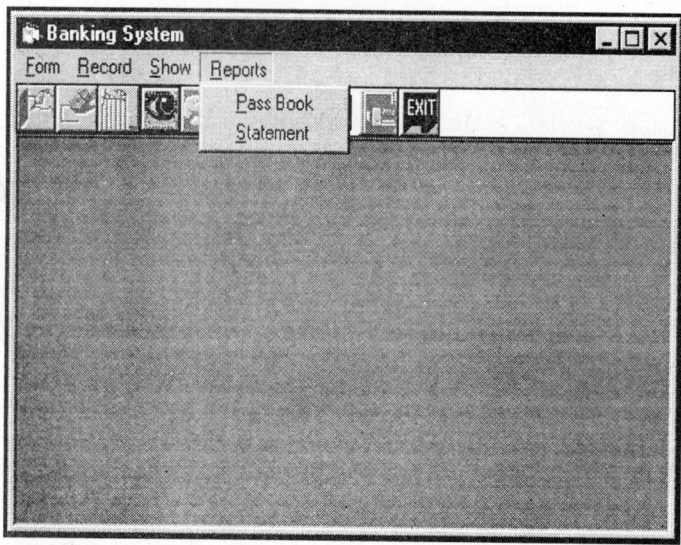

Diagram 6.3: Sub-options under the **Report** menu option

The sub menu options and the toolbar buttons used for data manipulation remain disabled untill a data entry form is not activated. Refer to diagram 6.4.

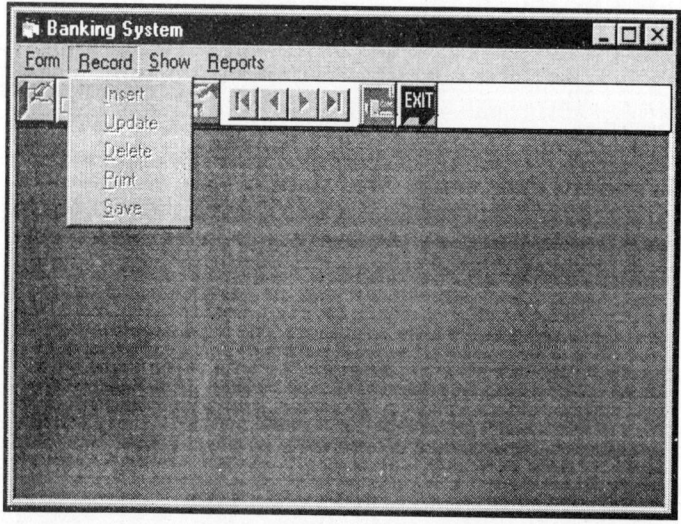

Diagram 6.4: Sub-options under the **Record** menu option

A COMMERCIAL BANKING SYSTEM: THE WORKING

The **View...** sub menu item also allows to select a data entry or reporting option. On click, a dialog box as shown in diagram 6.6 appears.

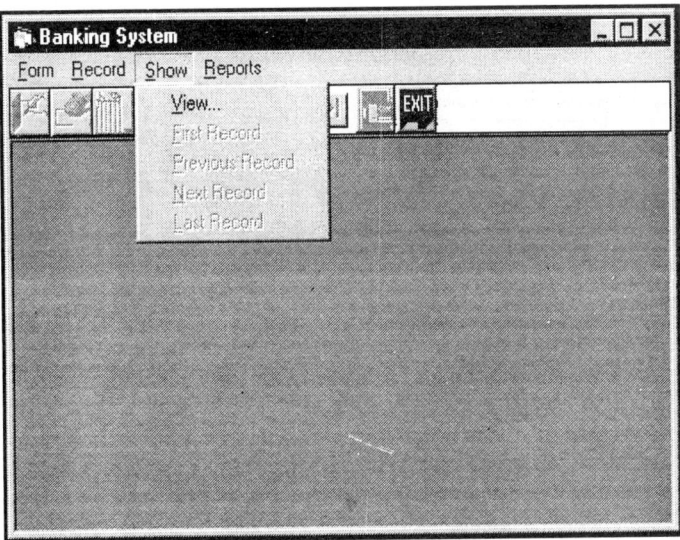

Diagram 6.5: Sub-options under the **Show** menu option

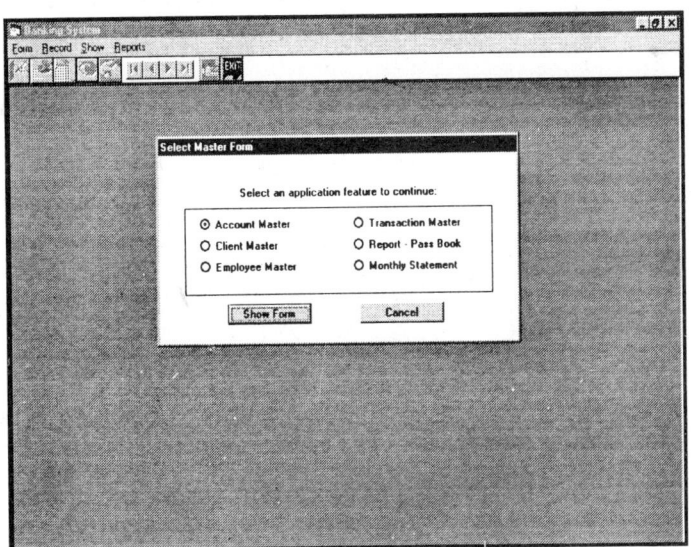

Diagram 6.6: Data entry screen for selecting a master form (frmOpenFrm.frm)

As user selects **Account Master** from the **Form** menu item, a form shown in diagram 6.7.1 appears. This form captures information regarding an account consisting of account type, account holders names, introducer's information and so on.

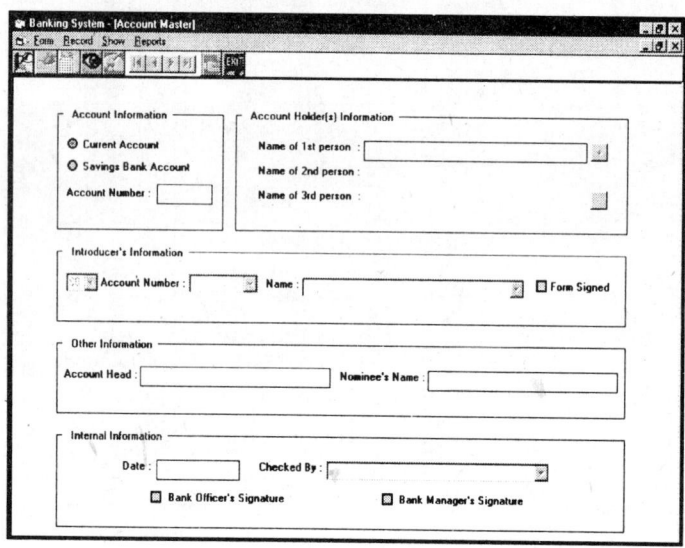

Diagram 6.7.1: Data entry screen for managing account's information (frmAcctMstr.frm)

The screen displayed in diagram 6.7.2 is displayed when a user opens a new account with the bank. This form avoids repetitive data entry while allowing an existing client to open an account.

If a client already has an account, by simply selecting the account type and number, the client's information can be added to open a new account.

If a client has been introduced for the first time, the dialog box allows to capture data for the same.

CHAP 06 A COMMERCIAL BANKING SYSTEM: THE WORKING

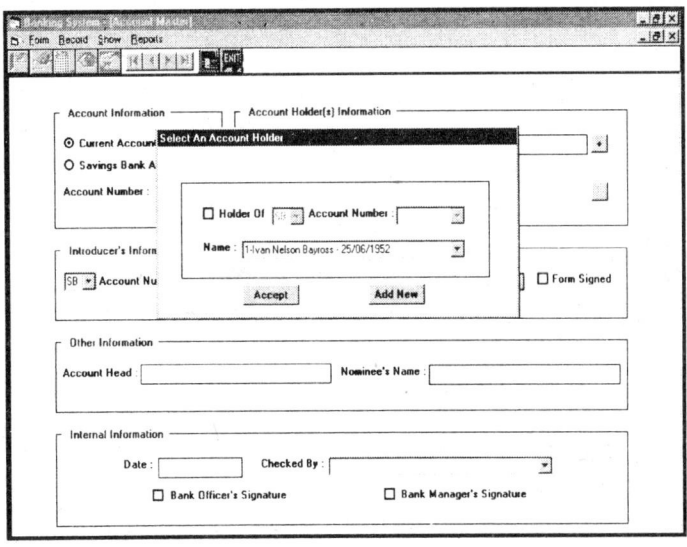

Diagram 6.7.2: Adding a client to the new account

While opening a new account, when a user clicks on the **Date** field, a calendar control is displayed on the screen. Refer to diagram 6.7.3. A user can select a date from this calendar control.

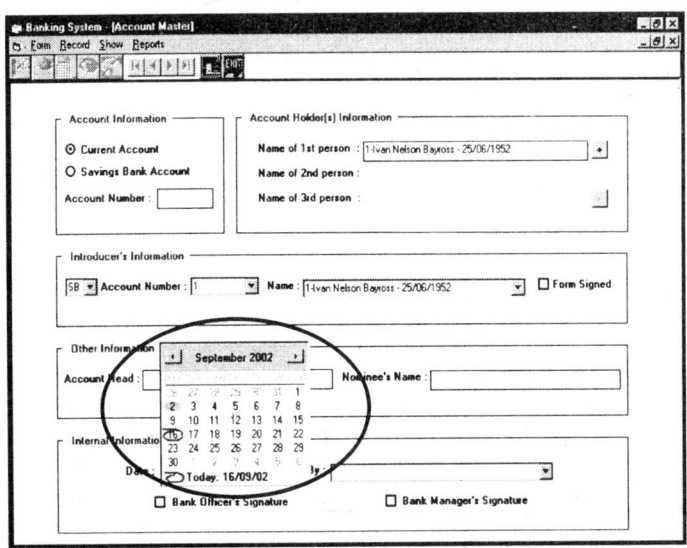

Diagram 6.7.3: Selecting the opening date through a calendar control

The screen displayed in diagram 6.8 is displayed, when a client comes to the bank to open an account. The form captures information consisting of name, postal address, birth date and contact information of a client.

In addition to the above, this form also confirms whether a client has submitted PAN information documents and information provided by a client is verified.

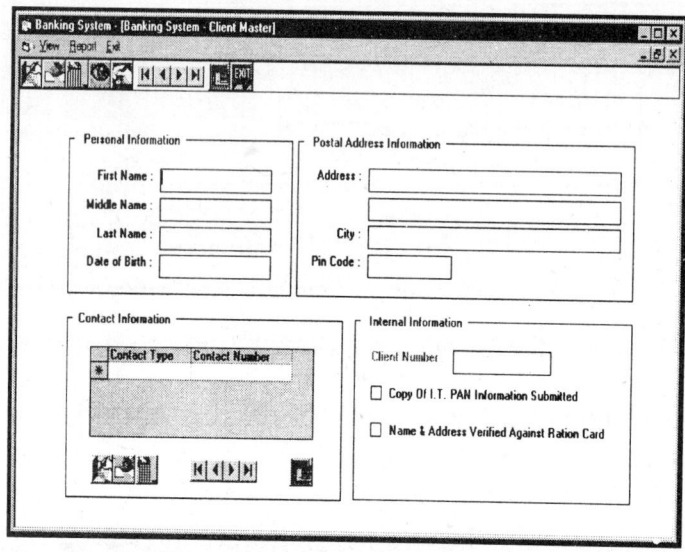

Diagram 6.8: Data entry screen for managing client's information (frmClntMstr.frm)

The screen displayed in diagram 6.9 is displayed that captures employee information. This form captures information such as name, postal address, and date of birth and telephone number of an employee.

In addition to the above, it also captures information consisting of employee code, department name and designation of an employee.

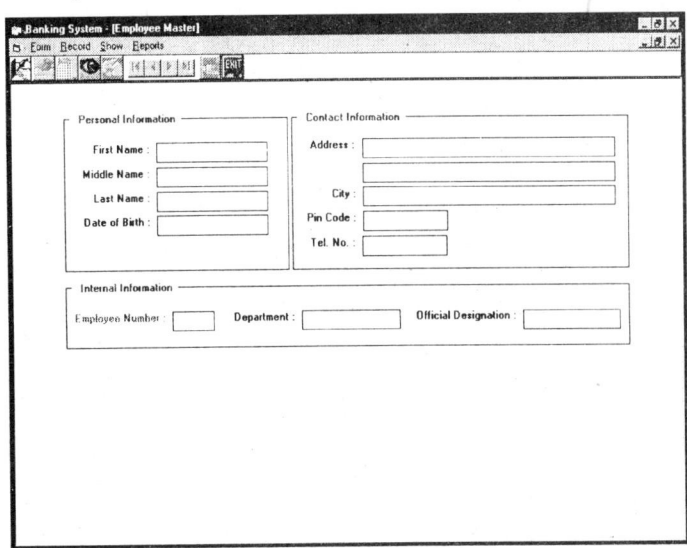

Diagram 6.9: Data entry screen for managing employee's information (frmEmpMstr.frm)

When the transaction's data entry form is activated, the screen as shown in diagram 6.10.1 appears. This screen allows only a data insert operation. While inserting a transaction, a user has to select an account type and number along with date, type and amount of a transaction.

It also captures details bound to a cheque transaction. The details section captures information such as cheque number, date on which it is drawn and MICR details. Refer to diagram 6.10.1.

In case of a cash transaction, the detail section of a data entry form is changed to appear as shown in diagram 6.10.2. Here, the details section captures information related to number of notes and coins of various denomination used during the transaction.

PRACTICAL VB 6 PROJECTS CHAP 06

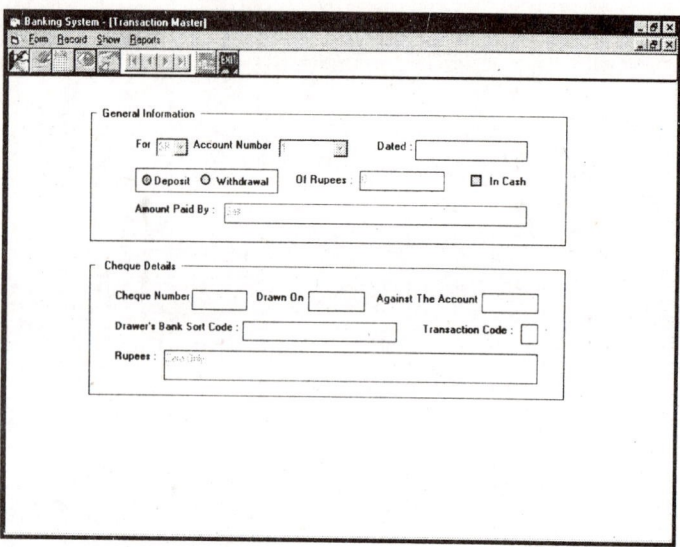

Diagram 6.10.1: Data entry screen for managing bank's cheque transaction (frmTransMstr.frm)

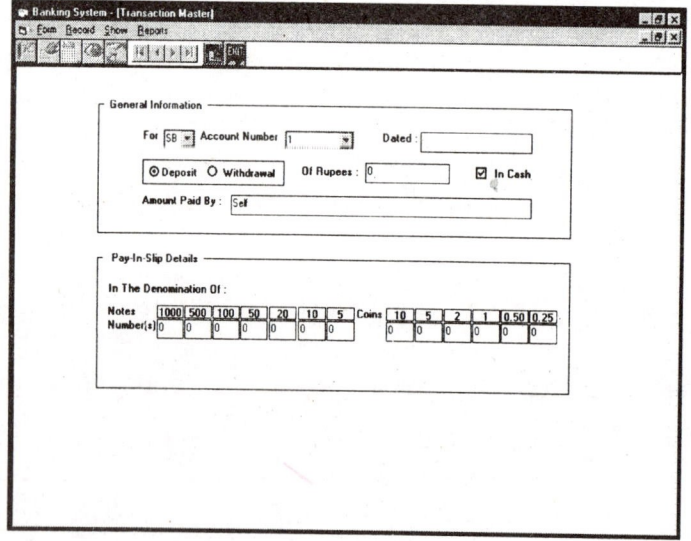

Diagram 6.10.2: Data entry screen for managing bank's cash transaction (frmTransMstr.frm)

When a user clicks on **Reports → Pass Book**, a screen as shown in diagram 6.11.1 appears. This screen captures data used to generate a passbook update for a specified period. It accepts the account type and number along with the starting and ending date of a period.

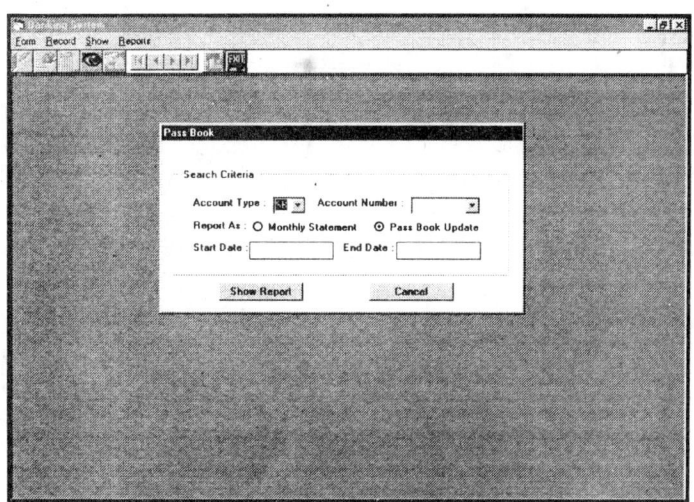

Diagram 6.11.1: Generating a passbook update

When a user clicks on **Reports → Statement**, a screen as shown in diagram 6.11.2 appears. This screen captures data used to generate a monthly statement for a specific account. It accepts the account type and number along with the month and the year of the statement.

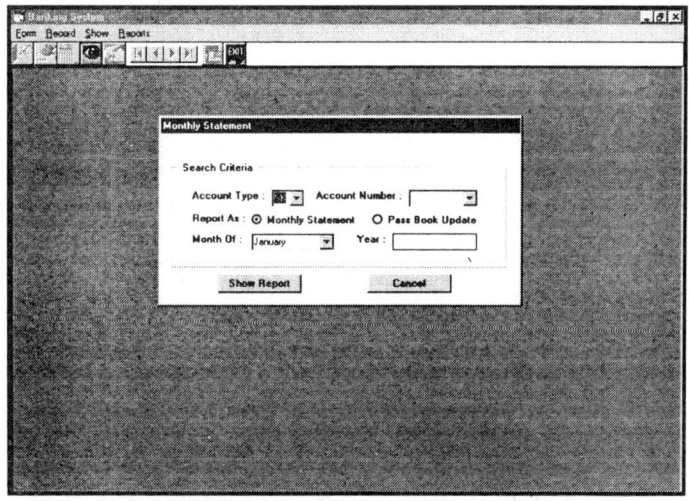

Diagram 6.11.2: Generating monthly statement

ADDITIONAL COMPONENTS AND REFERENCES

Along with the normal ActiveX control like the Labels, Textboxes, List boxes, Command button, etc the Commercial Banking System requires some additional components. These components are:

- Microsoft ADO Data Control 6.0 (OLEDB) (C:\Windows\System\MSADODC.ocx)
- Microsoft Data Grid Control 6.0 (OLEDB) (C:\Windows\System\MSDATGRD.ocx)
- Microsoft Windows Common Controls-2 6.0 (C:\Windows\System\MSCOMCT2.ocx)

In additions to these the following References are required:

- Microsoft ActiveX Data Object 2.0 library (C:\Program Files\Common Files\SYSTEM\msado20.tlb)
- Microsoft Data Reporter Designer v6.0 (C:\Windows\System\MSDBRPTR.dll)
- Microsoft Data Formatting Object Library (C:\Windows\System\MSSTDFMT.dll)

PROJECT CODE FOR frmMain.frm

The Form_Load() subroutine is called when the MDI form loads in memory. Before the MDI form is displayed on the screen, the subroutine initialises some global variables. It also establishes a permanent connection with the Access database by making a call to the Connect2DB() subroutine.

The call to the SetQuery() subroutine creates SQL queries used in other application functionalities. Finally, the call to the OptStatus() subroutine determines the state for the sub menu options and the toolbar buttons.

```
'***************************************************************
'******** FUNCTIONALITY FOR THE FORM SPECIFIC EVENTS BEGINS ********
```
The Form_Load() is called when the form loads

```
Public Sub MDIForm_Load()
'Storing initialisation values into global variables
    gObjId = ""
    gFrmName1 = ""
    gFrmName2 = ""
    gFrmName3 = ""
    gFrmRs1 = ""
    gFrmRs2 = ""
    gFrmRs3 = ""
'Calling Connect2DB to open up a connection to the database
    Call Connect2DB
'Calling SetQry to store SQL Queries into global variables
    Call SetQry
'Calling OptStatus to determine the state of the MDI's menubar and
'toolbar when all data entry forms are inactive
    Call OptStatus
End Sub
```

The **Form_Unload()** subroutine is called before the MDI form is actually destroyed from memory. The subroutine insures that the global variables are emptied and the permanent connection with database is terminated.

```
Public Sub Form_Unload(Cancel As Integer)
    gFrmName1 = ""
    gFrmName2 = ""
    gFrmName3 = ""
    gFrmRs1 = ""
    gFrmRs2 = ""
    gFrmRs3 = ""
'Closing the database connection
    mConnect.Close
End Sub
'********* FUNCTIONALITY FOR THE FORM SPECIFIC EVENTS ENDS *********
'******************************************************************
```

The following subroutines are bound to the CLICK event of a particular sub menu option on the menu bar. Depending on the sub menu option clicked an appropriate code block is executed.

```
'******************************************************************
'***** FUNCTIONALITY OF THE MDI FORM's MENU BAR OPTIONS BEGINS *****
```

The **mnuAcctMstr_Click()** subroutine is called when a sub menu item to load the Account Master's data entry form is clicked.

```
Public Sub mnuAcctMstr_Click()
    Call LoadChild(frmAcctMstr)
End Sub
```

The **mnuClntMstr_Click()** subroutine is called when a sub menu item to load the Client Master's data entry form is clicked.

```
Public Sub mnuClntMstr_Click()
    Call LoadChild(frmClntMstr)
End Sub
```

CHAP 06 — A COMMERCIAL BANKING SYSTEM: THE WORKING

The **mnuEmpMstr_Click()** subroutine is called when a sub menu item to load the Employee Master's data entry form is clicked.

```
Public Sub mnuEmpMstr_Click()
    Call LoadChild(frmEmpMstr)
End Sub
```

The **mnuTransMstr_Click()** subroutine is called when a sub menu item to load the Transaction Master's data entry form is clicked.

```
Public Sub mnuTransMstr_Click()
    Call LoadChild(frmTransMstr)
End Sub
```

The **mnuExit_Click()** subroutine is called when a sub menu item to unload the active form is clicked.

```
Public Sub mnuExit_Click()
    Unload GetActvFrm(gFrmName1)
End Sub
```

The **mnuInst_Click()** subroutine is called when a sub menu item to insert a Master record is clicked.

```
Public Sub mnuInst_Click()
    Call GetActvFrm(gFrmName1).InstMstrRecd
End Sub
```

The **mnuUpdt_Click()** subroutine is called when a sub menu item to update the record, displayed on the U.I., is clicked.

```
Public Sub mnuUpdt_Click()
    Call GetActvFrm(gFrmName1).UpdtMstrRecd
End Sub
```

The **mnuDel_Click()** subroutine is called when the sub menu item to delete the record, displayed on the U.I., is clicked.

```
Public Sub mnuDel_Click()
    Call GetActvFrm(gFrmName1).DelMstrRecd
End Sub
```

PRACTICAL VB 6 PROJECTS CHAP 06

The **mnuPrnt_Click()** subroutine is called when the sub menu item to print the record, displayed on the U.I., is clicked.

```
Public Sub mnuPrnt_Click()
    Call PrntMstrRecd(GetActvRs(gFrmRs1))
End Sub
```

The **mnuSave_Click()** subroutine is called when the sub menu item to save the changes made to the record, displayed on the U.I., is clicked.

```
Public Sub mnuSave_Click()
    Call GetActvFrm(gFrmName1).SaveMstrRecd
End Sub
```

The **mnuView_Click()** subroutine is called when the sub menu item **'View'** is clicked.

```
Public Sub mnuView_Click()
'Checking whether the variable 'gFrmName1' holds a value
    If gFrmName1 = "" Then
    'Calling Load to display the form with options to start a data entry
    'or reporting operation
        Load frmOpenFrm
        frmOpenFrm.Show vbModal   Else
    Else
    'Calling VuMstrRecd to View records in the active U.I.
        Call VuMstrRecd(GetActvRs(gFrmRs1))
    End If
End Sub
```

The **mnuFrst_Click()** subroutine is called when a sub menu item to display the first record from the active recordset, is clicked.

```
Public Sub mnuFrst_Click()
    Call VuFrstMstr(GetActvRs(gFrmRs1))
End Sub
```

The **mnuPrev_Click()** subroutine is called when a sub menu to display the previous record from the active recordset, is clicked.

```
Public Sub mnuPrev_Click()
    Call VuPrevMstr(GetActvRs(gFrmRs1))
End Sub
```

CHAP 06   A COMMERCIAL BANKING SYSTEM: THE WORKING

The **mnuNext_Click()** subroutine is called when a sub menu item to display the Next record from the active recordset, is clicked.

```
Public Sub mnuNext_Click()
    Call VuNextMstr(GetActvRs(gFrmRs1))
End Sub
```

The **mnuLast_Click()** subroutine is called when a sub menu item to display the last record from the active recordset, is clicked.

```
Public Sub mnuLast_Click()
    Call VuLastMstr(GetActvRs(gFrmRs1))
End Sub
```

The **mnuPassBk_Click()** subroutine is called when a sub menu item to load the Pass Book's report generator, is clicked.

```
Public Sub mnuPassBk_Click()
'Calling Load to display a form to generate a transaction report
'as a monthly statement
    gRprtType = "Monthly Statement"
    Load frmShowRprt
    frmShowRprt.Show vbModal
End Sub
```

The **mnuStmt_Click()** subroutine is called when a sub menu item to load the Monthly Statement's report generator, is clicked.

```
Public Sub mnuStmt_Click()
'Calling Load to display a form to generate a transaction report
'as a pass book update
    gRprtType = "Pass Book"
    Load frmShowRprt
    frmShowRprt.Show vbModal
End Sub
'****** FUNCTIONALITY OF THE MDI FORM's MENU BAR OPTIONS ENDS ******
'******************************************************************
```

PRACTICAL VB 6 PROJECTS

The following subroutines are bound to the CLICK event of a particular command button on the toolbar. Depending on the button clicked an appropriate code block is executed.

```
'*************************************************************
'***** FUNCTIONALITY OF THE MDI FORM's TOOLBAR BUTTONS BEGINS ******
```

The **cmdInst_Click()** subroutine is called when the toolbar button to insert a Master record, is clicked.

```
Public Sub cmdInst_Click()
    Call GetActvFrm(gFrmName1).InstMstrRecd
End Sub
```

The **cmdUpdt_Click()** subroutine is called when the toolbar button to update the record displayed on the U.I., is clicked.

```
Public Sub cmdUpdt_Click()
    Call GetActvFrm(gFrmName1).UpdtMstrRecd
End Sub
```

The **cmdDel_Click()** subroutine is called when the toolbar button to delete the record displayed on the U.I., is clicked.

```
Public Sub cmdDel_Click()
    Call GetActvFrm(gFrmName1).DelMstrRecd
End Sub
```

The **cmdView_Click()** subroutine is called when the toolbar button to view records, is clicked.

```
Public Sub cmdView_Click()
'Checking whether the variable 'gFrmName1' holds a value
    If gFrmName1 = "" Then
    'Calling Load to display the form with options to start a data entry
    'or reporting operation
        Load frmOpenFrm
        frmOpenFrm.Show vbModal   Else
    'Calling VuMstrRecd to view records on the U.I.
        Call VuMstrRecd(GetActvRs(gFrmRs1))
    End If
End Sub
```

CHAP 06 A COMMERCIAL BANKING SYSTEM: THE WORKING

The **cmdPrnt_Click()** subroutine is called when the toolbar button to print the record displayed on the U.I., is clicked.

```
Public Sub cmdPrnt_Click()
    Call PrntMstrRecd(GetActvRs(gFrmRs1))
End Sub
```

The **cmdFrst_Click()** subroutine is called when the toolbar button to display the first record from the active recordset, is clicked.

```
Public Sub cmdFrst_Click()
    Call VuFrstMstr(GetActvRs(gFrmRs1))
End Sub
```

The **cmdPrior_Click()** subroutine is called when the toolbar button to display the previous record from the active recordset, is clicked.

```
Public Sub cmdPrior_Click()
    Call VuPrevMstr(GetActvRs(gFrmRs1))
End Sub
```

The **cmdNext_Click()** subroutine is called when the toolbar button to display the next record from the active recordset, is clicked.

```
Public Sub cmdNext_Click()
    Call VuNextMstr(GetActvRs(gFrmRs1))
End Sub
```

The **cmdLast_Click()** subroutine is called when the toolbar button to display the last record from the active recordset, is clicked.

```
Public Sub cmdLast_Click()
    Call VuLastMstr(GetActvRs(gFrmRs1))
End Sub
```

The **cmdSave_Click()** subroutine is called when the toolbar button to save the changes made to the record displayed on the U.I., is clicked.

```
Public Sub cmdSave_Click()
    Call GetActvFrm(gFrmName1).SaveMstrRecd
End Sub
```

The **cmdExit_Click()** subroutine is called when the toolbar button to unload the active form is clicked.

```
Public Sub cmdExit_Click()
    Unload GetActvFrm(gFrmName1)
End Sub
'****** FUNCTIONALITY OF THE MDI FORM's TOOLBAR BUTTONS ENDS *******
'******************************************************************

'******************************************************************
'********* FUNCTIONALITY FOR MDI SPECIFIC SUBROUTINES BEGINS ********
```

The **SetQry()** subroutine is called to store SQL queries into the global variables.

```
Public Sub SetQry()
'Storing SQL Queries into global variables for later use
    gAcctSql = "SELECT * FROM Acct_Mstr"
    gClntSql = "SELECT * FROM Clnt_Mstr"
    gEmpSql = "SELECT * FROM Emp_Mstr"
    gTransSql = "SELECT * FROM Trans_Mstr"
End Sub
```

The **OptStatus()** subroutine is called to determine the state of the MDI's menubar and toolbar when all data entry forms are inactive.

```
Public Sub OptStatus()
'Calling SaveMstr to determine the state of the MDI's menubar
'and toolbar such as to allow only the Save operation
    Call SaveMstr
    mnuAcctMstr.Enabled = True
    mnuClntMstr.Enabled = True
    mnuEmpMstr.Enabled = True
    mnuTransMstr.Enabled = True
    mnuPassBk.Enabled = True
    mnuStmt.Enabled = True
    mnuSave.Enabled = False
    mnuView.Enabled = True
    cmdView.Enabled = True
    cmdSave.Enabled = False
End Sub
'********* FUNCTIONALITY FOR MDI SPECIFIC SUBROUTINES ENDS *********
'******************************************************************
```

PROJECT CODE FOR modBnkSys.bas

```vb
Option Explicit
'Declaring variables for later use
Public gFrmName1, gFrmName2, gFrmName3, gObjId As String
Public gFrmRs1, gFrmRs2, gFrmRs3 As String
Public gAcctSql, gClntSql, gEmpSql, gTransSql, gTemp1Sql As String
Dim mStrCheck, mStrCheck1 As String
Dim mStrLen, mPosition, gMsgResponse As Integer
'Declaring the Connection object variable
Public gConnect As Adodb.Connection
'Declaring the Recordset object variable
Public gAcctRs, gClntRs, gEmpRs, gTransRs As Adodb.Recordset
Public gChqRs, gCshRs, gContRs, gTemp1Rs, gTemp2Rs, gTemp3Rs As Adodb.Recordset

'*****************************************************************
'*********** APPLICATION's DATABASE CONNECTIVITY BEGINS ***********
```

The **Connect2DB()** subroutine is called to open a database connection. It also creates ADODB's Recordset object, which are globally accessible.

```vb
Public Sub Connect2DB()
'Initializing an ADODB Connection object
    Set gConnect = New Adodb.Connection
'Binding the connection object's Provider attribute
'to an Access database through an OLEDB provider
    gConnect.Provider = "Microsoft.Jet.OLEDB.4.0; Data Source = " & App.Path _
                    & "\Database\Bank.mdb"
    gConnect.Open
'Initialising the ADODB's Recordset objects
    Set gAcctRs = New Adodb.Recordset
    Set gClntRs = New Adodb.Recordset
    Set gEmpRs = New Adodb.Recordset
    Set gTransRs = New Adodb.Recordset
    Set gChqRs = New Adodb.Recordset
    Set gCshRs = New Adodb.Recordset
    Set gContRs = New Adodb.Recordset
    Set gTemp1Rs = New Adodb.Recordset
    Set gTemp2Rs = New Adodb.Recordset
    Set gTemp3Rs = New Adodb.Recordset
End Sub
'*********** APPLICATION's DATABASE CONNECTIVITY ENDS ************
'*****************************************************************
```

```
'****************************************************************
'******** FUNCTIONALITY FOR THE FORM SPECIFIC EVENTS BEGINS ********
```

The **LoadChild()** subroutine is called to load a child form passed as a parameter.

```
Public Sub LoadChild(frmName As Form)
'Resetting the Caption attribute for the MDI's sub menu option 'Exit'
    frmMain.mnuExit.Caption = "&Close"
'Resetting the ToolTipText attribute for MDI's toolbar button 'Exit'
    frmMain.cmdExit.ToolTipText = "Click to close the form"
    gFrmName3 = gFrmName2
    gFrmName2 = gFrmName1
'Checking that the global variable 'gFrmName1' is not empty
    If gFrmName1 <> "" Then
    'Calling DisableFrmOpt to disabling the MDI's menubar options used
    'to open a child form
        Call DisableFrmOpt
    End If
'Loading the child form passed as a parameter
    Load frmName
End Sub
```

The **GetActvFrm()** subroutine is called to returns a form object for the string passed as a parameter.

```
Public Function GetActvFrm(ByVal mFrmName As String) As Form
'Use the variable 'mFrmName' with the Select Case statement
'to returning an appropriate the data entry form
    Select Case mFrmName
    Case Is = "Account"           'If the variable holds 'Account'
        Set GetActvFrm = frmAcctMstr
    Case Is = "Client"            'If the variable holds 'Client'
        Set GetActvFrm = frmClntMstr
    Case Is = "Employee"          'If the variable holds 'Employee'
        Set GetActvFrm = frmEmpMstr
    Case Is = "Transaction"       'If the variable holds 'Transaction'
        Set GetActvFrm = frmTransMstr
    Case Is = "Pass Book"         'If the variable holds 'Pass Book'
        Set GetActvFrm = frmPassBk
    Case Is = "Monthly Statement" 'If the variable holds 'Monthly Statement'
        Set GetActvFrm = frmMthlyStmt
```

```
    Case Is = "Open Form"         'If the variable holds 'Open Form'
        Set GetActvFrm = frmOpenFrm
    Case Is = ""                   'If the variable is empty
        Set GetActvFrm = frmMain
    End Select
End Function
```

The **ResetMDI()** subroutine is called to reset a sequence of global variables used to identify an active child form or recordset object. It also determines the status for the objects on the MDI form.

```
Public Sub ResetMDI()
    gFrmName1 = gFrmName2
    gFrmName2 = gFrmName3
    gFrmName3 = ""
    gFrmRs1 = gFrmRs2
    gFrmRs2 = gFrmRs3
    gFrmRs3 = ""
'Checking if the variable 'gFrmName1' holds a value other than
'the string 'frmMain'
    If gFrmName1 = "" Then
    'Resetting the Caption attribute for the menu option 'Exit'
    'under the menubar option 'Form'
        frmMain.mnuExit.Caption = "&Exit"
    'Resetting the ToolTipText attribute for MDI's toolbar button 'Exit'
        frmMain.cmdExit.ToolTipText = "Click to exit the application"
    'Calling MDI's SetQry to reset SQL queries stored into the global
    'variables
        Call frmMain.SetQry
    'Calling MDI's OptStatus to determine the state of the MDI's menubar
    'and toolbar when all data entry forms are inactive
        Call frmMain.OptStatus
    End If
End Sub
'********* FUNCTIONALITY FOR THE FORM SPECIFIC EVENTS ENDS *********
'******************************************************************
```

PRACTICAL VB 6 PROJECTS

CHAP 06

```
'*************************************************************
'********** FUNCTIONALITY FOR FORM's DATA VIEWING BEGINS **********
```
The **VuMstrRecd()** subroutine is called to view a Master record.

```vb
Public Sub VuMstrRecd(mFrmRs As Adodb.Recordset)
    'Checking if the recordset passed as a parameter is empty
    If mFrmRs.RecordCount > 0 Then
        'Calling ChngMstr to allow data manipulation and navigation operations
        Call ChngMstr
        'Calling PopFrmFlds to populate the data capture fields on the U.I.
        Call GetActvFrm(gFrmName1).PopFrmFlds
    Else
        'Disabling MDI's View options
        frmMain.mnuView.Enabled = False
        frmMain.cmdView.Enabled = False
        'Checking if the global variable 'gFrmName1' refers to
        'the Client master data entry screen
        If gFrmName1 = "Client" Then
            'Calling Client Master's DisableDtls to disable data manipulation
            'in the U.I.'s Detail section
            Call frmClntMstr.DelDtlsRecd
        End If
        'Prompt the user about no records being available
        gMsgResponse = MsgBox("No " & gFrmName1 & " Information exists!!" & vbCrLf _
                        & vbCrLf & "Do you want to insert such information?", _
                        vbYesNo + vbDefaultButton1 + vbInformation, _
                        "Please Note")
        'Checking if the user chose to Insert a record.
        If gMsgResponse = 6 Then
            'Calling InstMstrRecd to insert a record
            Call GetActvFrm(gFrmName1).InstMstrRecd
        Else
            'Unloading the form returned by 'GetActvFrm'
            Unload GetActvFrm(gFrmName1)
        End If
    End If
End Sub
```
```
'********** FUNCTIONALITY FOR FORM's DATA VIEWING ENDS **********
'*************************************************************
```

CHAP 06   A COMMERCIAL BANKING SYSTEM: THE WORKING

```
'*************************************************************
'**************** DATA PRINTING FOR THE FORM BEGINS ***************
```

The **PrntMstrRecd()** subroutine is called to Prints the record displayed on the UI.

```
Public Sub PrntMstrRecd(mFrmRs As Adodb.Recordset)
    MsgBox "Printer not available!!", vbOKOnly
End Sub
'**************** DATA PRINTING FOR THE FORM ENDS *****************
'*************************************************************
```

The following set of subroutines are bound to the data entry form's navigation operations.

```
'*************************************************************
'************ FUNCTIONALITY FOR DATA NAVIGATION BEGINS *************
```

The **VuFrstMstr()** subroutine is called to display a recordset's FIRST record.

```
Public Sub VuFrstMstr(mFrmRs As Adodb.Recordset)
    mFrmRs.MoveFirst
    Call GetActvFrm(gFrmName1).PopFrmFlds
End Sub
```

The **VuPrevMstr()** subroutine is called to display a recordset's PREVIOUS record.

```
Public Sub VuPrevMstr(mFrmRs As Adodb.Recordset)
    mFrmRs.MovePrevious
'Checking if the recordset cursor has moved beyond the FIRST record
    If mFrmRs.BOF Then
        MsgBox "You are on the first record!!", vbExclamation, "PLEASE NOTE"
        mFrmRs.MoveNext
    Else
        Call GetActvFrm(gFrmName1).PopFrmFlds
    End If
End Sub
```

The **VuNextMstr()** subroutine is called to display a recordset's NEXT record.

```
Public Sub VuNextMstr(mFrmRs As Adodb.Recordset)
    mFrmRs.MoveNext
```

```vb
'Checking if the cursor has moved beyond the LAST record
    If mFrmRs.EOF Then
        MsgBox "You are on the last record!!", vbExclamation, "PLEASE NOTE"
        mFrmRs.MovePrevious
    Else
        Call GetActvFrm(gFrmName1).PopFrmFlds
    End If
End Sub
```

The **VuLastMstr()** subroutine is called to display a recordset's LAST record

```vb
Public Sub VuLastMstr(mFrmRs As Adodb.Recordset)
    mFrmRs.MoveLast
    Call GetActvFrm(gFrmName1).PopFrmFlds
End Sub
'************ FUNCTIONALITY FOR DATA NAVIGATION ENDS **************
'****************************************************************


'****************************************************************
'********* FUNCTIONALITY FOR FORM FIELD VALIDATIONS BEGINS *********
```

The **CharFound()** subroutine is called to check for a specific character in a string.

```vb
Public Function CharFound(mText As String, mChar As String) As Boolean
'Retrieving the position of the specific character in the string
    mPosition = InStr(1, mText, mChar, vbTextCompare)
'Checking the value of the variable 'mPosition' to return
'an appropriate Boolean value
    If mPosition > 0 Then
        CharFound = True
    Else
        CharFound = False
    End If
End Function
```

The **MinLen()** subroutine is called to check the minimum length of a string.

```vb
Public Function MinLen(mText As String, mMinLen As Integer) As Boolean
'Removing any spaces from the string passed as a parameter
    mText = Trim(mText)
'Retrieving the length of the string passed as a parameter
    mStrLen = Len(mText)
```

```vb
'Checking the length to returning an appropriate Boolean value
    If Not mStrLen < mMinLen Then
        MinLen = True
    Else
        MinLen = False
    End If
End Function
```

The **ValidTxt()** subroutine is called to check if the string contains anything other than alphabets or a single quote.

```vb
Public Function ValidTxt(mText As String) As Boolean
    mStrLen = Len(mText)
'Iterating to scan each character in the parameter string
    For mPosition = 1 To mStrLen
      'Retrieve each character from the parameter string
        mStrCheck1 = Mid(mText, mPosition, 1)
      'Checking the character to returning an appropriate Boolean value
        If (Asc(strCheck1) < 65 And Not Asc(strCheck1)) Or (Asc(strCheck1) > 90 _
            And Asc(strCheck1) < 97) Or Asc(strCheck1) > 122 Then
            ValidTxt = False
            Exit Function
        Else
            ValidTxt = True
        End If
    Next
End Function
'********** FUNCTIONALITY FOR FORM FIELD VALIDATIONS ENDS **********
'****************************************************************

'****************************************************************
'****** FUNCTIONALITY FOR APPLICATION's OTHER FEATURES BEGINS ******
```

The **ConvertAmt()** subroutine is called to return an amount in words.

```vb
Public Function ConvertAmt(mInt As String) As String
    mStr = ""
    mInt = Trim(Str(mInt))
    mStrLen = Len(mInt)
```

PRACTICAL VB 6 PROJECTS

```vb
'Creating an iterated process to scan each digit in the parameter
    For mPosition = 2 To mStrLen
    'Checking if the digit is not a zero or a dot symbol
        If Mid(mInt, mPosition, 1) <> 0 Or mPosition = 9 Then
        'Checking for the digit's position in the parameter
        'to concatenate a string accordingly
            If mPosition = 2 Or mPosition = 4 Or mPosition = 7 _
                Or mPosition = 10 Then
                Select Case Mid(mInt, mPosition, 1)
                Case "1"
                    If Mid(mInt, mPosition + 1, 1) = 0 Or (mPosition = mStrLen) Then
                        mStr = mStr & "Ten "
                    End If
                Case "2"
                    mStr = mStr & "Twenty "
                Case "3"
                    mStr = mStr & "Thirty "
                Case "4"
                    mStr = mStr & "Forty "
                Case "5"
                    mStr = mStr & "Fifty "
                Case "6"
                    mStr = mStr & "Sixty "
                Case "7"
                    mStr = mStr & "Seventy "
                Case "8"
                    mStr = mStr & "Eighty "
                Case "9"
                    mStr = mStr & "Ninety "
                End Select
            End If
            If ((mPosition = 3 Or mPosition = 5 Or mPosition = 8 Or mPosition = 11) _
                And (Not Mid(mInt, mPosition - 1, 1) = 1)) Or mPosition = 6 Then
                Select Case Mid(mInt, mPosition, 1)
                Case "1"
                    mStr = mStr & "One "
                Case "2"
                    mStr = mStr & "Two "
                Case "3"
                    mStr = mStr & "Three "
```

```
            Case "4"
                mStr = mStr & "Four "
            Case "5"
                mStr = mStr & "Five "
            Case "6"
                mStr = mStr & "Six "
            Case "7"
                mStr = mStr & "Seven "
            Case "8"
                mStr = mStr & "Eight "
            Case "9"
                mStr = mStr & "Nine "
        End Select
    ElseIf (Mid(mInt, mPosition - 1, 1) = 1) And (Not mPosition = 2) Then
        Select Case Mid(mInt, mPosition, 1)
            Case "1"
                mStr = mStr & "Eleven "
            Case "2"
                mStr = mStr & "Twelve "
            Case "3"
                mStr = mStr & "Thirteen "
            Case "4"
                mStr = mStr & "Fourteen "
            Case "5"
                mStr = mStr & "Fifteen "
            Case "6"
                mStr = mStr & "Sixteen "
            Case "7"
                mStr = mStr & "Seventeen "
            Case "8"
                mStr = mStr & "Eighteen "
            Case "9"
                mStr = mStr & "Nineteen "
        End Select
    End If
End If
```

```
        Select Case mPosition
        Case 3
            If Mid(mInt, 2, 2) <> 0 Then
                mStr = mStr & "Lakh "
            End If
        Case 5
            If Mid(mInt, 4, 2) <> 0 Then
                mStr = mStr & "Thousand "
            End If
        Case 6
            If Mid(mInt, 6, 1) <> 0 Then
                mStr = mStr & "Hundred "
            End If
        Case 9
            If Mid(mInt, 10, 2) <> 0 Then
                mStr = mStr & "And "
            End If
        End Select
    Next
'Checking if the length of the parameter exceeds 9 characters
    If mStrLen > 9 Then
        mStr = mStr & "Paise "
    End If
'Returning a concatenated string
    ConvertAmt = mStr & "Only"
End Function
```

The **GetActvRs()** subroutine is called to returns an appropriate ADODB's Recordset object for the parameter string passed.

```
Public Function GetActvRs(ByVal mFrmRs As String) As Adodb.Recordset
'Checking the value of the variable 'mFrmRs', by using
'the 'Select Case' statement
    Select Case mFrmRs
    Case Is = "gAcctRs"              'If the variable holds 'gAcctRs'
        Set GetActvRs = gAcctRs
    Case Is = "gClntRs"              'If the variable holds 'gClntRs'
        Set GetActvRs = gClntRs
    Case Is = "gEmpRs"               'If the variable holds 'gEmpRs'
        Set GetActvRs = gEmpRs
```

```
        Case Is = "gTransRs"           'If the variable holds 'gTransRs'
            Set GetActvRs = gTransRs
        End Select
End Function
```

The **GetAcctType()** subroutine is called to return an A/c type for an A/c number.

```
Public Function GetAcctType(mIdNo As Integer) As String
'Creating an SQL query string to retrieve the Account Type field
'from the Account's Master table
    gTemp1Sql = "SELECT AcctType FROM Acct_Mstr Where AcctNo = " & mIdNo
'Opening a temporary ADODB's Recordset by passing the SQL query
'and other parameters
    gTemp3Rs.Open gTemp1Sql, gConnect, adOpenKeyset, adLockPessimistic
'Storing the Account Type into a variable
    mStr = gTemp3Rs.Fields(0)
'Closing the temporary ADODB's recordset
    gTemp3Rs.Close
'Returning the Account Type
    GetAcctType = mStr
End Function
```

The **GetIdentity()** subroutine is called to return a client's full name.

```
Public Function GetIdentity(mTable As String, mIdNo As Integer) As String
'Creating an SQL query string to retrieve fields from the table passed
'as a parameter
    If mTable = "Clnt_Mstr" Then
        mStr = "SELECT ClientId, FName, MName, LName, DOB FROM Clnt_Mstr " & _
               "Where ClientId = " & mIdNo
    Else
        mStr = "SELECT EmpId, FName, MName, LName, DOB FROM Emp_Mstr " & _
               "Where EmpId = " & mIdNo
    End If
'Opening a temporary ADODB's Recordset by passing the SQL query
'and other parameters
    gTemp3Rs.Open mStr, gConnect, adOpenKeyset, adLockPessimistic
```

```vb
'Storing the concatenated Client's Id number, full name
'and date of birth into a variable
    mStr = gTemp3Rs.Fields(0) & "-" & gTemp3Rs.Fields(1) & " " & _
            gTemp3Rs.Fields(2) & " " & gTemp3Rs.Fields(3) & " - " & _
            Format(gTemp3Rs.Fields(4), "dd/mm/yyyy")
'Closing the temporary ADODB's recordset
    gTemp3Rs.Close
'Returning the concatenated Client's full name
    GetIdentity = mStr
End Function
```

The **GetNumber()** subroutine is called to return a person's identity number.

```vb
Public Function GetNumber(mStr As String) As Integer
'Getting the position of the hyphen (-) in the selected client's name
    mPosition = InStr(1, mStr, "-", vbTextCompare)
'Returning the Client's Id number from the selected name
    GetNumber = Mid(mStr, 1, mPosition - 1)
End Function
```

The **PopNameCmb()** subroutine is called to populate the combo box, passed as a parameter, listing client's name.

```vb
Public Function PopNameCmb(ByVal mSql As String, mStr As String, _
                    mCmb As ComboBox) As String
'Clearing the option list held in the combo box
    mCmb.Clear
'Opening the ADODB's Recordset object used for retrieving records
    gTemp2Rs.Open mSql, gConnect, adOpenKeyset, adLockPessimistic
'Checking if the active recordset contains records
    If gTemp2Rs.RecordCount > 0 Then
'Displaying a client's name in the combo box passed as a parameter
        mCmb.Text = GetIdentity(mStr, gTemp2Rs.Fields(0))
'Checking if the recordset contains three fields
        If gTemp2Rs.Fields.Count = 3 Then
            For mPosition = 0 To 2
                If gTemp2Rs.Fields(mPosition) > 0 Then
                    mCmb.AddItem (GetIdentity(mStr, gTemp2Rs.Fields(mPosition)))
                End If
            Next
```

```
        Else
            Do While Not gTemp2Rs.EOF
                mCmb.AddItem (GetIdentity(mStr, gTemp2Rs.Fields(0)))
                gTemp2Rs.MoveNext
            Loop
        End If
    End If
'Closing the active recordset
    gTemp2Rs.Close
'Returning the value displayed on the combo box
    PopNameCmb = mStr
End Function
```

The **PopNoCmb()** subroutine is called to populate a combo box passed a parameter.

```
Public Function PopNoCmb(mStr As String, mCmb As ComboBox) As String
'Clearing the option list held in the combo box
    mCmb.Clear
'Creating a SQL query string to retrieve all Account numbers
'for a specific account type
    mStr = "SELECT AcctNo FROM Acct_Mstr Where AcctType = '" & mStr & "'"
'Opening the ADODB's Recordset object used for retrieving records
    gTemp2Rs.Open mStr, gConnect, adOpenKeyset, adLockPessimistic
'Checking if the active recordset contains records
    If gTemp2Rs.RecordCount > 0 Then
        'Displaying an account number in the combo box passed as parameter
        mCmb.Text = gTemp2Rs.Fields(0)
        'Checking if the recordset's cursor has moved beyond the LAST record
        'in the recordset
        Do While Not gTemp2Rs.EOF
            'Adding an item to the combo box passed as parameter
            mCmb.AddItem (gTemp2Rs.Fields(0))
            gTemp2Rs.MoveNext
        Loop   'End of 'Do While ... Loop' iteration
    End If
'Closing the active recordset
    gTemp2Rs.Close
'Returning the value displayed on the combo box
    PopNoCmb = mStr
End Function
```

The **ReturnId()** subroutine is called to display a person's name in a form field passed as parameters.

```
Public Sub ReturnId(mVal As String, ByVal mFrmFld As String)
'Checking the value of the variable 'mFrmFld', using the 'Select Case'
statement, to decide on a form field for displaying the first parameter
    Select Case mFrmFld
    Case Is = "frmAcctMstr.txtHldrName(0)"
        frmAcctMstr.txtHldrName(0).Text = mVal
    Case Is = "frmAcctMstr.txtHldrName(1)"
        frmAcctMstr.txtHldrName(1).Text = mVal
    Case Is = "frmAcctMstr.txtHldrName(2)"
        frmAcctMstr.txtHldrName(2).Text = mVal
    Case Is = "frmAcctMstr.txtNomiName"
        frmAcctMstr.txtNomiName.Text = mVal
    Case Is = "frmAcctMstr.txtNomiName"
        frmAcctMstr.txtNomiName.Text = mVal
    End Select
End Sub
'******* FUNCTIONALITY FOR APPLICATION's OTHER FEATURES ENDS *******
'***************************************************************

'***************************************************************
'******** FUNCTIONALITY FOR MDI's OTHER SUBROUTINES BEGINS *********
```

The **DisableFrmOpt()** subroutine is called to disable the MDI's sub menu options used to open a child form.

```
Public Sub DisableFrmOpt()
'Disabling the sub menu options used to open a data entry form
    frmMain.mnuAcctMstr.Enabled = False
    frmMain.mnuClntMstr.Enabled = False
    frmMain.mnuEmpMstr.Enabled = False
    frmMain.mnuTransMstr.Enabled = False
'Disabling the sub menu options used to open a report generating form
    frmMain.mnuPassBk.Enabled = False
    frmMain.mnuStmt.Enabled = False
End Sub
```

The **DisableMstrNvgt()** subroutine is called to disable the data entry form's navigation options.

```
Public Sub DisableMstrNvgt()
'Disabling the sub menu options used for data navigation
    frmMain.mnuFrst.Enabled = False
    frmMain.mnuPrev.Enabled = False
    frmMain.mnuNext.Enabled = False
    frmMain.mnuLast.Enabled = False
'Disabling the toolbar buttons used for data navigation
    frmMain.cmdFrst.Enabled = False
    frmMain.cmdPrior.Enabled = False
    frmMain.cmdNext.Enabled = False
    frmMain.cmdLast.Enabled = False
End Sub
```

The **EnabledMstrNvgt()** subroutine is called to enable the data entry form's navigation options.

```
Public Sub EnableMstrNvgt()
'Enabling the sub menu options used for data navigation
    frmMain.mnuFrst.Enabled = True
    frmMain.mnuPrev.Enabled = True
    frmMain.mnuNext.Enabled = True
    frmMain.mnuLast.Enabled = True
'Enabling the toolbar buttons used for data navigation
    frmMain.cmdFrst.Enabled = True
    frmMain.cmdPrior.Enabled = True
    frmMain.cmdNext.Enabled = True
    frmMain.cmdLast.Enabled = True
End Sub
```

The **AddQuote()** subroutine is called to return a string passed as a parameter after replacing single quote with two single quotes.

```
Public Function AddQuote(mString As String)
'Calling the Replace() function to replace single quote
'with two single quotes
    AddQuote = Replace(mString, "'", "''")
End Function
'********* FUNCTIONALITY FOR MDI's OTHER SUBROUTINES ENDS **********
'*******************************************************************
```

```
'****************************************************************
'************* SUBROUTINES BASED ON TRUTH TABLE BEGINS *************
```

The **NoMode()** subroutine is called to determine the state of the MDI's menubar and toolbar such as to allow **Insert** or **View** operations only.

```
Public Sub NoMode()
'Calling DisableFrmOpt() to disable the MDI's sub menu options used
'to open a child form
    Call DisableFrmOpt
'Enabling sub menu options used to deactivate a form
    frmMain.mnuExit.Enabled = True
'Enabling or disabling sub menu options used for data manipulation
    frmMain.mnuInst.Enabled = True
    frmMain.mnuUpdt.Enabled = False
    frmMain.mnuDel.Enabled = False
    frmMain.mnuPrnt.Enabled = False
    frmMain.mnuSave.Enabled = False
    frmMain.mnuView.Enabled = True
'Enabling or disabling toolbar buttons used for data manipulation
    frmMain.cmdInst.Enabled = True
    frmMain.cmdUpdt.Enabled = False
    frmMain.cmdDel.Enabled = False
    frmMain.cmdView.Enabled = True
    frmMain.cmdPrnt.Enabled = False
    frmMain.cmdSave.Enabled = False
'Call DisableMstrNvgt to disable navigation options
    Call DisableMstrNvgt
'Call DisableFrmFlds to disable data entry form fields
    Call GetActvFrm(gFrmName1).DisableFrmFlds
End Sub
```

The **ChngMstr()** subroutine is called to determine the state of the MDI's menubar and toolbar such as to allow data manipulation and navigation operations only.

```
Public Sub ChngMstr()
'Enabling or disabling sub menu options used for data manipulation
    frmMain.mnuInst.Enabled = True
    frmMain.mnuUpdt.Enabled = True
    frmMain.mnuDel.Enabled = True
    frmMain.mnuPrnt.Enabled = True
    frmMain.mnuSave.Enabled = False
'Calling EnableMstrNvgt to enable navigation options
    Call EnableMstrNvgt
```

```
'Enabling or disabling toolbar buttons used for data manipulation
    frmMain.cmdInst.Enabled = True
    frmMain.cmdUpdt.Enabled = True
    frmMain.cmdDel.Enabled = True
    frmMain.cmdView.Enabled = False
    frmMain.cmdPrnt.Enabled = True
    frmMain.cmdSave.Enabled = False
    frmMain.cmdExit.Enabled = True
'Calling DisableFrmFlds to disable data entry form fields
    Call GetActvFrm(gFrmName1).DisableFrmFlds
End Sub
```

The **SaveMstr()** subroutine is called to determine the state of the MDI's menu bar and toolbar such as to allow only the Save operation.

```
Public Sub SaveMstr()
'Enabling or disabling sub menu options used for data manipulation
    frmMain.mnuInst.Enabled = False
    frmMain.mnuUpdt.Enabled = False
    frmMain.mnuDel.Enabled = False
    frmMain.mnuPrnt.Enabled = False
    frmMain.mnuSave.Enabled = True
    frmMain.mnuView.Enabled = False
'Enabling or disabling toolbar buttons used for data manipulation
    frmMain.cmdInst.Enabled = False
    frmMain.cmdUpdt.Enabled = False
    frmMain.cmdDel.Enabled = False
    frmMain.cmdView.Enabled = False
    frmMain.cmdPrnt.Enabled = False
    frmMain.cmdSave.Enabled = True
    frmMain.cmdExit.Enabled = True
'Calling DisableMstrNvgt to disable navigation options
    Call DisableMstrNvgt
'Checking if the variable 'gFrmName1' is not empty
    If gFrmName1 <> "" Then
        'Calling EnableFrmFlds to enable data entry form fields
        Call GetActvFrm(gFrmName1).EnableFrmFlds
    End If
End Sub
'************** SUBROUTINES BASED ON TRUTH TABLE ENDS **************
'******************************************************************
```

PROJECT CODE FOR frmOpenFrm.frm

```
'*************************************************************
'******** FUNCTIONALITY FOR THE FORM SPECIFIC EVENTS BEGINS ********
```

The **Form_Load()** subroutine is called when the MDI form loads in memory. Before the form is displayed on the screen, the **View** operation of the MDI's menu bar and toolbar are disabled.

```vb
Public Sub Form_Load()
    frmMain.mnuView.Enabled = False
    frmMain.cmdView.Enabled = False
End Sub
```

The **Form_Unload()** subroutine is called when the MDI form is destroyed from memory. Before the form is destroyed, the **View** operation from the MDI's menu bar and toolbar are enabled.

```vb
Public Sub Form_Unload(Cancel As Integer)
    frmMain.mnuView.Enabled = True
    frmMain.cmdView.Enabled = True
End Sub
```
```
'******** FUNCTIONALITY FOR THE FORM SPECIFIC EVENTS ENDS ********
'*************************************************************


'*************************************************************
'******** FUNCTIONALITY FOR THE FORM BUTTON's EVENTS BEGINS ********
```

The **cmdShowFrm_Click()** subroutine is called when the **Show Form** button on the form is clicked. A scan is made to find the option selected by the user and an appropriate form is displayed on the screen.

```vb
Public Sub cmdShowFrm_Click()
'Checking the value of each element in the control array 'optFrmOpt'
    If optFrmOpt(0).Value = True Then
        Call LoadChild(frmAcctMstr)  'Loading the Account's data entry form
    ElseIf optFrmOpt(1).Value = True Then
        Call LoadChild(frmClntMstr)  'Loading the Client's data entry form
    ElseIf optFrmOpt(2).Value = True Then
        Call LoadChild(frmEmpMstr)   'Loading the Employee's data entry form
```

```
    ElseIf optFrmOpt(3).Value = True Then
        Call LoadChild(frmTransMstr) 'Loading the Transaction's data entry form
    ElseIf optFrmOpt(4).Value = True Then
    'Calling Load to display a form to generate a transaction report
    'as a monthly statement
        gRprtType = "Pass Book"
        Load frmShowRprt
        frmShowRprt.Show vbModal
    ElseIf optFrmOpt(5).Value = True Then
    'Calling Load to display a form to generate a transaction report
    'as a monthly statement
        gRprtType = "Monthly Statement"
        Load frmShowRprt
        frmShowRprt.Show vbModal
    End If
    Unload frmOpenFrm
End Sub
```

The **cmdCncl_Click()** subroutine is called when the **Cancel** button on the form is clicked. The form is destroyed in memory, by calling the unload event.

```
Public Sub cmdCncl_Click()
'Calling Unload to terminate the form's functionality
    Unload frmOpenFrm
End Sub
'********* FUNCTIONALITY FOR THE FORM BUTTON's EVENTS ENDS *********
'******************************************************************
```

PRACTICAL VB 6 PROJECTS

CHAP 06

PROJECT CODE FOR frmEmpMstr.frm

```
'***************************************************************
'******** FUNCTIONALITY FOR THE FORM SPECIFIC EVENTS BEGINS ********
```

The **Form_Load()** subroutine is called when the data entry form used for capturing and displaying Employee's information loads in memory. Before the form is displayed on the screen, the maximum number of characters enterable is set for each form field.

The SQL query stored in a global variable named **gEmpSql** is used to retrieve records held in the **Emp_Mstr** table. After the recordset is created a call to the **NoMode()** subroutine is made to allow an **Insert** or **View** operations only.

```
Public Sub Form_Load()
    txtFName.MaxLength = 25
    txtMName.MaxLength = 25
    txtLName.MaxLength = 25
    txtAddr1.MaxLength = 40
    txtAddr2.MaxLength = 40
    txtCity.MaxLength = 25
    txtPin.MaxLength = 6
    txtRTel.MaxLength = 15
    txtDept.MaxLength = 20
    txtDesig.MaxLength = 20
'Storing the active child form's reference, into the global
'variable 'gFrmName1'
    gFrmName1 = "Employee"
'Hiding the frame 'fraDate' containing the MonthView control
    fraDate.Visible = False
'Opening the ADODB's Recordset object used for retrieving records
'from the Employee's Master table
    gEmpRs.Open gEmpSql, gConnect, adOpenKeyset, adLockPessimistic
    gFrmRs3 = gFrmRs2
    gFrmRs2 = gFrmRs1
'Storing the name of the ADODB's Recordset object, into 'gfrmRs1'
    gFrmRs1 = "gEmpRs"
'Calling NoMode to allow Insert or View operations only
    Call NoMode
End Sub
```

The **Form_Unload()** subroutine is called just before the data entry form used for capturing and displaying Employee's information is destroyed in memory. Before the form is destroyed, the recordset used to retrieve records from the **Emp_Mstr** table is destroyed. A call is made to the global subroutine **ResetMDI()**, used to reset a sequence which is used with the active child form.

```
Public Sub Form_Unload(Cancel As Integer)
    gEmpRs.Close
    Call ResetMDI
End Sub
'********* FUNCTIONALITY FOR THE FORM SPECIFIC EVENTS ENDS *********
'*****************************************************************

'*****************************************************************
'******* FUNCTIONALITY FOR CHANGE EVENTS ON FORM FIELD BEGINS *******
```

The **txtDOB_KeyPress()** subroutine is called when the value held in the Employee's date of birth field is changed.

```
Public Sub txtDOB_KeyPress(KeyAscii As Integer)
'Displaying the frame 'fraDate' containing a MonthView control
'to capture an Employee's date of birth
    fraDate.Visible = True
'Clearing the Employee's date of birth field
    txtDOB.Text = ""
'Placing the form cursor on a MonthView control to select
'the Employee's date of birth
    mvwDOB.SetFocus
End Sub
'********* FUNCTIONALITY FOR FOCUS EVENTS ON FORM FIELD ENDS *********
'*******************************************************************

'*******************************************************************
'******* FUNCTIONALITY FOR CALENDAR CONTROL's EVENTS BEGINS *******
```

The **mvwDOB_DateClick()** subroutine is called when the form cursor moves away from the MonthView control capturing an Employee's date of birth.

```
Public Sub mvwDOB_DateClick(ByVal DateClicked As Date)
'Setting the Text attribute of the Employee's date of birth field
    txtDOB.Text = mvwDOB.Value
'Hiding the frame 'fraDate' containing a MonthView control
'to capture an Employee's date of birth
    fraDate.Visible = False
```

```
'Placing the form cursor on the next enterable field
    txtAddr1.SetFocus
End Sub
'******** FUNCTIONALITY FOR CALENDAR CONTROL's EVENTS ENDS *********
'****************************************************************

'****************************************************************
'*********** FUNCTIONALITY FOR DATA MANIPULATION BEGINS ***********
```

The **InstMstrRecd( )** subroutine is called to Insert a Master record.

```
Public Sub InstMstrRecd()
    Call SaveMstr
    Call ClrFrmFlds
'Checking if the active recordset has records
    If gEmpRs.RecordCount > 0 Then
        txtFName.SetFocus
    End If
End Sub
```

The **UpdtMstrRecd()** subroutine is called to Update a Master record.

```
Public Sub UpdtMstrRecd()
    Call SaveMstr
'Disabling appropriate Master section form fields
    txtFName.Enabled = False
    txtMName.Enabled = False
    txtLName.Enabled = False
    txtDOB.Enabled = False
    txtAddr1.SetFocus
End Sub
```

The **DelMstrRecd()** subroutine is called to Delete a Master record.

```
Public Sub DelMstrRecd()
'Checking if the recordset cursor is on the first record
    If gEmpRs.AbsolutePosition = 1 Then
        MsgBox "The first record cannot be deleted!!", vbCritical + vbOKOnly, _
            "CAUTION"
        Exit Sub
    End If
```

```vb
'Prompting a user before deleting the master record
    gMsgResponse = MsgBox("The current employee record will be deleted!!!", _
                        vbOKCancel + vbCritical, "Delete Warning")
'Checking if the 'Cancel' button is clicked
    If gMsgResponse = 2 Then
        'Exiting from the delete subroutine
        Exit Sub
    Else
        'Deleting master table record
        gEmpRs.Delete
        'Checking if the 'gEmpRs' recordset is empty
        If gEmpRs.RecordCount = 0 Then
            'Calling NoMode to allow Insert or View operations only
            Call NoMode
        Else
            'Calling VuNextMstr to view Employee Master's next record
            Call VuNextMstr(GetActvRs(gEmpRs))
        End If
    End If
End Sub
'*********** FUNCTIONALITY FOR DATA MANIPULATION ENDS *************
'******************************************************************


'******************************************************************
'********** FUNCTIONALITY FOR SAVING MASTER DATA BEGINS ***********
```

The **SaveMstrRecd()** subroutine is called to save the data, captured by the active form, into the database.

```vb
Public Sub SaveMstrRecd()
'Checking if any mandatory form fields have been left empty
    If Trim(txtFName) = "" Or Trim(txtLName) = "" Or Trim(txtDOB) = "" _
        Or Trim(txtAddr1) = "" Or Trim(txtCity) = "" Or Trim(txtPin) = "" _
        Or Trim(txtRTel) = "" Or Trim(txtDept) = "" Or Trim(txtDesig) = "" Then
        MsgBox "All the fields are mandatory!!", vbCritical + vbOKOnly, "Caution"
    Else
        'Checking if the employee's Id number field is empty
        If Trim(txtEmpId.Text) = "" Then
            'Appending a blank record into the active recordset
            gEmpRs.AddNew
        End If
```

```vb
    'Inserting values, captured by the active form's fields, into the
    'active recordset after replacing every single quote with two quotes
        gEmpRs.Fields(1) = AddQuote(Trim(txtFName.Text))
        'Checking if the Employee's middle name field is empty, to avoid
        'storing an empty value into the active recordset
        If Trim(txtMName.Text) <> "" Then
            gEmpRs.Fields(2) = AddQuote(Trim(txtMName.Text))
        End If
        gEmpRs.Fields(3) = AddQuote(Trim(txtLName.Text))
        gEmpRs.Fields(4) = AddQuote(Trim(txtAddr1.Text))
    'Checking if the second field for address is empty to avoid storing
    'an empty value into the active recordset
        If Trim(txtAddr2.Text) <> "" Then
            gEmpRs.Fields(5) = AddQuote(txtAddr2.Text)
        End If
        gEmpRs.Fields(6) = AddQuote(Trim(txtCity.Text))
        gEmpRs.Fields(7) = Trim(txtPin.Text)
        gEmpRs.Fields(8) = Trim(txtRTel.Text)
        gEmpRs.Fields(9) = Trim(txtDOB.Text)
        gEmpRs.Fields(10) = AddQuote(Trim(txtDept.Text))
        gEmpRs.Fields(11) = AddQuote(Trim(txtDesig.Text))
    'Updating the table in the database with the new values inserted
        mEmpRs.Update
    'Assigning an auto generated employee's Id number into 'txtEmpId'
        txtEmpId.Text = gEmpRs.Fields(0)
        Call ChngMstr
    End If
End Sub
'*********** FUNCTIONALITY FOR SAVING MASTER DATA ENDS *************
'******************************************************************


'******************************************************************
'********* FUNCTIONALITY FOR FORM FIELD VALIDATIONS BEGINS *********
```

The **txtFName_Validate()** subroutine is called to validate data captured in the Employee's first name field.

```vb
Public Sub txtFName_Validate(Cancel As Boolean)
'Removing spaces from the Employee's first name field
    txtFName.Text = Trim(txtFName.Text)
'Checking if the Employee's first name field is empty
    If txtFName.Text = "" Then
        MsgBox "Employee's first name field cannot be left blank!!"
```

CHAP 06

A COMMERCIAL BANKING SYSTEM: THE WORKING

```
'Checking the value returned by ValidTxt while scanning
'the Employee's first name field for anything other than alphabets
    ElseIf Not ValidTxt(txtFName.Text) Then
        MsgBox "Only alphabetical characters are acceptable as a first name!!"
    Else
    'Placing the form cursor on the Employee's middle name field
    'and terminating the subroutine
        txtMName.SetFocus
        Exit Sub
    End If
'Placing the form's focus on the Employee's first name field
    Cancel = True
End Sub
```

The **txtMName_Validate()** subroutine is called to validate the data captured in the Employee's middle name field.

```
Public Sub txtMName_Validate(Cancel As Boolean)
'Removing spaces from the Employee's middle name field
    txtMName.Text = Trim(txtMName.Text)
'Checking if the Employee's middle name field is not empty
    If Not txtMName.Text = "" Then
        'Checking the value returned by ValidTxt while scanning
        'the Employee's middle name field for anything other than alphabets
        If Not ValidTxt(txtMName.Text) Then
            MsgBox "Only alphabetical characters are acceptable as a middle name!!"
        Else
        'Placing the form cursor on the Employee's last name field
        'and terminating the subroutine
            txtLName.SetFocus
            Exit Sub
        End If
    'Placing the form's focus on the Employee's middle name field
        Cancel = True
    End If
End Sub
```

The **txtLName_Validate()** subroutine is called to validate the data captured in the Employee's last name field.

```vb
Public Sub txtLName_Validate(Cancel As Boolean)
'Removing spaces from the Employee's last name field
    txtLName.Text = Trim(txtLName.Text)
'Checking if the Employee's last name field is empty
    If txtLName.Text = "" Then
        MsgBox "Employee's last name field cannot be left blank!!"
'Checking the value returned by ValidTxt while scanning
'the Employee's last name field for anything other than alphabets
    ElseIf Not ValidTxt(txtLName.Text) Then
        MsgBox "Only alphabetical characters are acceptable as a last name!!"
    Else
    'Placing the form cursor on the Employee's date of birth field
    'and terminating the subroutine
        txtDOB.SetFocus
        Exit Sub
    End If
'Placing the form's focus on the Employee's last name field
    Cancel = True
End Sub
```

The **txtAddr1_Validate()** subroutine is called to validate the data captured in the Employee's first address field.

```vb
Public Sub txtAddr1_Validate(Cancel As Boolean)
'Removing spaces from the Employee's first address field
    txtAddr1.Text = Trim(txtAddr1.Text)
'Checking if the Employee's first address field is empty
    If txtAddr1.Text = "" Then
        MsgBox "The address cannot be left blank!!"
    'Placing the form's focus on the Employee's first address field
        Cancel = True
    Else
    'Placing the form cursor on the Employee's second address field
        txtAddr2.SetFocus
    End If
End Sub
```

The **txtCity_Validate()** subroutine is called to validate the data captured in the Employee's city name field.

```
Public Sub txtCity_Validate(Cancel As Boolean)
'Removing spaces from the Employee's city name field
    txtCity.Text = Trim(txtCity.Text)
'Checking if the Employee's city name field is empty
    If txtCity.Text = "" Then
        MsgBox "The city name cannot be left blank!!"
'Checking the value returned by the ValidTxt while scanning the
'Employee's city name field for anything other than alphabets
    ElseIf Not ValidTxt(txtCity.Text) Then
        MsgBox "Only alphabetical characters are acceptable as a city name!!"
    Else
        'Placing the form cursor on the Employee's pin code field
        txtPin.SetFocus
        Exit Sub
    End If
'Placing the form's focus on the Employee's city name field
    Cancel = True
End Sub
```

The **txtPin_Validate()** subroutine is called to validate the data captured in the Employee's pin code field.

```
Public Sub txtPin_Validate(Cancel As Boolean)
'Checking the value returned by the MinLen function called to validate
'that the Employee's pin code field is not less than six digits
'in length
    If Not MinLen(txtPin.Text, 6) Then
        MsgBox "Pin code must consist of only 6 digits!!"
    Else
    'Checking the value returned by IsNumeric while scanning
    'the Employee's pin code field for non numeric characters
        If IsNumeric(txtPin.Text) Then
            'Checking the value returned by the CharFound function called to
            'scan the Employee's pin code field for a plus or minus sign
            If (Not CharFound(txtPin.Text, "+")) _
                And (Not CharFound(txtPin.Text, "-")) Then
                'Placing the form cursor on the contact number field
                'and terminating the subroutine
                txtRTel.SetFocus
                Exit Sub
            End If
        End If
```

```
        MsgBox "Only numeric data are acceptable as a pin code!!"
    End If
'Placing the form's focus on the Employee's pin code field
    Cancel = True
End Sub
```

The **txtRTel_Validate()** subroutine is called to validate the data captured in the Employee's contact number field.

```
Public Sub txtRTel_Validate(Cancel As Boolean)
'Checking the value returned by the MinLen function while validating
'the contact number field's length
    If Not MinLen(txtRTel.Text, 7) Then
        MsgBox "Contact number must consist of minimum 7 digits!!"
    Else
    'Checking the value returned by the IsNumeric function
    'while scanning the Employee's contact number field for
    'non numeric characters
        If IsNumeric(txtRTel.Text) Then
        'Checking the value returned by the CharFound function called to
        'scan the Employee's contact number field for a plus or
        'minus sign
            If (Not CharFound(txtRTel.Text, "+")) _
            And (Not CharFound(txtRTel.Text, "-")) Then
            'Placing the form cursor on the Employee's department field
            'and terminating the subroutine
                txtDept.SetFocus
                Exit Sub
            End If
        End If
        MsgBox "Only numeric data are acceptable as a contact number!!"
    End If
'Placing the form's focus on the Employee's contact number field
    Cancel = True
End Sub
```

The **txtDept_Validate()** subroutine is called to validate data captured in the Employee's department name field.

```
Public Sub txtDept_Validate(Cancel As Boolean)
'Removing spaces from the Employee's department name field
    txtDept.Text = Trim(txtDept.Text)
```

```
'Checking if the Employee's department name field is empty
    If txtDept.Text = "" Then
        MsgBox "Employee's department name field cannot be left blank!!"
'Checking the value returned by the ValidTxt function while scanning
'the Employee's department field for anything other than alphabets
    ElseIf Not ValidTxt(txtDept.Text) Then
        MsgBox "Only alphabetical characters are acceptable as a department name!!"
    Else
        'Placing the form cursor to the Employee's designation field
        'and terminating the subroutine
        txtDesig.SetFocus
        Exit Sub
    End If
'Placing the form's focus to the Employee's department name field
    Cancel = True
End Sub
```

The **txtDesig_Validate()** subroutine is called to validate data captured in the Employee's designation field.

```
Public Sub txtDesig_Validate(Cancel As Boolean)
'Removing any spaces from the Employee's designation field
    txtDesig.Text = Trim(txtDesig.Text)
'Checking if the Employee's designation field is empty
    If txtDesig.Text = "" Then
        MsgBox "Employee's designation field cannot be left blank!!"
'Checking the value returned by ValidTxt while scanning
'the Employee's designation field for non alphabetical characters
    ElseIf Not ValidTxt(txtDesig.Text) Then
        MsgBox "Only alphabetical characters are acceptable as a designation!!"
    Else
        'Placing the form cursor to the MDI toolbar's Save button
        'and terminating the subroutine
        frmMain.cmdSave.SetFocus
        Exit Sub
    End If
'Placing the form's focus to the Employee's designation field
    Cancel = True
End Sub
'********** FUNCTIONALITY FOR FORM FIELD VALIDATIONS ENDS **********
'*******************************************************************
```

```
'************************************************************
'******** FUNCTIONALITY FOR FORM's OTHER SUBROUTINES BEGINS ********
```

The **ClrFrmFlds()** subroutine is called to empty the form's data capture fields.

```vb
Public Sub ClrFrmFlds()
    txtEmpId.Text = ""
    txtDOB.Text = ""
    txtFName.Text = ""
    txtMName.Text = ""
    txtLName.Text = ""
    txtAddr1.Text = ""
    txtAddr2.Text = ""
    txtCity.Text = ""
    txtPin.Text = ""
    txtRTel.Text = ""
    txtDept.Text = ""
    txtDesig.Text = ""
End Sub
```

The **PopFrmFlds()** subroutine is called to populate form fields.

```vb
Public Sub PopFrmFlds()
    txtEmpId.Text = gEmpRs.Fields(0)
    txtFName.Text = gEmpRs.Fields(1)
'Checking if the recordset's field for Employee's middle name is empty
    If gEmpRs.Fields(2) <> "" Then
        txtMName.Text = gEmpRs.Fields(2)
    Else
        txtMName.Text = ""
    End If
    txtLName.Text = gEmpRs.Fields(3)
    txtAddr1.Text = gEmpRs.Fields(4)
    txtAddr2.Text = gEmpRs.Fields(5)
    txtCity.Text = gEmpRs.Fields(6)
    txtPin.Text = gEmpRs.Fields(7)
    txtRTel.Text = gEmpRs.Fields(8)
    txtDOB.Text = gEmpRs.Fields(9)
    txtDept.Text = gEmpRs.Fields(10)
    txtDesig.Text = gEmpRs.Fields(11)
End Sub
```

The **DisableFrmFlds()** subroutine is called to disable the form's data entry fields.

```
Public Sub DisableFrmFlds()
    txtEmpId.Enabled = False
    txtFName.Enabled = False
    txtMName.Enabled = False
    txtLName.Enabled = False
    txtAddr1.Enabled = False
    txtAddr2.Enabled = False
    txtCity.Enabled = False
    txtPin.Enabled = False
    txtRTel.Enabled = False
    txtDOB.Enabled = False
    txtDept.Enabled = False
    txtDesig.Enabled = False
End Sub
```

The **EnableFrmFlds()** subroutine is called to enable the form's data entry fields.

```
Public Sub EnableFrmFlds()
    txtFName.Enabled = True
    txtMName.Enabled = True
    txtLName.Enabled = True
    txtAddr1.Enabled = True
    txtAddr2.Enabled = True
    txtCity.Enabled = True
    txtPin.Enabled = True
    txtRTel.Enabled = True
    txtDOB.Enabled = True
    txtDept.Enabled = True
    txtDesig.Enabled = True
End Sub
'********* FUNCTIONALITY FOR FORM's OTHER SUBROUTINES ENDS *********
'******************************************************************
```

PROJECT CODE FOR frmClntMstr.frm

Option Explicit
```
'Declaring a variable for later use
```
Dim mMsgStr As String
```
'Declaring a variable, used as a flag, to indicate whether any changes
'have occurred in the details section or not
```
Dim mFlgDtlsChng As String

```
'***************************************************************
'******** FUNCTIONALITY FOR THE FORM SPECIFIC EVENTS BEGINS ********
```
The **Form_Load()** subroutine is called when the data entry form used for capturing and displaying Client's information loads in memory. Before the form is displayed on the screen, the maximum number of characters enterable is set for each form field.

The SQL query stored in a global variable named **gClntSql** is used to retrieve records held in the **Clnt_Mstr** table. After the recordset is obtained, a check is made to insure the form is not invoked through another data entry form.

If another data entry form has invoked this form, then depending on the existence of a record in the recordset an Insert or Update operation is called. During either of the operations, behaviour of the MDI form is such that it allows only **Save** as the next operation.

If the form has been invoked by another data entry form, a call to the **NoMode()** subroutine is made to allow an **Insert** or **View** operations only.

```
Public Sub Form_Load()
    txtFName.MaxLength = 25
    txtMName.MaxLength = 25
    txtLName.MaxLength = 25
    txtAddr1.MaxLength = 40
    txtAddr2.MaxLength = 40
    txtCity.MaxLength = 25
    txtPin.MaxLength = 6
    txtContNo.MaxLength = 15
'Storing the active child form's reference into
'the global variable 'gFrmName1'
    gFrmName1 = "Client"
```

```vb
'Setting the flag value as 'F' to indicate that no changes has occurred
'in the details section
    mFlgDtlsChng = "F"
'Hiding the frame 'fraDate' containing the MonthView control
    fraDate.Visible = False
'Hiding the form fields used for capturing a client's contact number
    cmbContType.Visible = False
    txtContNo.Visible = False
'Setting a attributes of the DataGrid
    dgContact.HeadFont.Bold = True
    dgContact.WrapCellPointer = True
'Opening the ADODB's Recordset object used for retrieving records from
'the Client's Master table
    gClntRs.Open gClntSql, gConnect, adOpenKeyset, adLockPessimistic
    gFrmRs3 = gFrmRs2
    gFrmRs2 = gFrmRs1
'Storing the name of the ADODB's Recordset object into 'gfrmRs1'
    gFrmRs1 = "gClntRs"
        'Calling DisableDtls to disable the form's Details section
            Call DisableDtls
'Checking if the variable 'gFrmRs2' holds a value
    If gFrmRs2 <> "" Then
        'Disabling the MDI's Exit options
            frmMain.mnuExit.Enabled = False
            frmMain.cmdExit.Enabled = False
        'Checking if the active recordset is empty
            If gClntRs.RecordCount = 0 Then
                'Calling InstMstrRecd to insert a new Master record
                    Call InstMstrRecd
            'Checking if the active recordset contains only one record
            ElseIf gClntRs.RecordCount = 1 Then
                'Calling PopFrmFlds to populate the form fields with data from
                'the active recordset
                    Call PopFrmFlds
                'Calling UpdtMstrRecd to update current Master record
                    Call UpdtMstrRecd
            End If
    Else
        'Calling NoMode to allow Insert or View operations only
            Call NoMode
    End If
End Sub
```

The **Form_Unload()** subroutine is called just before the data entry form used for capturing and displaying Client's information is destroyed from memory. Before the form is destroyed, the recordset used to retrieve records from the **Clnt_Mstr** table is destroyed. A call is made to the global subroutine **ResetMDI()**, used to reset a sequence which is used with active child form.

```
Public Sub Form_Unload(Cancel As Integer)
    gClntRs.Close
    Call ResetMDI
End Sub
'********* FUNCTIONALITY FOR THE FORM SPECIFIC EVENTS ENDS *********
'******************************************************************


'******************************************************************
'******* FUNCTIONALITY FOR CHANGE EVENTS ON FORM FIELD BEGINS *******
```

The **txtDOB_KeyPress()** subroutine is called when the value held in the Client's date of birth field is changed.

```
Public Sub txtDOB_KeyPress(KeyAscii As Integer)
'Displaying the frame 'fraDate' containing a MonthView control
'to capture the Client's date of birth
    fraDate.Visible = True
'Clearing the Client's date of birth field
    txtDOB.Text = ""
'Placing the form cursor on a MonthView control to select
'the Client's date of birth
    mvwDOB.SetFocus
End Sub
'******** FUNCTIONALITY FOR FOCUS EVENTS ON FORM FIELD ENDS ********
'******************************************************************


'******************************************************************
'******* FUNCTIONALITY FOR CALENDAR CONTROL's EVENTS BEGINS ********
```

The **mvwDOB_DateClick()** subroutine is called when form cursor moves away from the MonthView control capturing an Client's date of birth.

```
Public Sub mvwDOB_DateClick(ByVal DateClicked As Date)
'Setting the Text attribute of the Client's date of birth field
    txtDOB.Text = mvwDOB.Value
```

```vb
'Hiding the frame 'fraDate' containing a MonthView control
'to capture the Client's date of birth
    fraDate.Visible = False
'Placing the form cursor on the next enterable field
    txtAddr1.SetFocus
End Sub
'******** FUNCTIONALITY FOR CALENDAR CONTROL's EVENTS ENDS *********
'******************************************************************


'******************************************************************
'*** FUNCTIONALITY OF THE DETAILS SECTION TOOLBAR BUTTONS BEGINS ***
```

The **cmdDgInst_Click()** subroutine is called when the button to Insert a contact information is clicked.

```vb
Public Sub cmdDgInst_Click()
'Appending blank record into the Client's details recordset
    AdodcCont.Recordset.AddNew
'Setting the flag value as 'T' to indicate that a changes has occurred
'in the details section
    mFlgDtlsChng = "T"
'Calling ChngDtlsRecd to prepare the form to accept a client's contact
'information
    Call ChngDtlsRecd
'Clearing the client's contact number field within the UI
    txtContNo.Text = ""
'Populating the Data Grid's first column with the client's Id number
    dgContact.Columns(0).Text = txtClntId.Text
End Sub
```

The **cmdDgUpdt_Click()** subroutine is called when the button to Update a contact information is clicked.

```vb
Public Sub cmdDgUpdt_Click()
'Setting the flag value as 'T' to indicate that a changes has occurred
'in the details section
    mFlgDtlsChng = "T"
'Displaying the contact number that the user wishes to change
    txtContNo.Text = dgContact.Columns(2).Text
'Calling ChngDtlsRecd to accept a client's contact information
    Call ChngDtlsRecd
End Sub
```

PRACTICAL VB 6 PROJECTS — CHAP 06

The **cmdDgDel_Click()** subroutine is called when the Details section's Delete button is clicked.

```vb
Public Sub cmdDgDel_Click()
'Checking if details table's recordset contains just one record
    If AdodcCont.Recordset.RecordCount = 1 Then
      'Prompt to confirm the user's wishes to delete
        gMsgResponse = MsgBox("Client's last contact number will be Deleted .... " & _
                            "Proceed? Yes/No", vbYesNo + vbCritical _
                            + vbDefaultButton2, "Details Deletion Warning")
      'Processing detail record deletion based on user instructions
        If gMsgResponse = 6 Then
          'Disabling the details section's Update and Delete buttons
            cmdDgUpdt.Enabled = False
            cmdDgDel.Enabled = False
        Else
            Exit Sub
        End If
    End If
'Checking if details table's recordset contains just two record
    If AdodcCont.Recordset.RecordCount = 2 Then
      'Calling DisableDgNvgt()is called to disable the navigation buttons
      'within the UI's Details section
        Call DisableDgNvgt
    End If
'Deleting the current Details record and refreshing the data grid
    AdodcCont.Recordset.Delete
    dgContact.Refresh
End Sub
```

The **cmdDgFrst_Click()** subroutine is called when the button to move the data grid's cursor to the First contact information record is clicked.

```vb
Public Sub cmdDgFrst_Click()
'Placing the details table's recordset cursor on the First record
    AdodcCont.Recordset.MoveFirst
End Sub
```

CHAP 06   A COMMERCIAL BANKING SYSTEM: THE WORKING

The **cmdDgPrior_Click()** subroutine is called when the button to move the data grid's cursor to the Previous contact information record is clicked.

```
Public Sub cmdDgPrior_Click()
'Placing the details table's recordset cursor on the Previous record
    AdodcCont.Recordset.MovePrevious
'Checking if the detail table's recordset cursor has moved beyond
'the First record
    If AdodcCont.Recordset.BOF Then
        MsgBox "You are on the first record for client's contact information", _
            vbExclamation, "PLEASE NOTE"
        'Placing the details table's recordset cursor on the Next record
        AdodcCont.Recordset.MoveNext
    End If
End Sub


'The cmdDgNext_Click() is called when the button to move the
'data grid's cursor to the Next contact information record is clicked
Public Sub cmdDgNext_Click()
'Placing the details table's recordset cursor on the Next record
    AdodcCont.Recordset.MoveNext
'Checking if the detail table's recordset cursor has moved beyond the
'Last record
    If AdodcCont.Recordset.EOF Then
        MsgBox "You are on the last record for client's contact information", _
            vbExclamation, "PLEASE NOTE"
        'Placing the details table's recordset cursor on the Previous record
        AdodcCont.Recordset.MovePrevious
    End If
End Sub
```

The **cmdDgLast_Click()** subroutine is called when the button to move the data grid's cursor to the Last contact information record is clicked.

```
Public Sub cmdDgLast_Click()
'Placing the details table's recordset cursor on the Last record
    AdodcCont.Recordset.MoveLast
End Sub
```

The **cmdDgSave_Click()** subroutine is called when the button to Save changes made to the data grid holding contact information is clicked.

```
Public Sub cmdDgSave_Click()
'Calling SaveDtlsRecd to save changes made in the details recordset
'to the Database
    Call SaveDtlsRecd
End Sub
'************ FUNCTIONALITY FOR DETAILS BUTTONS ENDS **************
'******************************************************************


'******************************************************************
'*********** FUNCTIONALITY FOR DATA MANIPULATION BEGINS ***********
```

The **InstMstrRecd()** subroutine is called to Insert a Master record.

```
Public Sub InstMstrRecd()
'Calling SaveMstr to allow only the Save operation
    Call SaveMstr
'Calling ClrFrmFlds to clear the Master form fields
    Call ClrFrmFlds
'Enabling the Insert button within the details section
    cmdDgInst.Enabled = True
'Calling ChkDtlsRecd to populate the contact information's data grid
    Call ChkDtlsRecd
'Checking if the active recordset has records
    If gClntRs.RecordCount > 0 Then
        txtFName.SetFocus
    End If
End Sub
```

The **UpdtMstrRecd()** subroutine is called to Update a Master record.

```
Public Sub UpdtMstrRecd()
    Call SaveMstr
'Disabling appropriate Master section form fields
    txtFName.Enabled = False
    txtMName.Enabled = False
    txtLName.Enabled = False
    txtDOB.Enabled = False
```

```vb
'Enabling the Insert buttons within the UI's details section
    cmdDgInst.Enabled = True
'Checking if the detail table's recordset have records
    If AdodcCont.Recordset.RecordCount > 0 Then
        'Enabling the Insert buttons within the UI's details section
            cmdDgUpdt.Enabled = True
            cmdDgDel.Enabled = True
    End If
    Call ChkDtlsRecd
    txtAddr1.SetFocus
End Sub
```

The **DelMstrRecd()** subroutine is called to Delete a Master record.

```vb
Public Sub DelMstrRecd()
'Checking if the recordset cursor is on the first record
    If gClntRs.AbsolutePosition = 1 Then
        MsgBox "The first record cannot be deleted!!", vbCritical + vbOKOnly, "CAUTION"
        Exit Sub
    End If
'Prompt to confirm the user's wishes to perform a cascade delete
    gMsgResponse = MsgBox("Click [ Yes ] to delete Client Personal and Contact " & _
                        "Information together   " & vbCrLf & "OR" & vbCrLf & _
                        "Click [ No ] to delete Client Contact information " & _
                        "exclusively.   " & vbCrLf & vbCrLf & vbCrLf & _
                        "NOTE" & vbCrLf & "To Delete Client Contact " & _
                        "Information individually [ Cancel ] this process" & _
                        vbCrLf & "and use the Delete Button in Client " & _
                        "Contact Information section", vbYesNoCancel + _
                        vbCritical + vbDefaultButton3, "Delete Warning")
'Checking if the 'Cancel' button is clicked
    If gMsgResponse = 2 Then
        Exit Sub
    Else
    'Deleting any contact information for the current Master record
        Do While AdodcCont.Recordset.RecordCount > 0
            'Setting recordset cursor of the detail table to its last record
                AdodcCont.Recordset.MoveLast
            'Deleting the current record in the detail recordset
                AdodcCont.Recordset.Delete
        Loop    'End of 'Do While ... Loop' iteration
    'Disabling the details frame's navigation buttons
        DisableDgNvgt
```

```
        'Checking whether the 'Yes' button is clicked
        If gMsgResponse = 6 Then
            'Deleting master table record
                gClntRs.Delete
            'Checking if the Client Master's recordset is empty
            If gClntRs.RecordCount = 0 Then
                'Calling NoMode to allow Insert or View operations only
                    Call NoMode
                'Calling DisableDtls to disable the detail section
                    Call DisableDtls
            Else
                gClntRs.MoveNext
                'Checking whether the cursor has moved beyond the LAST record
                'in the recordset
                If gClntRs.EOF Then
                    gClntRs.MovePrevious
                End If
                'Calling PopFrmFlds to populate the active form's fields
                    Call PopFrmFlds
            End If
        End If
    End If
End Sub
'*********** FUNCTIONALITY FOR DATA MANIPULATION ENDS *************
'*****************************************************************


'*****************************************************************
'*********** FUNCTIONALITY FOR SAVING MASTER DATA BEGINS ************
```

The **SaveMstrRecd()** subroutine is called to save the data captured by the form.

```
Public Sub SaveMstrRecd()
'Checking if any mandatory form fields have been left empty
    If Trim(txtFName) = "" Or Trim(txtLName) = "" Or Trim(txtDOB) = "" Or _
        Trim(txtAddr1) = "" Or Trim(txtCity) = "" Or Trim(txtPin) = "" Then
        MsgBox "All the fields are mandatory!!", vbCritical + vbOKOnly, "Caution"
    Else
        'Checking if the Client's Id number field is empty
        If txtClntId.Text = "" Then
            'Appending a blank record into the active recordset
                gClntRs.AddNew
        End If
```

```vb
'Inserting values, captured by the active form's fields, into the
'active recordset after replacing every single quote with two quotes
    gClntRs.Fields(1) = AddQuote(Trim(txtFName.Text))
'Checking if the Employee's middle name field is empty
    If Trim(txtMName.Text) <> "" Then
        gClntRs.Fields(2) = AddQuote(Trim(txtMName.Text))
    End If
    gClntRs.Fields(3) = AddQuote(Trim(txtLName.Text))
    gClntRs.Fields(4) = AddQuote(Trim(txtAddr1.Text))
'Checking if the second field for address is empty to avoid storing
'an empty value into the active recordset
    If Trim(txtAddr2.Text) <> "" Then
        gEmpRs.Fields(5) = AddQuote(txtAddr2.Text)
    End If
    gClntRs.Fields(6) = AddQuote(Trim(txtCity.Text))
    gClntRs.Fields(7) = Trim(txtPin.Text)
    gClntRs.Fields(8) = Trim(txtDOB.Text)
'Checking if the Client has submitted the I.T. PAN Information
    If chkPAN.Value = 1 Then
        gClntRs.Fields(9) = True
    Else
        gClntRs.Fields(9) = False
    End If
'Checking if the Client's name and address has been verified
    If chkVerified.Value = 1 Then
        gClntRs.Fields(10) = True
    Else
        gClntRs.Fields(10) = False
    End If
'Updating the table in the database with the new values
    gClntRs.Update
'Assigning an auto generated client's Id number to its form field
    txtClntId.Text = gClntRs.Fields(0)
'Checking if the flag 'mFlgDtlsChng' indicates a change
'in the details section
    If mFlgDtlsChng = "T" Then
        'Checking if the details section's Save button is enabled
        If cmdDgSave.Enabled = True Then
            MsgBox "Click [Save] under Contact Information first!!"
        End If
        Exit Sub
    End If
```

```vb
    'Checking if the variable 'gEmpRs2' is empty
    If gFrmRs2 = "" Then
        'Calling ChngMstr to allow data manipulation and navigation
            Call ChngMstr
        'Disabling the details section's data manipulation buttons
            cmdDgInst.Enabled = False
            cmdDgUpdt.Enabled = False
            cmdDgDel.Enabled = False
        Else
            gClntSql = "SELECT * FROM Clnt_Mstr"
        'Enabling the MDI's Exit options
            frmMain.mnuExit.Enabled = True
            frmMain.cmdExit.Enabled = True
        'Calling ReturnId to display a person's identification
            mMsgStr = gClntRs.Fields(0) & "-" & gClntRs.Fields(1) & " " & _
                    gClntRs.Fields(2) & " " & gClntRs.Fields(3) & " - " & _
                    gClntRs.Fields(8)
        'Unloading the active child form
            Unload frmClntMstr
        End If
    End If
End Sub
'*********** FUNCTIONALITY FOR SAVING MASTER DATA ENDS *************
'******************************************************************


'******************************************************************
'**************** DETAIL DATA GRID SAVING BEGINS ******************
```

The **SaveDtlsRecd()** subroutine is called to Save the changes made in the Details' recordset into the Database.

```vb
Public Sub SaveDtlsRecd()
'Checking if the value held in the contact number field is not less
'than seven digits
    If MinLen(txtContNo.Text, 7) Then
    'Checking the contact number field for non numeric characters
        If IsNumeric(txtContNo.Text) Then
        'Checking the contact number field for a plus or minus sign
            If (Not CharFound(txtContNo.Text, "+")) _
                And (Not CharFound(txtContNo.Text, "-")) Then
            'Hiding the Contact Information's data capture objects
                cmbContType.Visible = False
                txtContNo.Visible = False
```

```vb
'Enabling the details section's data manipulation buttons
    cmdDgInst.Enabled = True
    cmdDgUpdt.Enabled = True
    cmdDgDel.Enabled = True
'Disabling the Save button within the UI's details section
    cmdDgSave.Enabled = False
'Checking if the Data Grid's Client Id column is empty
    If dgContact.Columns(0).Text = "" Then
        'Appending blank record into the Client's details recordset
        AdodcCont.Recordset.AddNew
        'Populating the Data Grid's first column with the Client's
        'Id number
        dgContact.Columns(0).Text = txtClntId.Text
    End If
'Using the 'Select Case' statement to decide a value for
'the Data Grid's second column
    Select Case cmbContType.Text
    Case Is = "Residence"
        dgContact.Columns(1).Text = "R"
    Case Is = "Office"
        dgContact.Columns(1).Text = "O"
    Case Is = "Mobile"
        dgContact.Columns(1).Text = "M"
    Case Is = "Pager"
        dgContact.Columns(1).Text = "P"
    Case Is = "Fax"
        dgContact.Columns(1).Text = "F"
    End Select
'Populating the Data Grid's third column with the value held
'in the contact number field
    dgContact.Columns(2).Text = txtContNo.Text
'Refreshing the Data Grid
    dgContact.Refresh
'Setting the flag value as 'F' to indicate that no changes has
'occurred in the details section
    mFlgDtlsChng = "F"
'Checking the details table's recordset for just two record
    If AdodcCont.Recordset.RecordCount = 2 Then
        Call EnableDgNvgt
    End If
```

```
            'Updating the Details table in the database and terminating
            'the subroutine
                AdodcCont.Recordset.Update
                Exit Sub
            End If
        End If
        MsgBox "Only numeric data are acceptable as a contact number!!"
    Else
        MsgBox "Contact number must consist of minimum 7 digits!!"
    End If
'Placing the form's focus to the Client's contact number field
    txtContNo.SetFocus
End Sub
'***************** DETAIL DATA GRID SAVING ENDS ******************
'****************************************************************


'****************************************************************
'********* FUNCTIONALITY FOR FORM FIELD VALIDATIONS BEGINS *********
```

The **txtFName_Validate()** subroutine is called to validate data captured in the Client's first name field.

```
Public Sub txtFName_Validate(Cancel As Boolean)
'Removing any spaces from the Client's first name field
    txtFName.Text = Trim(txtFName.Text)
'Checking if the Client's first name field is empty
    If txtFName.Text = "" Then
        MsgBox "Client's first name field cannot be left blank!!"
'Checking the first name field for anything other than alphabets
    ElseIf Not ValidTxt(txtFName.Text) Then
        MsgBox "Only alphabetical characters are acceptable as a first name!!"
    Else
        'Placing the form cursor on the middle name field
        txtMName.SetFocus
        Exit Sub
    End If
'Placing the form's focus on the Client's first name field
    Cancel = True
End Sub
```

The **txtMName_Validate()** subroutine is called to validate data captured in the Client's middle name field.

```
Public Sub txtMName_Validate(Cancel As Boolean)
'Removing any spaces from the Client's middle name field
    txtMName.Text = Trim(txtMName.Text)
'Checking if the Client's middle name field is not empty
    If Not txtMName.Text = "" Then
        'Checking the middle name field for anything other than alphabets
        If Not ValidTxt(txtMName.Text) Then
            MsgBox "Only alphabetical characters are acceptable as a middle name!!"
        Else
        'Placing the form cursor on the last name field
            txtLName.SetFocus
            Exit Sub
        End If
    'Placing the form's focus on the Client's middle name field
        Cancel = True
    End If
End Sub
```

The **txtLName_Validate()** subroutine subroutine is called to validate data captured in the Client's last name field.

```
Public Sub txtLName_Validate(Cancel As Boolean)
'Removing any spaces from the Client's last name field
    txtLName.Text = Trim(txtLName.Text)
'Checking if the Client's last name field is empty
    If txtLName.Text = "" Then
        MsgBox "Client's last name field cannot be left blank!!"
'Checking the last name field for anything other than alphabets
    ElseIf Not ValidTxt(txtLName.Text) Then
        MsgBox "Only alphabetical characters are acceptable as a last name!!"
    Else
    'Placing the form cursor on the date of birth field
        txtDOB.SetFocus
        Exit Sub
    End If
'Placing the form's focus on the Employee's last name field
    Cancel = True
End Sub
```

The **txtAddr1_Validate()** subroutine is called to validate data captured in the Client's first address field.

```
Public Sub txtAddr1_Validate(Cancel As Boolean)
'Removing any spaces from the Client's first address field
    txtAddr1.Text = Trim(txtAddr1.Text)
'Checking if the Client's first address field is empty
    If txtAddr1.Text = "" Then
        MsgBox "The address cannot be left blank!!"
        Cancel = True
    Else
    'Placing the form cursor on the Client's second address field
        txtAddr2.SetFocus
    End If
End Sub
```

The **txtCity_Validate()** subroutine is called to validate data captured in the Client's city name field.

```
Public Sub txtCity_Validate(Cancel As Boolean)
'Removing any spaces from the Client's city name field
    txtCity.Text = Trim(txtCity.Text)
'Checking if the Client's city name field is empty
    If txtCity.Text = "" Then
        MsgBox "The city name cannot be left blank!!"
'Checking the city's name field for anything other than alphabets
    ElseIf Not ValidTxt(txtCity.Text) Then
        MsgBox "Only alphabetical characters are acceptable as a city name!!"
    Else
    'Placing the form cursor on the Client's pin code field
        txtPin.SetFocus
        Exit Sub
    End If
'Placing the form's focus on the Client's city name field
    Cancel = True
End Sub
```

The **txtPin_Validate()** subroutine is called to validate data captured in the Client's pin code field.

```
Public Sub txtPin_Validate(Cancel As Boolean)
'Checking if the pin code field is not less than six digits in length
    If Not MinLen(txtPin.Text, 6) Then
        MsgBox "Pin code must consist of only 6 digits!!"
    Else
    'Checking the pin code field for non numeric characters
        If IsNumeric(txtPin.Text) Then
        'Checking the pin code field for a plus or minus sign
            If (Not CharFound(txtPin.Text, "+")) _
                Or (Not CharFound(txtPin.Text, "-")) Then
                Exit Sub
            End If
        End If
        MsgBox "Only numeric data are acceptable as a pin code!!"
    End If
'Placing the form's focus on the Client's pin code field
    Cancel = True
End Sub
'********** FUNCTIONALITY FOR FORM FIELD VALIDATIONS ENDS **********
'******************************************************************

'******************************************************************
'********* FUNCTIONALITY FOR FORM's OTHER SUBROUTINES BEGINS *********
```

The **ClrFrmFlds()** subroutine is called to empty the form's data capture fields.

```
Public Sub ClrFrmFlds()
    txtClntId.Text = ""
    txtDOB.Text = ""
    txtFName.Text = ""
    txtMName.Text = ""
    txtLName.Text = ""
    txtAddr1.Text = ""
    txtAddr2.Text = ""
    txtCity.Text = ""
    txtPin.Text = ""
    chkPAN.Value = 0
    chkVerified.Value = 0
End Sub
```

The **PopFrmFlds()** subroutine is called to populate form fields.

```vb
Public Sub PopFrmFlds()
    txtClntId.Text = gClntRs.Fields(0)
    txtFName.Text = gClntRs.Fields(1)
'Checking if the recordset's field for Employee's middle name is empty
    If gClntRs.Fields(2) <> "" Then
        txtMName.Text = gClntRs.Fields(2)
    Else
        txtMName.Text = ""
    End If
    txtLName.Text = gClntRs.Fields(3)
    txtAddr1.Text = gClntRs.Fields(4)
    txtAddr2.Text = gClntRs.Fields(5)
    txtCity.Text = gClntRs.Fields(6)
    txtPin.Text = gClntRs.Fields(7)
    txtDOB.Text = gClntRs.Fields(8)
'Checking the value of the PANCopy field for the current record
    If gClntRs.Fields(9) Then
        chkPAN.Value = 1
    Else
        chkPAN.Value = 0
    End If
'Checking the value of the VerifiedData field for the current record
    If gClntRs.Fields(10) Then
        chkVerified.Value = 1
    Else
        chkVerified.Value = 0
    End If
'Calling ChkDtlsRecd to populate the contact information's data grid
    Call ChkDtlsRecd
End Sub
```

The **DisableFrmFlds()** subroutine is called to disable the form's data entry fields.

```vb
Public Sub DisableFrmFlds()
    txtClntId.Enabled = False
    txtFName.Enabled = False
    txtMName.Enabled = False
    txtLName.Enabled = False
```

```
    txtAddr1.Enabled = False
    txtAddr2.Enabled = False
    txtCity.Enabled = False
    txtPin.Enabled = False
    txtDOB.Enabled = False
    chkPAN.Enabled = False
    chkVerified.Enabled = False
End Sub
```

The **EnableFrmFlds()** subroutine is called to enable the form's data entry fields.

```
Public Sub EnableFrmFlds()
    txtFName.Enabled = True
    txtMName.Enabled = True
    txtLName.Enabled = True
    txtAddr1.Enabled = True
    txtAddr2.Enabled = True
    txtCity.Enabled = True
    txtPin.Enabled = True
    txtDOB.Enabled = True
    chkPAN.Enabled = True
    chkVerified.Enabled = True
End Sub
```

The **ChkDtlsRecd()** subroutine is called to set the details section' behaviour.

```
Public Sub ChkDtlsRecd()
'Checking if the form field for the Client's Id number is empty to pass
'an appropriate SQL query to the ADODC control
    If txtClntId.Text = "" Then
        AdodcCont.RecordSource = "SELECT * FROM Clnt_Dtls WHERE ClientId = 0"
    Else
        AdodcCont.RecordSource = "SELECT * FROM Clnt_Dtls WHERE ClientId = " _
                                    & txtClntId.Text
    End If
'Refreshing the Detail table's ADODC recordset
    AdodcCont.Refresh
'Checking if the detail table's recordset contains more than on records
'to decide the behaviour of the details section's navigation buttons
    If AdodcCont.Recordset.RecordCount > 1 Then
        Call EnableDgNvgt
```

```vb
        Else
            Call DisableDgNvgt
        End If
'Refreshing the data grid with data from the detail table's recordset
        dgContact.Refresh
End Sub
```

The **ChngDtlsRecd()** subroutine is called to accept a client's contact information.

```vb
Public Sub ChngDtlsRecd()
'Checking if the Client's Id number field is empty
    If txtClntId.Text = "" Then
        'Calling SaveMstrRecd to save data held in the master section
        Call SaveMstrRecd
    End If
'Disabling data manipulation buttons within the UI's details section
    cmdDgInst.Enabled = False
    cmdDgUpdt.Enabled = False
    cmdDgDel.Enabled = False
'Enabling the Save button within the UI's details section
    cmdDgSave.Enabled = True
'Showing the Contact Information's data capture objects
    cmbContType.Visible = True
    txtContNo.Visible = True
'Placing the form focus on combobox to select type of contact number
    cmbContType.SetFocus
End Sub
```

The **DisableDtls()** subroutine is called to disable the UI's Details section.

```vb
Public Sub DisableDtls()
'Disabling the detail frame's command buttons
    cmdDgInst.Enabled = False
    cmdDgUpdt.Enabled = False
    cmdDgDel.Enabled = False
    cmdDgSave.Enabled = False
'Disabling the detail frame's navigation buttons
    DisableDgNvgt
```

```
'Disabling the Insert; update and delete property of the DataGrid
'in the detail section
    dgContact.AllowAddNew = False
    dgContact.AllowUpdate = False
    dgContact.AllowDelete = False
End Sub
```

The **EnableDltlsFrmFldsNvgt()** subroutine is called to enable data manipulation within the UI's Details section.

```
Public Sub EnableDtlsFrmFlds()
'Disabling data manipulation within the data grid
    dgContact.AllowAddNew = True
    dgContact.AllowUpdate = True
    dgContact.AllowDelete = True
'Enabling the data manipulation buttons within the Details section
    cmdDgDel.Enabled = True
    cmdDgUpdt.Enabled = True
    cmdDgInst.Enabled = True
End Sub
```

The **DisableDltlsFrmFldsNvgt()** subroutine is called to disable data manipulation within the Details section.

```
Public Sub DisableDtlsFrmFlds()
'Enabling data manipulation within the data grid
    dgContact.AllowAddNew = False
    dgContact.AllowUpdate = False
    dgContact.AllowDelete = False
'Disabling the data manipulation buttons within the Details section
    cmdDgInst.Enabled = False
    cmdDgUpdt.Enabled = False
    cmdDgDel.Enabled = False
End Sub
```

The **EnableDgNvgt()** subroutine is called to enable the navigation buttons within the Details section.

```
Public Sub EnableDgNvgt()
    cmdDgFrst.Enabled = True
    cmdDgPrior.Enabled = True
    cmdDgNext.Enabled = True
    cmdDgLast.Enabled = True
End Sub
```

The **DisableDgNvgt()** subroutine is called to disable the navigation buttons within the UI's Details section.

```
Public Sub DisableDgNvgt()
    cmdDgFrst.Enabled = False
    cmdDgPrior.Enabled = False
    cmdDgNext.Enabled = False
    cmdDgLast.Enabled = False
End Sub
'********* FUNCTIONALITY FOR FORM's OTHER SUBROUTINES ENDS *********
'******************************************************************
```

PROJECT CODE FOR FrmSlctclnt.frm

Option Explicit
```
'Declaring variables for later use
```
Dim mAcctType, mAcctNo, mClntName, mSqlStr As String
```
'***************************************************************
'********* FUNCTIONALITY FOR THE FORM SPECIFIC EVENTS BEGINS ********
```
The **Form_Load()** subroutine is called to load a form to add a client as an account holder.

Public Sub Form_Load()
```
'Disabling data capture objects which binds a client to an account
```
   cmbAcctType.Enabled = False
   cmbAcctNo.Enabled = False
```
'Creating an SQL query string to retrieve records
'from the Client's master table
```
   mSqlStr = "SELECT ClientId FROM Clnt_Mstr"
```
'Storing the value returned by PopNameCmd while populating the
'combobox listing client's name
```
   mClntName = PopNameCmb(mSqlStr, "Clnt_Mstr", cmbName)
End Sub
```
'********* FUNCTIONALITY FOR THE FORM SPECIFIC EVENTS ENDS *********
'***************************************************************


'***************************************************************
'******* FUNCTIONALITY OF THE FORM's CHECKBOX BUTTONS BEGINS *******
```
The **chkAcctHldr_Click()** subroutine is called when the option to select client, bound to an account as an account holder, is clicked.

Public Sub chkAcctHldr_Click()
```
'Checking if the option for the cash transaction is checked
```
   If chkAcctHldr.Value = 1 Then
```
      'Setting initial values into a variable local to the form
```
     mAcctType = ""
```
      'Enabling some data capture objects
```
     cmbAcctType.Enabled = True
     cmbAcctNo.Enabled = True
```
      'Calling cmbAcctType_Click to refresh the combo box listing
      'account type
```
     Call cmbAcctType_Click

```vb
    Else
    'Disabling some data capture objects
        cmbAcctType.Enabled = False
        cmbAcctNo.Enabled = False
    'Creating an SQL query string to retrieve records
    'from the Client's master table
        mSqlStr = "SELECT ClientId FROM Clnt_Mstr"
    'Storing the value returned by PopNameCmd while populating the
    'combobox listing client's name
        mClntName = PopNameCmb(mSqlStr, "Clnt_Mstr", cmbName)
    End If
End Sub
'******** FUNCTIONALITY OF THE FORM's CHECKBOX BUTTONS ENDS ********
'*****************************************************************


'*****************************************************************
'******** FUNCTIONALITY OF THE FORM's OPTION BUTTONS BEGINS ********
```

The **cmbAcctType_Click()** subroutine is called when the combo box listing account types get clicked.

```vb
Public Sub cmbAcctType_Click()
'Checking if the user has selected a different account type
    If cmbAcctType.Text <> mAcctType Then
    'Storing the value returned by PopNoCmd while populating the
    'combobox listing account numbers
        mAcctType = PopNoCmb(cmbAcctType.Text, cmbAcctNo)
    'Clearing the variable holding the last selected account number
        mAcctNo = ""
    'Calling cmbAcctNo_Click to refresh the combo box listing
    'account numbers
        Call cmbAcctNo_Click
    End If
End Sub
```

The **cmbAcctNo_Click()** subroutine is called when the combo box listing account numbers get clicked.

```vb
Public Sub cmbAcctNo_Click()
'Checking if the user has selected a different account type
    If cmbAcctNo.Text <> mAcctNo Then
```

CHAP 06
A COMMERCIAL BANKING SYSTEM: THE WORKING

```
'Creating an SQL query string to retrieve records
'from the Account master table
    mSqlStr = "SELECT ClientId1, ClientId2, ClientId3 FROM Acct_Mstr " & _
              "Where AcctNo = " & cmbAcctNo.Text
'Storing the value returned by PopNameCmd
'while populating the combobox listing client's name
    mClntName = PopNameCmb(mSqlStr, "Clnt_Mstr", cmbName)
    End If
End Sub
'********* FUNCTIONALITY OF THE FORM's OPTION BUTTONS ENDS *********
'******************************************************************
```

'********* FUNCTIONALITY FOR THE FORM BUTTON's EVENTS BEGINS ********

The **cmdAdd_Click()** subroutine is called when the button to add a new client is clicked.

```
Public Sub cmdAdd_Click()
'Storing a new SQL query to retrieve records from the Client's master
'recordset
    gClntSql = "SELECT * FROM Clnt_Mstr Where ClientId = 0"
'Calling Unload to terminate the form's functionality
    Unload frmSlctClnt
'Calling LoadChild to load the Client Master form
'by passing a parameter of the Form object type
    Call LoadChild(frmClntMstr)
End Sub
```

The **cmdAccept_Click()** subroutine is called when the button 'OK' is clicked.

```
Public Sub cmdAccept_Click()
'Calling ReturnId to pass a client's name,
'to be displayed in the data entry form field
    Call ReturnId(cmbName.Text, gObjId)
    Unload frmSlctClnt
End Sub
'********* FUNCTIONALITY FOR THE FORM BUTTON's EVENTS ENDS *********
'*******************************************************************
```

PROJECT CODE FOR frmAcctMstr.frm

Option Explicit
'Declaring object variables for later use
Dim mHldrName1, mHldrName2, mHldrName3 As String
Dim mIntroAcctType, mIntroAcctNo As String
Dim mNominName As String
Dim mSqlStr As String
Dim mObjCount, mPosition As Integer

'***
'******** FUNCTIONALITY FOR THE FORM SPECIFIC EVENTS BEGINS ********

The **Form_Load()** subroutine is called when the data entry form used for capturing and displaying Account's information loads in memory. The SQL query stored in a global variable named **gAcctSql** is used to retrieve records held in the **Acct_Mstr** table.

A call is made to the **NoMode()** subroutine which allows **Insert** or **View** operations only. Finally, the Employee's Name field (combo box) is populated with a list of bank employees' names.

```vb
Public Sub Form_Load()
'Storing initial values into a variable local to the form
    mObjCount = 0
'Storing a reference to the active child form's into the global
'variable 'gFrmName1'
    gFrmName1 = "Account"
'Hiding some of the U.I. objects
    fraDate.Visible = False
'Opening the ADODB's Recordset object used for retrieving records from
'the Employee's Master table
    gAcctRs.Open gAcctSql, gConnect, adOpenKeyset, adLockPessimistic
    gFrmRs3 = gFrmRs2
    gFrmRs2 = gFrmRs1
'Storing the name of the ADODB's Recordset object in 'gfrmRs1'
    gFrmRs1 = "gAcctRs"
'Calling NoMode to allow Insert or View operations only
    Call NoMode
```

```
'Creating an SQL query string to retrieve records
'from the Employee's master table
    mSqlStr = "SELECT EmpId FROM Emp_Mstr"
'Storing the value returned by PopNameCmd while populating the combobox
'listing employee's name
    mSqlStr = PopNameCmb(mSqlStr, "Emp_Mstr", cmbChkdBy)
End Sub
```

The **Form_Unload()** subroutine is called just before the data entry form used for capturing and displaying an Account's information is destroyed from memory. Before the form is destroyed, the recordset used to retrieve record from the **Acct_Mstr** table is destroyed and a call is made to the global subroutine **ResetMDI()**, used to reset a sequence which is used with active child form.

```
Public Sub Form_Unload(Cancel As Integer)
    gAcctRs.Close
    Call ResetMDI
End Sub
'********* FUNCTIONALITY FOR THE FORM SPECIFIC EVENTS ENDS *********
'*****************************************************************


'*****************************************************************
'********* FUNCTIONALITY OF THE BUTTON CLICK EVENT BEGINS *********
```

The **cmdAddPrsn()** subroutine is called when the button to add a new account holder is clicked.

```
Public Sub cmdAddPrsn_Click()
'Incrementing the counter bound to the number of account holders
    mObjCount = mObjCount + 1
'Showing the form field used to capture an identification
'for the next account holder
    txtHldrName(mObjCount).Visible = True
'Enabling the button to remove an existing account holder
    cmdRmvPrsn.Enabled = True
'Checking the counter to limit the number of account holders to three
    If mObjCount = 2 Then
        cmdAddPrsn.Enabled = False
    End If
'Placing the form cursor on the field just displayed
    txtHldrName(mObjCount).SetFocus
End Sub
```

The **cmdRmvPrsn()** subroutine is called when the button to remove an existing account holder is clicked.

```
Public Sub cmdRmvPrsn_Click()
'Hiding the form field used to capture identification
    txtHldrName(mObjCount).Visible = False
'Disabling the button used to add a new account holder
    cmdAddPrsn.Enabled = True
'Decrementing the counter, bound to the number of account holders
    mObjCount = mObjCount - 1
'Checking the counter to prevent losing information
'of the first account holder
    If mObjCount = 0 Then
        cmdRmvPrsn.Enabled = False
        cmdAddPrsn.SetFocus
    End If
End Sub
'*************************************************************
'********** FUNCTIONALITY OF THE BUTTON CLICK EVENT ENDS **********


'*************************************************************
'******** FUNCTIONALITY FOR FOCUS EVENTS ON FORM FIELD BEGINS ********
```

The **txtHldrName_GotFocus()** subroutine is called when the form's cursor moves onto one of the account holder's name field.

```
Public Sub txtHldrName_GotFocus(Index As Integer)
    gObjId = "frmAcctMstr.txtHldrName(" & Index & ")"
    Load frmSlctClnt
    frmSlctClnt.Show vbModal
End Sub
```

The **txtNomiName_GotFocus()** subroutine is called when the form cursor moves onto the nominee's name field.

```
Public Sub txtNomiName_GotFocus()
    gObjId = "frmAcctMstr.txtNomiName"
    Load frmSlctClnt
    frmSlctClnt.Show vbModal
End Sub
'******** FUNCTIONALITY FOR FOCUS EVENTS ON FORM FIELD ENDS ********
'*************************************************************
```

CHAP 06   A COMMERCIAL BANKING SYSTEM: THE WORKING

```
'*****************************************************************
'******* FUNCTIONALITY FOR CHANGE EVENTS ON FORM FIELD BEGINS *******
```

The **txtDate_KeyPress()** subroutine is called when the value held in the Account's opening date field is changed.

```
Public Sub txtDate_KeyPress(KeyAscii As Integer)
'Displaying the 'fraDate' frame containing a MonthView control
'to capture the Account's opening date
    fraDate.Visible = True
'Clearing the Account's opening date field
    txtDate.Text = ""
'Placing the form cursor on a MonthView control
'to select the Account's opening date
    mvwDate.SetFocus
End Sub
'******** FUNCTIONALITY FOR CHANGE EVENTS ON FORM FIELD ENDS *******
'*****************************************************************



'*****************************************************************
'******** FUNCTIONALITY OF THE FORM's OPTION BUTTONS BEGINS *******
```

The **cmbIntroType_Click()** subroutine is called when the combo box listing account types get clicked.

```
Public Sub cmbIntroType_Click()
'Checking if the user has selected a different account type
    If cmbIntroType.Text <> mIntroAcctType Then
    'Storing the value returned by PopNoCmd while populating the combo
    'box listing account numbers
        mIntroAcctType = PopNoCmb(cmbIntroType.Text, cmbIntroAcct)
    'Clearing the variable holding the last selection for an account
    'number
        mIntroAcctNo = ""
    'Calling cmbIntroAcct_Click to refresh the combo box listing account
    'numbers
        Call cmbIntroAcct_Click
    End If
End Sub
```

The **cmbIntroAcct_Click()** subroutine is called when the combo box listing account numbers get clicked.

```vb
Public Sub cmbIntroAcct_Click()
'Checking if the user has selected a different account type
    If cmbIntroAcct.Text <> mIntroAcctNo Then
    'Creating an SQL query string to retrieve records from the Account
    'master table
        mSqlStr = "SELECT ClientId1, ClientId2, ClientId3 FROM Acct_Mstr " & _
                  "Where AcctNo = " & cmbIntroAcct.Text
    'Storing the value returned by PopNameCmd while populating the combo
    'box listing client's name
        mIntroAcctNo = PopNameCmb(mSqlStr, "Clnt_Mstr", cmbIntroName)
    End If
End Sub
'********* FUNCTIONALITY OF THE FORM's OPTION BUTTONS ENDS *********
'*****************************************************************



'*****************************************************************
'******* FUNCTIONALITY FOR CALENDAR CONTROL's EVENTS BEGINS ********
```

The **mvwDate_DateClick()** subroutine is called when form cursor moves away from the MonthView control capturing an Account's opening date.

```vb
Public Sub mvwDate_DateClick(ByVal DateClicked As Date)
'Setting the Text attribute of the Account's opening date field
    txtDate.Text = mvwDate.Value
'Hiding the 'fraDate' frame containing a MonthView control
'to capture the Account's opening date
    fraDate.Visible = False
'Placing the form cursor on the next enterable field
    cmbChkdBy.SetFocus
End Sub
'******** FUNCTIONALITY FOR CALENDAR CONTROL's EVENTS ENDS *********
'*****************************************************************



'*****************************************************************
'************ FUNCTIONALITY FOR DATA MANIPULATION BEGINS ************
```

The **InstMstrRecd()** subroutine is called to Insert a Master record.

```vb
Public Sub InstMstrRecd()
'Calling ClrFrmFlds to clear the Master form fields
    Call ClrFrmFlds
'Calling SaveMstr to allow only the Save operation
    Call SaveMstr
```

```
'Placing the form cursor on the first account holder's name field
    txtHldrName(0).SetFocus
End Sub
```

The **UpdtMstrRecd()** subroutine is called to Update a Master record.

```
Public Sub UpdtMstrRecd()
'Calling SaveMstr to allow only the Save operation
    Call SaveMstr
End Sub
```

The **DelMstrRecd()** subroutine is called to Delete a Master record.

```
Public Sub DelMstrRecd()
'Checking if the recordset cursor is on the first record
    If gAcctRs.AbsolutePosition = 1 Then
        MsgBox "The first record cannot be deleted!!", vbCritical + vbOKOnly, _
                "CAUTION"
        Exit Sub
    End If
'Prompting a user before deleting the master record
    gMsgResponse = MsgBox("All information for this account will be deleted!!", _
                    vbOKCancel + vbCritical, "Delete Warning")
'Checking if the 'Cancel' button is clicked
    If gMsgResponse = 2 Then
        'Exiting from the delete subroutine
        Exit Sub
    Else
    'Creating a SQL query string to retrieve records from the
    'Transaction's master table
        mSqlStr = "SELECT * FROM Trans_Mstr WHERE AcctNo = " & gAcctRs.Fields(0)
    'Opening the ADODB's Recordset object used for retrieving records
    'from the Employee's Master table
        gTemp2Rs.Open mSqlStr, gConnect, adOpenKeyset, adLockPessimistic
    'Checking if there are any transactions for the account that will
    'be deleted
        Do While gTemp2Rs.RecordCount > 0
            'Placing the cursor on the Last record
            gTemp2Rs.MoveLast
```

```vb
        'Checking for a cash transaction, to decide on a SQL query
            If gTemp2Rs.Fields(4) Then
                mSqlStr = "SELECT * FROM Trans_Dtls_Cash WHERE TransId = " & _
                    gTemp2Rs.Fields(0)
            Else
                mSqlStr = "SELECT * FROM Trans_Dtls_Chq WHERE TransId = " & _
                    gTemp2Rs.Fields(0)
            End If
        'Opening the ADODB's Recordset object used for retrieving records
        'from the Employee's Master table
            gTemp3Rs.Open mSqlStr, gConnect, adOpenKeyset, adLockPessimistic
        'Checking if there is any cheques information for the account
        'that will be deleted
            Do While gTemp3Rs.RecordCount > 0
                gTemp3Rs.Delete
            Loop   'End of inner 'Do While ... Loop' iteration
        'Closing the recordset bound to the transaction's cash or cheque
        'table and deleting the current record for transaction's master
            gTemp3Rs.Close
            gTemp2Rs.Delete
        Loop   'End of 'Do While ... Loop' iteration
    'Closing the recordset bound to the transaction's master table
        gTemp2Rs.Close
    'Deleting the current record for the account's master table
        gAcctRs.Delete
    'Checking if the recordset bound to the account's master table
    'is empty
        If gAcctRs.RecordCount = 0 Then
        'Calling NoMode to allow Insert or View operations only
            Call NoMode
        Else
        'Calling VuNextMstr to view the next record
        'in the account's master table
            Call VuNextMstr(GetActvRs("gAcctRs"))
        End If
    End If
End Sub
'************ FUNCTIONALITY FOR DATA MANIPULATION ENDS *************
'******************************************************************
```

CHAP 06 A COMMERCIAL BANKING SYSTEM: THE WORKING

```
'*****************************************************************
'*********** FUNCTIONALITY FOR SAVING MASTER DATA BEGINS ************
```
The **SaveMstrRecd()** subroutine is called to save the data captured by the active form into the Database.

```vb
Public Sub SaveMstrRecd()
'Checking if any mandatory form fields have been left empty
    If Trim(txtHldrName(0)) = "" Or Trim(txtDate) = "" Or _
      Trim(cmbIntroName.Text) = "" Or Trim(cmbChkdBy.Text) = "" Then
        MsgBox "All the fields are mandatory!!", vbCritical + vbOKOnly, "Caution"
    ElseIf Trim(txtHldrName(1)) = "" And Trim(txtNomiName) = "" Then
        MsgBox "Enter a nominee's information for the Self account!!", vbCritical + _
             vbOKOnly, "Please Note"
    Else
    'Accepting an account head if the account is operated by joint
    'holders
        If txtAcctHead.Text = "" And mObjCount > 0 Then
            txtAcctHead.Text = Trim(InputBox("Enter a account head for the joint _
                           account!!", "Please Note"))
        End If
    'Checking if the account number field is empty
        If Trim(txtAcctNo.Text) = "" Then
        'Appending a blank record into the active recordset
            gAcctRs.AddNew
        End If
'Inserting values captured by the active form's fields into the
'Account's master recordset
    'Checking the option selected for an account type
        If optAcctType(0) Then
            gAcctRs.Fields(1) = "CA"
        Else
            gAcctRs.Fields(1) = "SB"
        End If
    'Checking if the Account Head's field is empty
        If txtAcctHead.Text <> "" Then
            gAcctRs.Fields(2) = txtAcctHead.Text
        End If
```

```vb
'Creating an iterated process to store account holder's information
    For mPosition = 0 To mObjCount
    'Checking if the form field is empty
        If txtHldrName(mPosition).Text <> "" Then
            gAcctRs.Fields(mPosition + 3) = _
                GetNumber(txtHldrName(mPosition).Text)
        End If
    Next
'Creating an iterated process to remove clients who are no longer
'account holders
    For mPosition = mObjCount + 1 To 2
        If Not (mPosition > 2) Then
            gAcctRs.Fields(mPosition + 3) = 0
        End If
    Next
'Checking if the field for Nominee's information is empty
    If txtNomiName.Text <> "" Then
        gAcctRs.Fields(6) = GetNumber(txtNomiName.Text)
    End If
'Storing introducer's information into the recordset
    gAcctRs.Fields(7) = cmbIntroAcct.Text
    gAcctRs.Fields(8) = GetNumber(cmbIntroName.Text)
'Checking if the field for the introducer's sign is selected
    If chkIntroSign.Value = 1 Then
        gAcctRs.Fields(9) = True
    Else
        gAcctRs.Fields(9) = False
    End If
'Storing the bank officer's information into the recordset
    gAcctRs.Fields(10) = GetNumber(cmbChkdBy.Text)
'Checking if the field for the bank officer's sign is selected
    If chkChkdSign.Value = 1 Then
        gAcctRs.Fields(11) = True
    Else
        gAcctRs.Fields(11) = False
    End If
'Checking if the field for the bank manager's sign is selected
    If chkMngrSign.Value = 1 Then
        gAcctRs.Fields(12) = True
    Else
        gAcctRs.Fields(12) = False
    End If
```

```vb
    'Storing the date on which the account was created
        gAcctRs.Fields(13) = txtDate.Text
    'Updating the table in the database with the new values captured
        gAcctRs.Update
    'Checking if the account number field is empty
        If Trim(txtAcctNo.Text) = "" Then
            'Assigning an auto generated account number to 'txtAcctNo' on the
            'U.I.
                txtAcctNo.Text = gAcctRs.Fields(0)
            'Storing a new SQL query to retrieve the table structure from the
            'Transaction's master table
                gTransSql = "SELECT * FROM Trans_Mstr WHERE TransId = 0"
            'Calling LoadChild to load the Transaction Master child form by
            'passing a parameter of the Form object type
                Call LoadChild(frmTransMstr)
        Else
            'Calling ChngMstr to allow manipulation and navigational
            'operations
                Call ChngMstr
        End If
    End If
End Sub
'*********** FUNCTIONALITY FOR SAVING MASTER DATA ENDS *************
'******************************************************************


'******************************************************************
'******** FUNCTIONALITY FOR FORM's OTHER SUBROUTINES BEGINS ********
```

The **ClrFrmFlds()** subroutine is called to empty the form's data capture fields.

```vb
Public Sub ClrFrmFlds()
    txtAcctHead.Text = ""
    optAcctType(0).Value = True
    txtAcctNo.Text = ""
    txtHldrName(0).Text = ""
    txtHldrName(1).Text = ""
    txtHldrName(2).Text = ""
    txtHldrName(1).Visible = False
    txtHldrName(2).Visible = False
    cmdAddPrsn.Enabled = True
    cmdRmvPrsn.Enabled = False
    cmbIntroType.Text = "SB"
```

```vb
'Calling cmbIntroType_Click to refresh the combo box listing account
'number under Introducer's information section
    Call cmbIntroType_Click
    chkIntroSign.Value = False
    txtNomiName.Text = ""
    txtDate.Text = ""
    cmbChkdBy.Text = ""
    chkChkdSign.Value = 0
    chkMngrSign.Value = 0
End Sub
```

The **PopFrmFlds()** subroutine is called to populate form fields using the active recordset.

```vb
Public Sub PopFrmFlds()
    txtAcctNo.Text = gAcctRs.Fields(0)
'Checking the 'AcctType' field to decide the account type for the
'current record
    If gAcctRs.Fields(1) = "CA" Then
        optAcctType(0).Value = True
    Else
        optAcctType(1).Value = True
    End If
'Checking if the Account Head field in the recordset is not empty
    If gAcctRs.Fields(2) <> "" Then
        txtAcctHead.Text = gAcctRs.Fields(2)
    Else
        txtAcctHead.Text = ""
    End If
'Creating an iterating process to populate the client's name fields
    For mPosition = 0 To 2
        'Checking if a client's Id is present in the recordset's Account
        'Holder(s) field
        If gAcctRs.Fields(mPosition + 3) > 0 Then
            'Displaying the account holder's name returned by GetIdentity, on
            'passing a client's Id
            txtHldrName(mPosition).Text = GetIdentity("Clnt_Mstr", _
                    gAcctRs.Fields(mPosition + 3))
            txtHldrName(mPosition).Visible = True
            mObjCount = mPosition
```

```
        Else
            'Clearing the account holder's name field on the U. I.
                txtHldrName(mPosition).Text = ""
                txtHldrName(mPosition).Visible = False
        End If
    Next
'Checking if a client's Id is present in the recordset's Nominee field
    If gAcctRs.Fields(6) > 0 Then
        'Displaying the nominee name returned by GetIdentity
            txtNomiName.Text = GetIdentity("Clnt_Mstr", gAcctRs.Fields(6))
    Else
        'Clearing the nominee name field on the U. I.
            txtNomiName.Text = ""
    End If
'Displaying the introducer's information on the U. I.
    cmbIntroType.Text = GetAcctType(gAcctRs.Fields(7))
    cmbIntroAcct.Text = gAcctRs.Fields(7)
    cmbIntroName.Text = GetIdentity("Clnt_Mstr", gAcctRs.Fields(8))
'Placing a tick sign if the recordset field for the introducer's
'signature hold a True
    If gAcctRs.Fields(9) Then
        chkIntroSign = 1
    Else
        chkIntroSign = 0
    End If
'Displaying the Bank Officer's name returned by GetIdentity
    cmbChkdBy.Text = GetIdentity("Emp_Mstr", gAcctRs.Fields(10))
'Placing a tick sign if the recordset field for the Bank Officer's
'signature hold a True
    If gAcctRs.Fields(11) Then
        chkChkdSign.Value = 1
    Else
        chkChkdSign.Value = 0
    End If
'Placing a tick sign if the recordset field for the Bank Manager's
'signature hold a True
    If gAcctRs.Fields(12) Then
        chkMngrSign.Value = 1
```

```
    Else
        chkMngrSign.Value = 0
    End If
    txtDate.Text = gAcctRs.Fields(13)
End Sub
```

The **DisableFrmFlds()** subroutine is called to disable the form's data entry fields.

```
Public Sub DisableFrmFlds()
    optAcctType(0).Enabled = False
    optAcctType(1).Enabled = False
    txtAcctNo.Enabled = False
    txtHldrName(0).Enabled = False
    txtHldrName(1).Enabled = False
    txtHldrName(2).Enabled = False
    cmdAddPrsn.Enabled = False
    cmdRmvPrsn.Enabled = False
    cmbIntroType.Enabled = False
    cmbIntroAcct.Enabled = False
    chkIntroSign.Enabled = False
    cmbIntroName.Enabled = False
    txtAcctHead.Enabled = False
    txtNomiName.Enabled = False
    txtDate.Enabled = False
    cmbChkdBy.Enabled = False
    chkChkdSign.Enabled = False
    chkMngrSign.Enabled = False
End Sub
```

The **EnableFrmFlds()** subroutine is called to enable the form's data entry fields.

```
Public Sub EnableFrmFlds()
    optAcctType(0).Enabled = True
    optAcctType(1).Enabled = True
    txtHldrName(0).Enabled = True
    txtHldrName(1).Enabled = True
    txtHldrName(2).Enabled = True
```

```
        If mObjCount < 2 Then
            cmdAddPrsn.Enabled = True
        End If
        If mObjCount = 2 Then
            cmdRmvPrsn.Enabled = True
        End If
        cmbIntroType.Enabled = True
        cmbIntroAcct.Enabled = True
        cmbIntroName.Enabled = True
        chkIntroSign.Enabled = True
        txtNomiName.Enabled = True
        txtDate.Enabled = True
        cmbChkdBy.Enabled = True
        chkChkdSign.Enabled = True
        chkMngrSign.Enabled = True
End Sub
'********* FUNCTIONALITY FOR FORM's OTHER SUBROUTINES ENDS *********
'******************************************************************
```

PROJECT CODE FOR frmTransMstr.frm

Option Explicit
'Declaring object variables for later use
Dim mAcctType, mAmt, mAmtStr, mParty As String
Dim mSqlStr As String
Dim mObjCount, mTotAmt As Integer

'***
'******** FUNCTIONALITY FOR THE FORM SPECIFIC EVENTS BEGINS ********

The **Form_Load()** subroutine is called when the data entry form used for capturing Transaction's information loads in memory. Before the form is displayed on the screen, the maximum number of characters enterable is set for each form field.

The SQL query stored in a global variable named **gTransSql** is used to retrieve records held in the **Trans_Mstr** table. After the recordset is obtained, a check is made to insure that the form is not invoked through another data entry form.

If another data entry form invokes this form, data Insert operation is called. During the insert operations, the behaviour of the MDI form is such that it allows **Save** as the only next operation.

If the form has been invoked by another data entry form, a call is made to the **NoMode()** subroutine to allow an **Insert** operation only.

```
Public Sub Form_Load()
    txtTransAmt.MaxLength = 10
    txtParty.MaxLength = 50
    txtChqNo.MaxLength = 6
    txtDrawerAcct.MaxLength = 6
    txtSortCode.MaxLength = 9
    txtTransCode.MaxLength = 2
'Storing initial values into a variable local to the form
    mAcctType = ""
    mAmt = "0"
    mAmtStr = "Zero only"
    mParty = ""
    mObjCount = 0
    mTotAmt = 0
```

```vb
'Setting the Text property for form fields
    cmbAcctNo.Text = "1"
    txtParty.Text = "Self"
'Storing a reference pointing to the active child form
    gFrmName1 = "Transaction"
'Hiding form objects by setting their Visible property to 'False'
    lblTransId.Visible = False
    txtTransId.Visible = False
'Hiding the frames containing the MonthView control
    fraDate.Visible = False
    fraChqDate.Visible = False
'Opening the ADODB's Recordset object used for retrieving records
'from the Employee's Master table
    gTransRs.Open gTransSql, gConnect, adOpenKeyset, adLockPessimistic
    gFrmRs3 = gFrmRs2
    gFrmRs2 = gFrmRs1
'Storing the name of the ADODB's Recordset object in 'gfrmRs1'
    gFrmRs1 = "gTransRs"
'Checking if the variable 'gFrmRs2' holds a value
    If gFrmRs2 <> "" Then
        'Disabling the MDI's Exit options
            frmMain.mnuExit.Enabled = False
            frmMain.cmdExit.Enabled = False
        'Calling InstMstrRecd to insert a new Master record
            Call InstMstrRecd
    Else
        'Calling NoMode to allow Insert or View operations only
            Call NoMode
    End If
'Disabling View operation
    frmMain.mnuView.Enabled = False
    frmMain.cmdView.Enabled = False
End Sub
```

PRACTICAL VB 6 PROJECTS

The **Form_Unload()** subroutine is called just before the data entry form used for capturing a Transaction's information is destroyed from memory. Before the form is destroyed, the recordset used to retrieve record from the **Trans_Mstr** table is destroyed and a call is made to the global subroutine **ResetMDI()**, used to reset a sequence which is used with active child form.

```
Public Sub Form_Unload(Cancel As Integer)
    gTransRs.Close
    Call ResetMDI
End Sub
'********* FUNCTIONALITY FOR THE FORM SPECIFIC EVENTS ENDS *********
'******************************************************************


'******************************************************************
'******** FUNCTIONALITY OF THE FORM's OPTION BUTTONS BEGINS ********
```

The **cmbAcctType_Click()** subroutine is called when the combo box listing account types get clicked.

```
Public Sub cmbAcctType_Click()
'Checking if the user has selected a different account type
    If cmbAcctType.Text <> mAcctType Then
    'Clearing the option list held in the combo box for account number
        cmbAcctNo.Clear
    'Storing a SQL query to retrieve Account numbers
    'based on a specific account type
        mSqlStr = "SELECT AcctNo FROM Acct_Mstr Where AcctType = '" _
                & cmbAcctType.Text & "'"
    'Opening the ADODB's Recordset object used for retrieving records
    'from the Account's Master table
        gTemp1Rs.Open mSqlStr, gConnect, adOpenKeyset, adLockPessimistic
    'Checking if the active recordset contains records
        If gTemp1Rs.RecordCount > 0 Then
            'Displaying the 1st record in the Account number combo box
            cmbAcctNo.Text = gTemp1Rs.Fields(0)
            'Checking if the recordset cursor has moved beyond the LAST record
            Do While Not gTemp1Rs.EOF
                'Adding an item to the Account number combo box
                cmbAcctNo.AddItem (gTemp1Rs.Fields(0))
                'Placing the active recordset cursor on the Next record
                gTemp1Rs.MoveNext
            Loop    'End of 'Do While ... Loop' iteration
```

CHAP 06 A COMMERCIAL BANKING SYSTEM: THE WORKING

```
            mAcctType = cmbAcctType.Text
        Else
        'Clearing the account number from the Account number combo box
            MsgBox "No accounts exist for the selected account type!!", _
                    vbCritical + vbOKOnly, "CAUTION"
            cmbAcctType.Text = mAcctType
        End If
     'Closing the active recordset
        gTemp1Rs.Close
     End If
End Sub
'********* FUNCTIONALITY OF THE FORM's OPTION BUTTONS ENDS *********
'******************************************************************


'******************************************************************
'******* FUNCTIONALITY FOR CHANGE EVENTS ON FORM FIELD BEGINS *******
```

The **txtTransDate_KeyPress()** subroutine is called when the value in the Transaction's date field is changed.

```
Public Sub txtTransDate_KeyPress(KeyAscii As Integer)
'Displaying the 'fraDate' frame containing a MonthView control
'to capture the Transaction's date
    fraDate.Visible = True
'Clearing the Transaction's date field
    txtTransDate.Text = ""
'Placing the form cursor on a MonthView control
'to select the Transaction's date
    mvwTransDate.SetFocus
End Sub
```

The **txtTransDate_KeyPress()** subroutine is called when the value in the Cheque's date field is changed.

```
Public Sub txtChqDate_KeyPress(KeyAscii As Integer)
'Displaying the 'fraDate' frame containing a MonthView control
'to capture the Cheque's date
    fraChqDate.Visible = True
'Clearing the Cheque's date field
    txtChqDate.Text = ""
```

```vb
'Placing the form cursor on a MonthView control
'to select the Cheque's date
    mvwChqDate.SetFocus
End Sub
'******** FUNCTIONALITY FOR FOCUS EVENTS ON FORM FIELD ENDS ********
'*****************************************************************



'*****************************************************************
'******** FUNCTIONALITY FOR CALENDAR CONTROL's EVENTS BEGINS ********
```

The **mvwTransDate_DateClick()** subroutine is called when form cursor moves away from the MonthView control capturing the Transaction's date.

```vb
Public Sub mvwTransDate_DateClick(ByVal DateClicked As Date)
'Setting the Text attribute of the Transaction's date field
    txtTransDate.Text = mvwTransDate.Value
'Placing the form cursor on the next enterable field
    optTransType(0).SetFocus
'Hiding the 'fraDate' frame containing a MonthView control
'to capture the Transaction's date
    fraDate.Visible = False
End Sub
```

The **mvwChqDate_DateClick()** subroutine is called when form cursor moves away from the MonthView control capturing the Cheque's date.

```vb
Public Sub mvwChqDate_DateClick(ByVal DateClicked As Date)
'Setting the Text attribute of the Transaction's date field
    txtChqdate.Text = mvwChqDate.Value
'Placing the form cursor on the next enterable field
    txtDrawerAcct.SetFocus
'Hiding the 'fraChqDate' frame containing a MonthView control
'to capture the Cheque's date
    fraChqDate.Visible = False
End Sub
'********* FUNCTIONALITY FOR CALENDAR CONTROL's EVENTS ENDS *********
'*****************************************************************
```

CHAP 06   A COMMERCIAL BANKING SYSTEM: THE WORKING

```
'*************************************************************
'********  FUNCTIONALITY OF THE FORM's OPTION BUTTONS BEGINS  ********
```

The **optTransType_Click()** subroutine is called when a transaction type is clicked.

```
Public Sub optTransType_Click(Index As Integer)
'Checking if the option button for the Deposit option is selected
    If Index = 0 Then
      'Assigning a new Caption value to some form objects
        fraCashDtls.Caption = " Pay-In-Slip Details "
        lblParty.Caption = "Paid By :"
      'Assigning new ToolTipText values to the some form objects
        lblTransAmt.ToolTipText = "The amount of rupees deposited (in figures)"
        txtTransAmt.ToolTipText = "Enter the amount of rupees deposited (in figures)"
        lblSumOf.ToolTipText = "The amount of rupees deposited (in words)"
        txtSumOf.ToolTipText = "Enter the amount of rupees deposited (in words)"
      'Checking if the option for the cash transaction is checked
        If chkCashTrans.Value = 1 Then
          'Assigning a new Text value to the Party's name field
            txtParty.Text = "Self"
        End If
    Else
      'Assigning a new Caption value to some form objects
        fraCashDtls.Caption = " Withdrawal-Slip Details "
        lblParty.Caption = "Pay To :"
      'Assigning new ToolTipText values to the some form objects
        lblTransAmt.ToolTipText = "The amount of rupees withdrawn (in figures)"
        txtTransAmt.ToolTipText = "Enter the amount of rupees withdrawn (in figures)"
        lblSumOf.ToolTipText = "The amount of rupees withdrawn (in words)"
        txtSumOf.ToolTipText = "Enter the amount of rupees withdrawn (in words)"
      'Checking if the option for the cash transaction is unchecked
        If chkCashTrans.Value = 0 Then
          'Assigning a new Text value to the Party's name field
            txtParty.Text = "Self"
        End If
    End If
End Sub
'*********  FUNCTIONALITY OF THE FORM's OPTION BUTTONS ENDS  *********
'*************************************************************
```

'***
'******* FUNCTIONALITY OF THE FORM's CHECKBOX BUTTONS BEGINS *******

The **chkCashTrans_Click()** subroutine is called when the option for cash transaction is clicked.

```
Public Sub chkCashTrans_Click()
'Checking if the option for the cash transaction is checked
    If chkCashTrans.Value = 1 Then
       'Showing the 'fraCashDtls' frame within the U.I.
        fraCashDtls.Visible = True
       'Hiding the 'fraChqDtls' frame from the U.I.
        fraChqDtls.Visible = False
    Else
       'Hiding the 'fraCashDtls' frame from the U.I.
        fraCashDtls.Visible = False
       'Showing the 'fraChqDtls' frame within the U.I.
        fraChqDtls.Visible = True
    End If
End Sub
```
'******** FUNCTIONALITY OF THE FORM's CHECKBOX BUTTONS ENDS ********
'***

'***
'*********** FUNCTIONALITY FOR DATA MANIPULATION BEGINS ************

The **InstMstrRecd()** subroutine is called to Insert a Master record.

```
Public Sub InstMstrRecd()
'Enabling or disabling the MDI's sub menu options and toolbar button
'so as to allow only the Save operation
    frmMain.mnuInst.Enabled = False
    frmMain.cmdInst.Enabled = False
    frmMain.mnuSave.Enabled = True
    frmMain.cmdSave.Enabled = True
'Calling ClrFrmFlds to clear the Master form fields
    Call ClrFrmFlds
'Calling EnableFrmFlds to enable U.I.'s form fields
    Call EnableFrmFlds
```

CHAP 06   A COMMERCIAL BANKING SYSTEM: THE WORKING

```vb
'Checking if the active recordset is empty
    If gTransRs.RecordCount = 0 Then
    'Providing preset values for some form fields
        cmbAcctType.Text = ""
        cmbAcctNo.Text = frmAcctMstr.txtAcctNo.Text
        txtTransDate.Text = frmAcctMstr.txtDate.Text
        optTransType(0) = True
        txtTransAmt.Text = "500"
        chkCashTrans.Value = 1
        txtParty.Text = "Self"
    'Disabling some form fields
        cmbAcctType.Enabled = False
        cmbAcctNo.Enabled = False
        txtTransDate.Enabled = False
        optTransType(0).Enabled = False
        optTransType(1).Enabled = False
        txtTransAmt.Enabled = False
        chkCashTrans.Enabled = False
        txtParty.Enabled = False
    'Calling chkCashTrans_Click to display a frame to capture cash
    'transaction details
        Call chkCashTrans_Click
    Else
'Placing the form cursor on the combo box to select an account type
        cmbAcctType.SetFocus
    End If
End Sub
'*********** FUNCTIONALITY FOR DATA MANIPULATION ENDS *************
'******************************************************************


'******************************************************************
'********** FUNCTIONALITY FOR SAVING MASTER DATA BEGINS ***********
```

The **SaveMstrRecd()** subroutine is called to save the data captured by the active form into the Database.

```vb
Public Sub SaveMstrRecd()
'Checking if the transaction's date field have been left empty
    If Trim(txtTransDate.Text) = "" Then
    'Placing the form cursor on the Transaction's date field
        txtTransDate.SetFocus
        Exit Sub
    End If
```

```vb
'Checking if the transaction amount field have been left empty
    If Trim(txtTransAmt) = 0 Then
        MsgBox "The amount fields is mandatory!!", vbCritical + vbOKOnly, "Caution"
    'Placing the form cursor on the Transaction's amount field
        txtTransAmt.SetFocus
        Exit Sub
    End If
'Checking if the transaction is in cash
    If chkCashTrans.Value = 1 Then
        'Adding the total cash value in various denominations
        mTotAmt = mTotAmt + (Trim(txtDeno(1).Text) * 1000)
        mTotAmt = mTotAmt + (Trim(txtDeno(2).Text) * 500)
        mTotAmt = mTotAmt + (Trim(txtDeno(3).Text) * 100)
        mTotAmt = mTotAmt + (Trim(txtDeno(4).Text) * 50)
        mTotAmt = mTotAmt + (Trim(txtDeno(5).Text) * 20)
        mTotAmt = mTotAmt + (Trim(txtDeno(6).Text) * 10)
        mTotAmt = mTotAmt + (Trim(txtDeno(7).Text) * 5)
        mTotAmt = mTotAmt + (Trim(txtDeno(8).Text) * 10)
        mTotAmt = mTotAmt + (Trim(txtDeno(9).Text) * 5)
        mTotAmt = mTotAmt + (Trim(txtDeno(10).Text) * 2)
        mTotAmt = mTotAmt + (Trim(txtDeno(11).Text) * 1)
        mTotAmt = mTotAmt + (Trim(txtDeno(12).Text) * 0.5)
        mTotAmt = mTotAmt + (Trim(txtDeno(13).Text) * 0.25)
    'Terminating the subroutine if the total cash value in various
    'denominations does not equal the transaction amount
        If Trim(txtTransAmt.Text) <> mTotAmt Then
            MsgBox "Total of all cash denominations does not equals " & _
                    "the transaction amount!!", vbCritical + vbOKOnly, "Caution"
            mTotAmt = 0
            Exit Sub
        End If
    Else
    'Checking if any mandatory form fields bound to a cheque transaction
    'have been left empty
        If (Trim(txtChqNo.Text) = "") Or (Trim(txtChqdate.Text) = "") Or _
           (Trim(txtParty.Text) = "") Or (Trim(txtDrawerAcct.Text) = "") Or _
           (Trim(txtSortCode.Text) = "") Or (Trim(txtTransCode.Text) = "") Then
            MsgBox "All the fields are mandatory for a cheque transaction!!", _
                    vbCritical + vbOKOnly, "Caution"
            Exit Sub
        End If
    End If
```

```vb
'Appending a blank record into the active recordset
    gTransRs.AddNew
'Posting values captured by the form fields into the active recordset
    gTransRs.Fields(1) = cmbAcctNo.Text
    gTransRs.Fields(2) = txtTransDate.Text
'Checking if the transaction is in the form of a deposit
    If optTransType(0) = True Then
        gTransRs.Fields(3) = "D"
        mParty = "By "
    Else
        gTransRs.Fields(3) = "W"
        mParty = "To "
    'Converting the account number effected by the transaction into a six
    'digit format and displaying it in the Drawer's Account number field
        txtDrawerAcct.Text = Mid(Format(cmbAcctNo.Text, "1000000"), 2)
    End If
'Checking if the transaction is in cash
    If chkCashTrans.Value = 1 Then
        gTransRs.Fields(4) = True
    Else
        gTransRs.Fields(4) = False
        mParty = mParty & AddQuote(Trim(txtParty.Text))
    End If
    gTransRs.Fields(5) = txtTransAmt.Text
'Updating the table in the database with the recordset's new values
    gTransRs.Update
'Assigning a form field with an auto generated transaction's Id
    txtTransId.Text = gTransRs.Fields(0)
'Checking if the transaction is in cash
    If chkCashTrans.Value = 1 Then
    'Creating an SQL query string to retrieve a empty recordset
    'from a table storing information for Cash Transactions
        mSqlStr = "SELECT * FROM Trans_Dtls_Cash WHERE TransId = 0"
        gCshRs.Open mSqlStr, gConnect, adOpenKeyset, adLockPessimistic
    'Appending a blank record into the active recordset
        gCshRs.AddNew
    'Transferring data captured by the form fields into the recordset
        gCshRs.Fields(0) = txtTransId.Text
        gCshRs.Fields(1) = Trim(txtDeno(1).Text)
        gCshRs.Fields(2) = Trim(txtDeno(2).Text)
        gCshRs.Fields(3) = Trim(txtDeno(3).Text)
```

```vb
        gCshRs.Fields(4) = Trim(txtDeno(4).Text)
        gCshRs.Fields(5) = Trim(txtDeno(5).Text)
        gCshRs.Fields(6) = Trim(txtDeno(6).Text)
        gCshRs.Fields(7) = Trim(txtDeno(7).Text)
        gCshRs.Fields(8) = Trim(txtDeno(8).Text)
        gCshRs.Fields(9) = Trim(txtDeno(9).Text)
        gCshRs.Fields(10) = Trim(txtDeno(10).Text)
        gCshRs.Fields(11) = Trim(txtDeno(11).Text)
        gCshRs.Fields(12) = Trim(txtDeno(12).Text)
        gCshRs.Fields(13) = Trim(txtDeno(13).Text)
    'Updating the table in the database with the recordset's new values
        gCshRs.Update
    'Closing the active recordset
        gCshRs.Close
    Else
    'Creating an SQL query string to retrieve a empty recordset
    'from a table storing information for Cheque Transactions
        mSqlStr = "SELECT * FROM Trans_Dtls_Chq WHERE TransId = 0"
        gChqRs.Open mSqlStr, gConnect, adOpenKeyset, adLockPessimistic
    'Appending a blank record into the active recordset
        gChqRs.AddNew
    'Transferring data captured by the form fields into the recordset
        gChqRs.Fields(0) = txtTransId.Text
        gChqRs.Fields(1) = Trim(txtChqNo.Text)
        gChqRs.Fields(2) = txtChqdate.Text
        gChqRs.Fields(3) = mParty
        gChqRs.Fields(4) = Trim(txtSortCode.Text)
        gChqRs.Fields(5) = Trim(txtDrawerAcct.Text)
        gChqRs.Fields(6) = Trim(txtTransCode.Text)
    'Updating the table in the database with the new values
    'in the recordset
        gChqRs.Update
        gChqRs.Close
    End If
'Checking if the active recordset contains only one record
    If gTransRs.RecordCount = 1 Then
        gTransSql = "SELECT * FROM Trans_Mstr"
    'Enabling the MDI's Exit options
        frmMain.mnuExit.Enabled = True
        frmMain.cmdExit.Enabled = True
```

CHAP 06   A COMMERCIAL BANKING SYSTEM: THE WORKING

```
        'Unloading the active child form
            Unload frmTransMstr
        Else
        'Calling DisableFrmFlds to disable the U.I.'s form fields
            Call DisableFrmFlds
        'Disabling or enabling the MDI's sub menu options and toolbar button
        'so as to allow only the Insert operation
            frmMain.mnuInst.Enabled = True
            frmMain.cmdInst.Enabled = True
            frmMain.mnuSave.Enabled = False
            frmMain.cmdSave.Enabled = False
        End If
End Sub
'*********** FUNCTIONALITY FOR SAVING MASTER DATA ENDS ************
'******************************************************************


'******************************************************************
'********* FUNCTIONALITY FOR FORM FIELD VALIDATIONS BEGINS *********
```

The **txtTransAmt_Validate()** subroutine is called to validate data captured in the Transaction's amount field.

```
Public Sub txtTransAmt_Validate(Cancel As Boolean)
'Removing any spaces from the Transaction's amount field
    txtTransAmt.Text = Trim(txtTransAmt.Text)
'Checking if the Transaction's amount field is not empty
    If txtTransAmt.Text = "" Then
        txtTransAmt.Text = 0
    End If
'Checking if the Transaction's amount field is not holding a value zero
    If Not txtTransAmt.Text = 0 Then
        'Checking the value returned by IsNumeric while scanning
        'for non numeric characters
        If IsNumeric(txtTransAmt.Text) Then
            'Checking the value returned by the function CharFound while
            'scanning the Transaction's amount field for a plus or minus sign
            If (Not CharFound(txtTransAmt.Text, "+")) _
                And (Not CharFound(txtTransAmt.Text, "-")) Then
                'Checking if the amount is below one crore
                If txtTransAmt.Text < 10000000 Then
```

```vb
            'Checking if the transaction amount has been changed
                If txtTransAmt.Text <> mAmt Then
                    'Placing the form cursor on the next enterable field
                        txtParty.SetFocus
                    'Storing the value of the form field in a ten digit format
                        mAmt = Format(txtTransAmt.Text, "10000000.00")
                    'Displaying textual format, returned by ConvertAmt,
                    'for the value passed in the ten digit format
                        txtSumOf.Text = ConvertAmt(Format(mAmt))
                    'Dropping the first digit from 'mAmt' and displaying it
                        mAmt = Mid(mAmt, 2)
                        txtTransAmt.Text = mAmt
                End If
            Else
                MsgBox "Transaction amount is limited below Rs. One Crore!!", _
                        vbInformation + vbOKOnly, "PLEASE NOTE"
                'Placing the form's focus to the Transaction's amount field
                    Cancel = True
            End If
            Exit Sub
        End If
    End If
End If
MsgBox "Only a non-zero number is acceptable as an amount!!", _
        vbCritical + vbOKOnly, "CAUTION"
'Placing the form focus on the Transaction's amount field
    Cancel = True
End Sub
```

The **txtParty_Validate()** subroutine is called to validate data captured in the Party's name field.

```vb
Public Sub txtParty_Validate(Cancel As Boolean)
'Removing spaces from the Party's name field
    txtParty.Text = Trim(txtParty.Text)
'Checking if the transaction is done through cheque
    If chkCashTrans.Value = 0 Then
        'Checking if the Party's name field is empty
            If txtParty.Text = "" Then
                MsgBox "The depositor's or payee's name cannot be left blank!!"
```

```
            'Placing the form's focus to the Party's name field
            Cancel = True
            Exit Sub
        End If
        txtChqNo.SetFocus
    Else
        txtDeno(1).SetFocus
        'Displaying the value held in the Party's name field
        txtParty.Text = "Self"
    End If
End Sub
```

The **txtChqNo_Validate()** subroutine is called to validate data captured in the Cheque number field.

```
Public Sub txtChqNo_Validate(Cancel As Boolean)
'Checking the value returned by function MinLen, called to validate
'the length of the Cheque number field
    If Not MinLen(txtChqNo.Text, 6) Then
        MsgBox "Cheque number must consist of only 6 digits!!"
    Else
        'Checking the value returned by IsNumeric while scanning
        'the Cheque number field for non numeric characters
        If IsNumeric(txtChqNo.Text) Then
            'Checking the value returned by function CharFound while scanning
            'the Cheque number field for a plus or minus sign
            If (Not CharFound(txtChqNo.Text, "+")) _
                And (Not CharFound(txtChqNo.Text, "-")) Then
                'Placing the form cursor to the Drawer's account number field
                txtDrawerAcct.SetFocus
                Exit Sub
            End If
        End If
        MsgBox "Only numeric data are acceptable as a cheque number!!"
    End If
'Placing the form focus on the Cheque number field
    Cancel = True
End Sub
```

The **txtDrawerAcct_Validate()** subroutine is called to validate data captured in the Drawer's account number field.

```vb
Public Sub txtDrawerAcct_Validate(Cancel As Boolean)
'Checking the value returned by function MinLen, called to validate
'the length of the Drawer's account number field
    If Not MinLen(txtDrawerAcct.Text, 6) Then
        MsgBox "Drawer's account number must consist of only 6 digits!!"
    Else
    'Checking the value returned by IsNumeric while scanning
    'the Drawer's account number field for non numeric characters
        If IsNumeric(txtDrawerAcct.Text) Then
            'Checking the value returned by the CharFound function while
            'scanning the Drawer's account number for a plus or minus sign
            If (Not CharFound(txtDrawerAcct.Text, "+")) _
                And (Not CharFound(txtDrawerAcct.Text, "-")) Then
                'Placing the form cursor on the Bank's Sort Code field
                txtSortCode.SetFocus
                Exit Sub
            End If
        End If
        MsgBox "Only numeric data are acceptable as the drawer's account number!!"
    End If
'Placing the form focus on the Drawer's account number code field
    Cancel = True
End Sub
```

The **txtSortCode_Validate()** subroutine is called to validate data captured in the Bank's Sort Code field.

```vb
Public Sub txtSortCode_Validate(Cancel As Boolean)
'Checking the value returned by the MinLen function, called to validate
'the length of the Bank's Sort Code field
    If Not MinLen(txtSortCode.Text, 9) Then
        MsgBox "Bank's sort code must consist of only 9 digits!!"
    Else
    'Checking the value returned by IsNumeric while scanning
    'the Bank's Sort Code field for non numeric characters
        If IsNumeric(txtSortCode.Text) Then
            'Checking the value returned by the CharFound function while
            'scanning
            'the Bank's Sort Code field for a plus or minus sign
            If (Not CharFound(txtSortCode.Text, "+")) _
                And (Not CharFound(txtSortCode.Text, "-")) Then
```

CHAP 06   A COMMERCIAL BANKING SYSTEM: THE WORKING

```
            'Placing the form cursor on the Cheque's Transaction Code field
                txtTransCode.SetFocus
                Exit Sub
            End If
          End If
          MsgBox "Only numeric data are acceptable as a bank's sort code!!"
      End If
'Placing the form focus on the Bank's Sort Code field
      Cancel = True
End Sub
```

The **txtTransCode_Validate()** subroutine is called to validate data captured in the Cheque's Transaction Code field.

```
Public Sub txtTransCode_Validate(Cancel As Boolean)
'Checking the value returned by the MinLen function, called to validate
'the length of the Cheque's Transaction Code field
    If Not MinLen(txtTransCode.Text, 2) Then
        MsgBox "Cheque's transaction code must consist of only 2 digits!!"
    Else
'Checking the value returned by IsNumeric while scanning
'the Cheque's Transaction Code field for non numeric characters
        If IsNumeric(txtTransCode.Text) Then
            'Checking the value returned by the CharFound function while
            'scanning the Employee's pin code field for a plus or minus sign
            If (Not CharFound(txtTransCode.Text, "+")) _
                And (Not CharFound(txtTransCode.Text, "-")) Then
                'Placing the form cursor on the MDI's Save button
                frmMain.cmdSave.SetFocus
                Exit Sub
            End If
        End If
        MsgBox "Only numeric data are acceptable as a cheque's transaction code!!"
    End If
'Placing the form focus on the Cheque's Transaction Code field
    Cancel = True
End Sub
```

The **txtDeno_Validate()** subroutine is called to validate data captured in any one of the Cash denomination number fields.

```vb
Public Sub txtDeno_Validate(Index As Integer, Cancel As Boolean)
'Removing spaces from the Cash denomination number field
    txtDeno(Index).Text = Trim(txtDeno(Index).Text)
'Setting the Cash denomination number as zero if the field is empty
    If txtDeno(Index).Text = "" Then
        txtDeno(Index).Text = "0"
        Exit Sub
    End If
'Checking the value returned by IsNumeric while scanning
'a Cash denomination field for non numeric characters
    If IsNumeric(txtDeno(Index).Text) Then
        'Checking the value returned by the CharFound function while
        'scanning the Cash denomination number for a plus or minus sign
        If (Not CharFound(txtDeno(Index).Text, "+")) _
            And (Not CharFound(txtDeno(Index).Text, "-")) Then
            Exit Sub
        End If
    End If
    MsgBox "Only numeric data are acceptable as a cash denomination number!!"
'Placing the form focus on the Cash denomination number field
    Cancel = True
End Sub
'********** FUNCTIONALITY FOR FORM FIELD VALIDATIONS ENDS **********
'*****************************************************************


'*****************************************************************
'********* FUNCTIONALITY FOR FORM's OTHER SUBROUTINES BEGINS ********
```

The **ClrFrmFlds()** subroutine is called to empty the form's data capture fields.

```vb
Public Sub ClrFrmFlds()
    txtTransId.Text = ""
    cmbAcctType.Text = "SB"
    cmbAcctNo.Text = "1"
    txtTransDate.Text = ""
    optTransType(0).Value = True
    optTransType(1).Value = False
    txtTransAmt.Text = "0"
    chkCashTrans.Value = 0
    txtParty.Text = "Self"
```

```
    txtChqNo.Text = ""
    txtDrawerAcct.Text = ""
    txtChqdate.Text = ""
    txtSortCode.Text = ""
    txtTransCode.Text = ""
    txtSumOf.Text = mAmtStr
    For mObjCount = 1 To 13
    'Resetting all form field for capturing cash denomination
        txtDeno(mObjCount).Text = 0
    Next
End Sub
```

The **DisableFrmFlds()** subroutine is called to disable the form's data entry fields.

```
Public Sub DisableFrmFlds()
    cmbAcctType.Enabled = False
    cmbAcctNo.Enabled = False
    txtTransDate.Enabled = False
    optTransType(0).Enabled = False
    optTransType(1).Enabled = False
    txtTransAmt.Enabled = False
    chkCashTrans.Enabled = False
    txtParty.Enabled = False
    txtChqNo.Enabled = False
    txtDrawerAcct.Enabled = False
    txtChqdate.Enabled = False
    txtSumOf.Enabled = False
    txtSortCode.Enabled = False
    txtTransCode.Enabled = False
    For mObjCount = 1 To 13
    'Disabling all form field to capture cash denomination information
        txtDeno(mObjCount).Enabled = False
    Next
End Sub
```

The **EnableFrmFlds()** subroutine is called to enable the form's data entry fields.

```vb
Public Sub EnableFrmFlds()
    cmbAcctType.Enabled = True
    cmbAcctNo.Enabled = True
    txtTransDate.Enabled = True
    optTransType(0).Enabled = True
    optTransType(1).Enabled = True
    txtTransAmt.Enabled = True
    chkCashTrans.Enabled = True
    txtParty.Enabled = True
    txtChqNo.Enabled = True
    txtDrawerAcct.Enabled = True
    txtChqdate.Enabled = True
    txtSortCode.Enabled = True
    txtTransCode.Enabled = True
    For mObjCount = 1 To 13
    'Enabling all form field for capturing cash denomination information
        txtDeno(mObjCount).Enabled = True
    Next
End Sub
'********* FUNCTIONALITY FOR FORM's OTHER SUBROUTINES ENDS *********
'*****************************************************************
```

Chapter 06

Self Evaluation

In This Chapter We Learned:

- **Behaviour Of The Commercial Banking System**
  Its Working Through Visual Basic 6

- **Built-In Components And References Required While Designing**

- **Project Source Codes**
  frmMain.frm
  modBnkSys.bas
  frmOpenFrm.frm
  frmEmpMstr.frm
  frmClntMstr.frm
  frmSlctClnt.frm
  frmAcctMstr.frm
  frmTransMstr.frm

Chapter 07

Creating Reports In VB 6

In This Chapter:

- **Crystal Reports**

- **Microsoft Data Reports**

- **Understanding Microsoft Data Report**
  The Report Header section
  The Page Header section
  The Detail section
  The Page Footer section
  The Report Footer section
  Separating the Label and Textbox

- **Project Source Codes**
  frmShowRprt.frm
  rptStatement.dsr
  rptAccHolderInfo.dsr

7. CREATING REPORTS IN VB 6

We have learned how to capture, manipulate, validate and finally **store** data in a database / table in the earlier chapters.

It's now time to learn how to extract this data from the Database/table, format it as required and display this formatted data on the VDU screen for viewing. Alternatively, dispatch this formatted data to a printer to obtain hard copy. The process of providing such functionality to commercial applications is known as '**Report Extraction**'.

With Visual Basic 6 there are **two** traditional techniques used for developing reports (**i.e.** Extracting and formatting data from a Database/table).

- Reports can be created within the Visual Basic development environment by using Microsoft Data Reports.

- By using the version of Crystal Reports included with Visual Basic by accessing Crystal Report's '**.RPT**' file via Crystal Reports ActiveX control.

Additionally, there are several third party tools available today that permit the extraction of reports from Database/tables.

Microsoft Data Reports

With Microsoft Data Reports a programmer can add a report directly to a Visual Basic Project. The report can be designed, saved and compiled with a Visual Basic project just like any form or class can.

This feature integrates well with the Visual Basic IDE and reports can be created as intuitively and easily as any Visual Basic form or menu would.

The major differences between creating reports with Microsoft Data Reports and creating forms are:

- The Data Report's, unit of measurement, is based on a printed page, whereas a form's unit of measurement is based on **twips**.

- The Data Report **does not use** the intrinsic controls or ActiveX controls that Visual Basic forms use. They have their **own report intrinsic controls**.

Using Microsoft Data Reports, a report can be displayed on the VDU screen in a Print Preview window.

From the print preview window:
- A report can be dispatched to a printer for printing

Or
- Exported to a file (including HTML)

Crystal Reports

Crystal Reports is included in Visual Basic 6. This includes the Crystal Reports Designer, ActiveX control and necessary runtimes. Visual Basic 6 is backward compatible with projects which have reports created using Crystal Reports, which was a part of an earlier version of Visual Basic.

Any Crystal Report must be created through the Report Designer. Certain elements of a report can be changed at runtime through the Crystal Report's OLE custom control but this control does not have the ability to create a report from scratch.

The Crystal Reports Designer works as a separate process from Visual Basic. The file created by the Crystal Report's Designer has a '**.RPT**' extension. It is a good application design to keep the report definition files created by Crystal Reports in the same subdirectory as the Visual Basic project. This helps make project management and program distribution a lot easier.

When To Use Microsoft Data Reports

Data Reports integrates very well into the Visual Basic environment. Reports are generated directly in the Visual Basic IDE. There are no separate report files. Report definitions are stored in an ActiveX designer form with the Visual Basic project. This means that when a project is compiled the report definition is compiled within the Visual Basic executable file (.**EXE**).

The report retrieves the data to be used from a Data Connection within a Data Environment. Thus reports created using Microsoft Data Reports retrieve data from a powerful new feature in Visual Basic.

Microsoft Data Reports is great for basic reports, however it does not have the options or the advanced features found in the more mature Crystal Reports and is not backward compatible with Crystal Reports '.**RPT**' files.

When To Use Crystal Reports

Crystal Reports takes a totally different approach to creating reports to use with an application created using Visual Basic. A separate application creates report definitions. These are stored in a .RPT file. The .RPT files need to be distributed along with the application's .EXE file.

Additionally, a few DLLs and an OCX control must be included in the Visual Basic application if Crystal Reports are used as the main report extraction tool. The application's distribution requirements are therefore heavier than those of Microsoft Data Reports.

Crystal Reports uses ODBC to connect to a data source and cannot access the new and powerful Data Environment object available in Visual Basic 6.

Crystal Reports is much more mature than Microsoft Data Reports and has a much wider set of features. It can generate cross-tab and sub reports. Crystal Reports has a much more powerful formula and number crunching features.

Crystal Reports is a mature and proven product. It might be heavier than Microsoft Data Reports but it offers a richer feature set and is really scalable.

CREATING A REPORT USING MICROSOFT DATA REPORTS

A Data Environment must be defined. This is the gateway that the Data Reports object will use to connect to a Database/table. Once the Data Environment is created, creating a report consists of three simple steps.

First, a Data Connection must be created. This is a child to the Data Environment. The Data Connection is the object that the report will use to retrieve data from a Database/table. Data can be accessed from any ODBC compliant data source, such as MS Access, MS SQL server or Oracle.

The second step is to bind a report to the Data Connector. Use the **retrieve structure** option of the Data Report (Right click the Data Report and select this from the sticky menu that appears) so that the report section matches the data connection.

The third step is to bind **report controls** to the report. These controls will display the data the report retrieves from the Data Environment via its Data Connector.

Controls can range from simple textboxes that display static data retrieved from fields in the database/table to textboxes with a formula bound to it, which can summarize and/or manipulate table data in hundred different ways.

Creating a simple columnar type report using Microsoft Data Reports will help in clarifying the three simple steps described above.

Start **Visual Basic** and select a new '`Standard EXE`' project. Please refer to diagram 7.1.

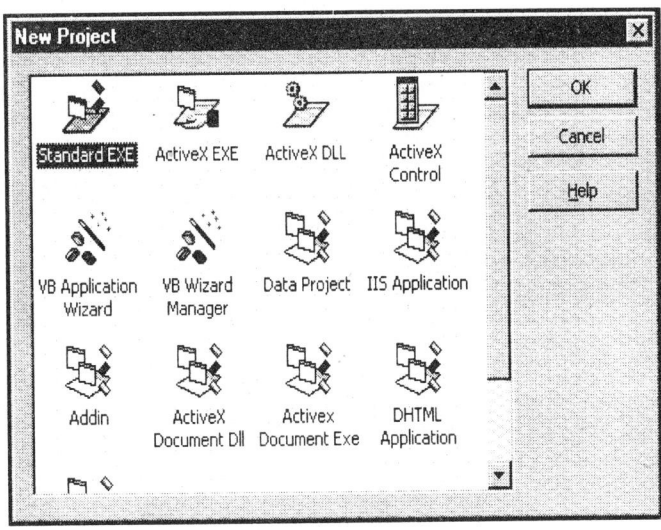

Diagram 7.1

The **Visual Basic IDE** will provide a standard form to work with as shown in diagram 7.2.

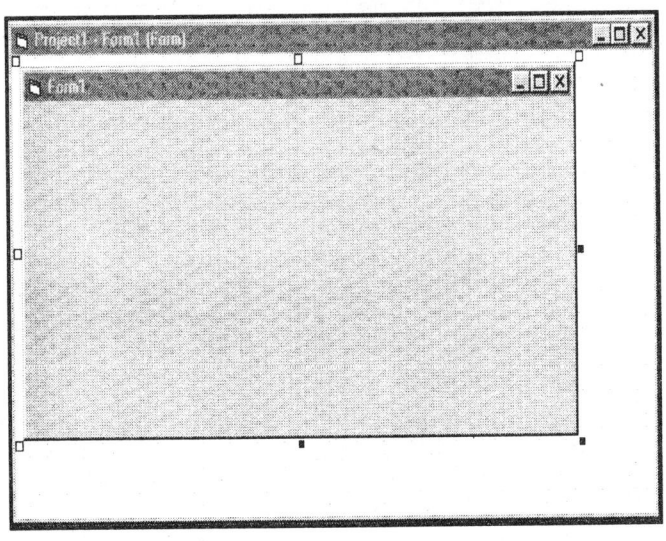

Diagram 7.2

Select 'Project' → 'More ActiveX Designers' → 'Data Environment' and add a Data Environment to the project. This opens up the **Data Environment** user interface to work with as shown in diagram 7.3.

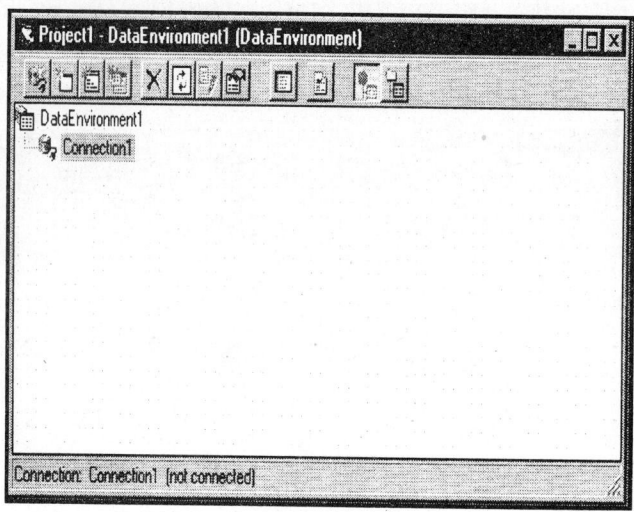

Diagram 7.3

Right click on 'Connection1' in displayed in the Data Environment user interface. From the sticky menu that appears select Properties, as shown in diagram 7.4.

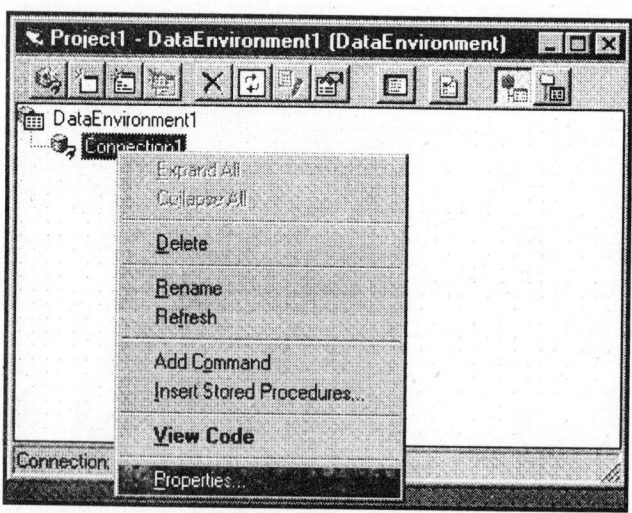

Diagram 7.4

From the **Data Link Window** that appears select the `Microsoft Jet 4.0 OLEDB Provider` as shown in diagram 7.5. This **OLEBD** provider is used for an MS Access 2000 database. Click `Next` to continue.

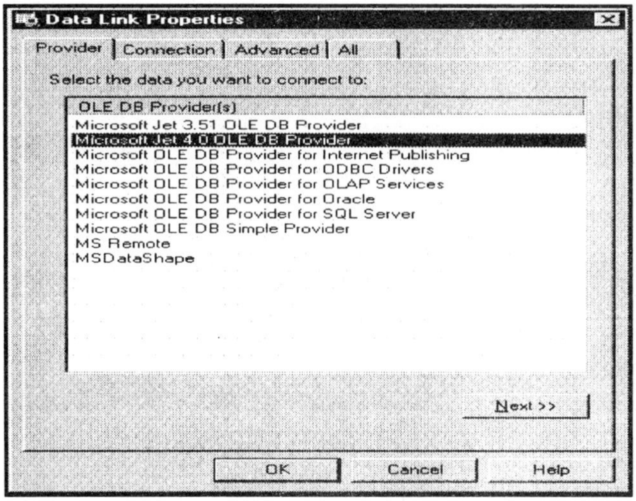

Diagram 7.5

Use the **Browse** button to browse the hard disk directory tree structure to locate the appropriate M.S. Access database file `biblio.mdb` as shown in diagram 7.6.

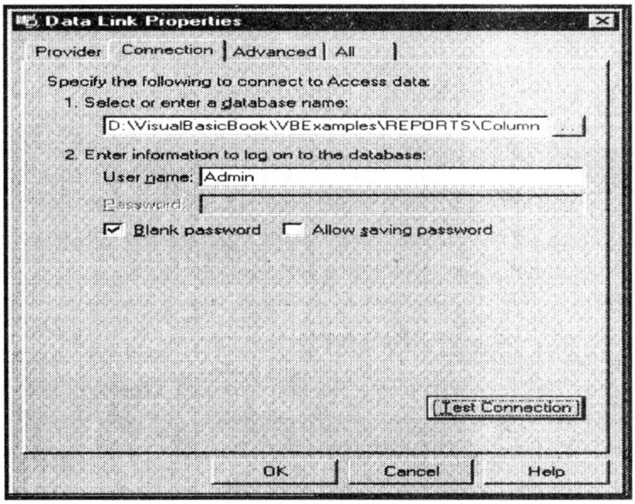

Diagram 7.6

Click on the 'Test Connection' 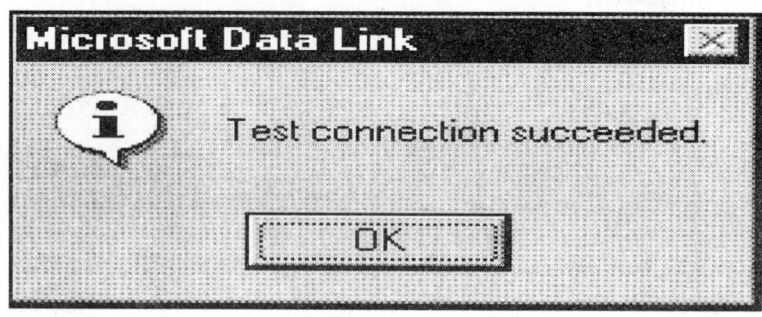 command button to test the link. A test OK screen should appear to indicate that all is well. Please refer to diagram 7.7.

Diagram 7.7

Click on 'OK' button of the message box that popped up as shown in diagram 7.7. Then click the 'OK' button on the **Data Link Properties window**.

Next, right click on 'Connection1' in the **Data Environment**. From the sticky menu that appears click on 'Add Command' as shown in diagram 7.8.

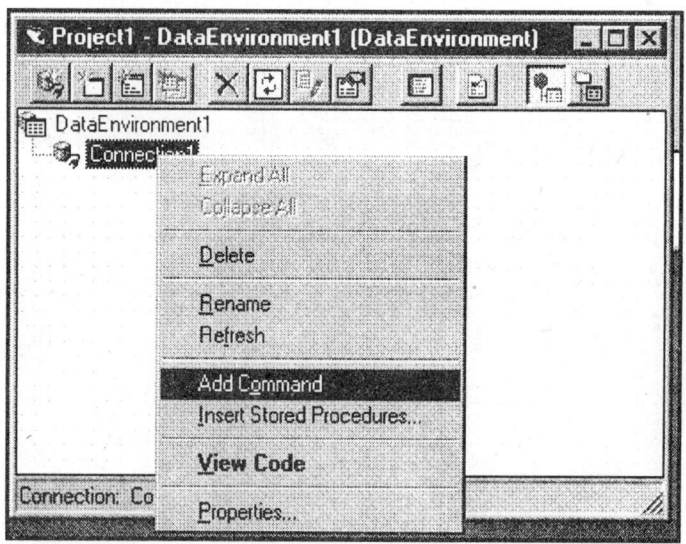

Diagram 7.8

A command object named 'Command1' is added to the **Data Environment** as shown in diagram 7.9.

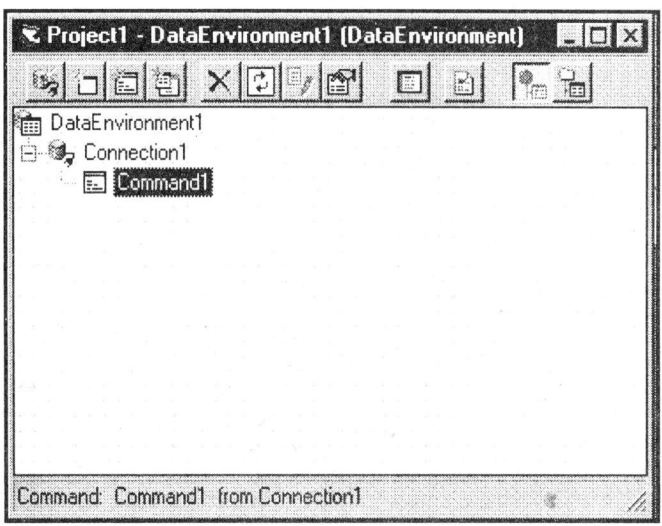

Diagram 7.9

Right click on 'Connection1' and from the sticky menu that appears select **Properties** as shown in diagram 7.10.

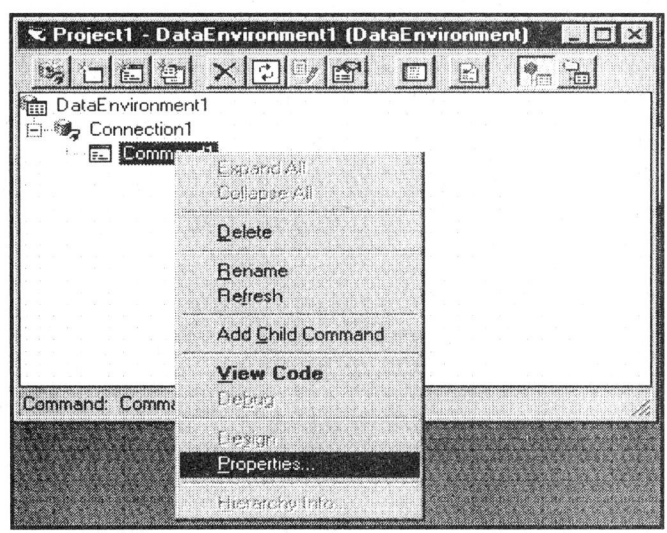

Diagram 7.10

In the **Command Properties window** that appears, click on the 'Connection' drop down list box and select '**Connection1**'. From the 'Database Object' drop down list box select '**Table**'. From the 'Object Name' drop down list box select '**Authors**'. Refer to diagram 7.11.

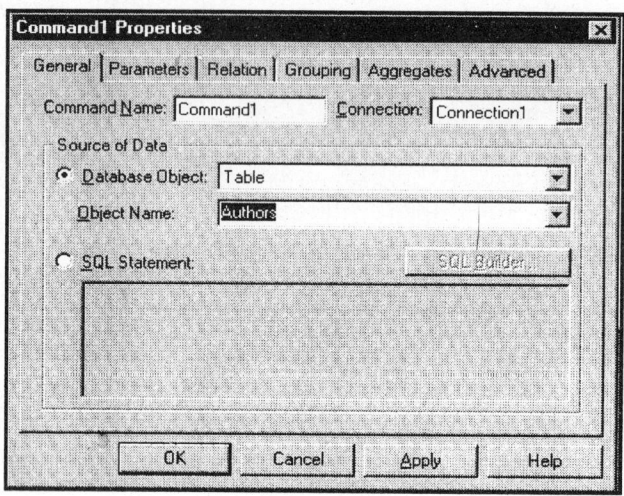

Diagram 7.11

From the Visual Basic's **Main Menu** select 'Project' → 'Add Data Report'. A **Data Report** is added as shown in diagram 7.12.

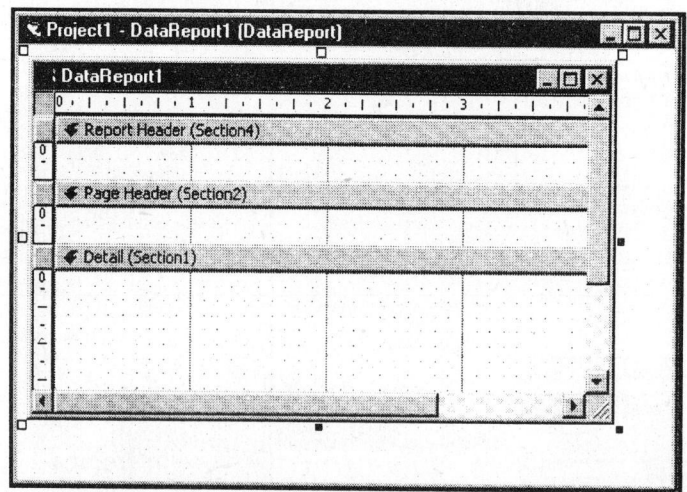

Diagram 7.12

CHAP 07   CREATING REPORTS IN VB 6

Set the following properties of the Data Report object.

Object	Property	Setting
DataReport	Name	drBasic
	DataMember	Command1
	DataSource	DataEnvironment1

Table 7.1

The fields of the Database/table (i.e. Biblio/Authors) can be displayed in one of two ways. The first method is to draw the fields on the report, then assign the proper **DataMember** and **DataField** properties to them.

The second method is to open the **Data Environment Window** and **Drag** and **Drop** the fields directly on the report. The fields and their captions will be shown in the report. Once visible, arrange the items as shown in diagram 7.13.

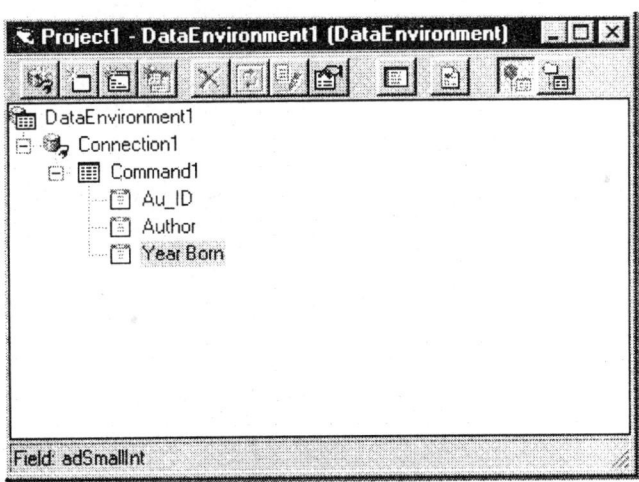

Diagram 7.13

Simply click on the ⊞ sign next to 'Command1'. The fields that are bound in 'Command1' will be visible. Select these fields and drag and drop them on the report. Refer to diagram 7.14

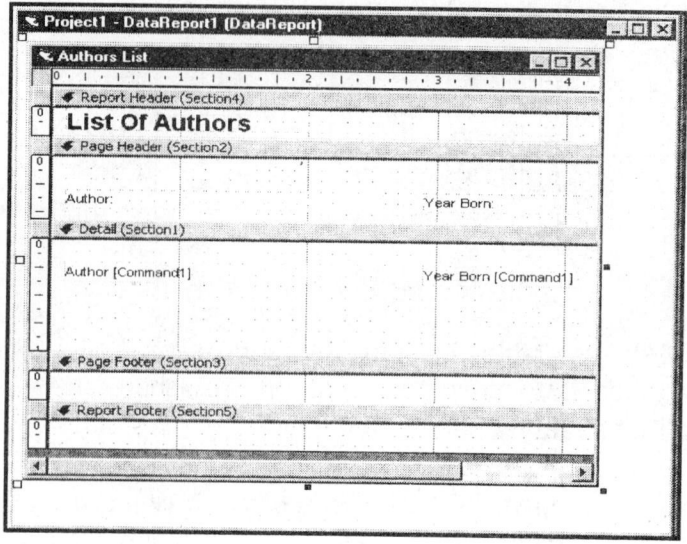

Diagram 7.14

Pick up a **Report label** from the toolbar on the left hand side of the **IDE**. Drop this in the **Report Header** section of the 'DataReport1'. Set the following properties:

Object	Property	Setting
ReportLabel	Name	rptLblAuthorNames
	Font	Arial, Bold, 14

Table 7.2

Next, **remove** 'Form1' that was automatically created when the project was started.

Tip

Go to the **Project Explorer**, locate 'Form1' in it. **Right click** 'Form1', from the sticky menu that appears click 'Remove'.

Next, **right click** 'Project1' in the Project Explorer. From the sticky menu that appears click on 'Project1 Properties ...' In the **Project Properties window** that appears click on the 'Startup Object' drop down list box and select **DataReport1**.

Save the project appropriately and run the report. The author's list will appear as shown in diagram 7.15.

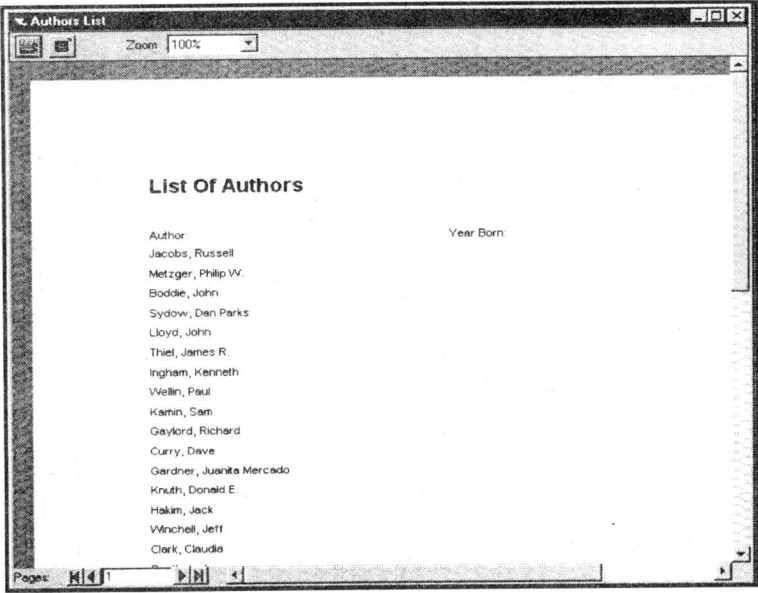

Diagram 7.15

Note

The reason why **nothing appears** under the Year Born Label is because there are no entries in the column **Year Born** in Authors table in the Biblio database.

Understanding Microsoft Data Report

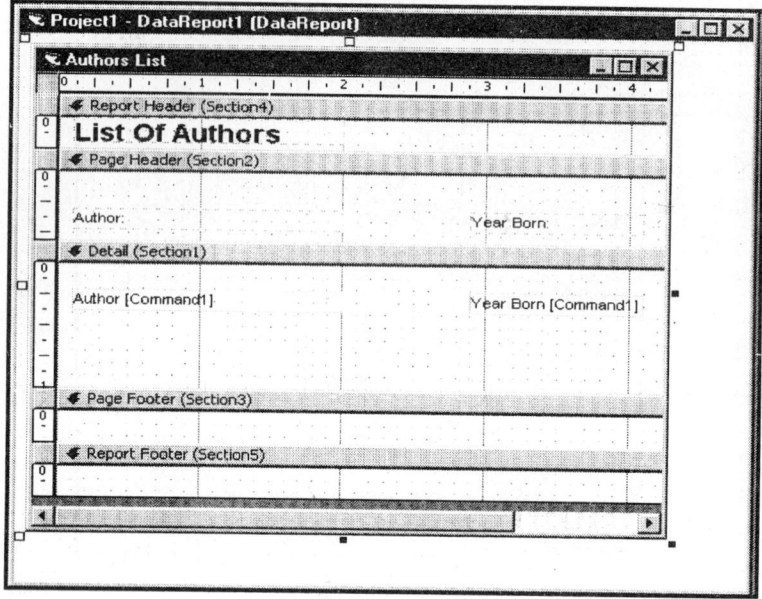

Diagram 7.16

The **Data Report** object (as shown in diagram 7.16 above) is really a container with five unique sections, they are:

Report Header	Section**4**
Page Header	Section**2**
Detail	Section**1**
Page Footer	Section**3**
Report Footer	Section**5**

Table 7.3

Each section of the report object can hold data display objects (meant especially for reports) from the toolbar on the left hand side of the Visual Basic IDE. The behavior of each section however is different.

The Report Header Section

Whatever is placed in this section will be displayed only once, at the very start of the report. This section can hold a **Label** with appropriate attributes set or a **Textbox**, which is bound to a column in the database table.

The Page Header Section

Whatever is placed in this section will be displayed once at the top of every page in the report. In a standard columnar type report the table's column names are generally displayed in this section of the data report.

The Detail Section

Whatever is placed in this section is tightly bound to the ResultSet retrieved from the Database/table. The ResultSet will have a number of rows and columns. It is always **row data** that is displayed in the **Detail section** of a report. Only one set of data display objects need to be placed in the reports Detail section.

The Detail section of the Data Report will loop through the ResultSet and spawn the data display objects as many times as is necessary to display all the data retrieved from the Database/table and held in the ResultSet.

The Detail section will also automatically take care of placing appropriate page breaks in the data displayed, bound to standard paper sizes such as A4, A3 and so on.

The Page Footer Section

Whatever is placed in this section will be displayed once at the bottom of every page in the report. Column, sub totals and so on are what are generally displayed in this section of the Data Report.

The Report Footer Section

Whatever is placed in this section will be displayed only once, at the very end of the report. Column totals and so on are generally displayed in this section of the Data Report.

Separating The Label And Textbox

When a field from the Command object (Command1) is dragged and dropped on the **Data Report** (in any section) both a **Label** and **Textbox** (the data display object) will be spawned in that section.

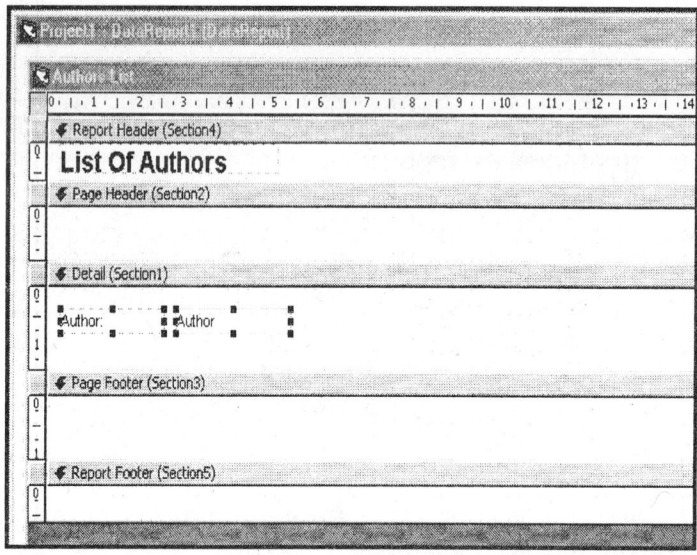

Diagram 7.17

These two objects will be **selected** and apparently joined together (refer to diagram 7.17). Click anywhere in the **Data Report** to **deselect** these objects. Then select **only** the **Label object** and cut this away from the data display object (`Ctrl X`).

To decide which is the Label object and which is the Data object simply **expand** each object **horizontally**, the object that contains the word **command1** internally is the **data** object, the other is the label.

Paste the **Label** in the Header section of the Data Report. **Align** the Label object and the Data display objects as required (refer to diagram 7.16). Run the report the output should be as shown in diagram 7.15.

AN ADODB'S RECORDSET VS A DATA ENVIRONMENT

A Data Environment object is not the only option for a data source to generate a report. An ADODB's Recordset object can be used as the data source for a report as well.

Using an ADODB's Recordset is advantageous in situations where a report needs to be drawn from multiple tables within a database. Once the record set is created with appropriate columns drawn from various tables, VB's Report object can be used to present its content in an aesthetically pleasing format.

In situations where a report is based on User input, a VB's Form object could be used to capture report extraction criteria. Based on this criteria, the recordset can be populated.

This technique is simpler and widely used by programmers when compared to the conventional method of using a VB Data Environment object as the Data Source for a VB's Report object.

The technique to create reports using an ADODB's Recordset has been used in the report source code that follows.

PROJECT CODE FOR frmShowRprt.frm

```vb
Option Explicit
'Declaring variables for later use
Public mConnection As ADODB.Connection
Public TempRs As ADODB.Recordset
Public TempBal As ADODB.Recordset
Public mAcctType, mSqlStr, mFlgGetRprt As String
Public strSql, mSql, mBalSql, mFlag As String
Public mFname, mMname, mLname, mAddr1, mAddr2, mCity, mPinCode As String
Public mAcct, mAcctNo, mSdate, mEdate, mTransType As String
Public mTransId, mCount, i, mOpBalance, mBalance As Integer
Public mDeposit, mWithdraw, mTransAmt, mCurBal, mTrack, As Integer
Public mMonth, mYear, mLDate As Integer
```

'***
'******** FUNCTIONALITY FOR THE FORM SPECIFIC EVENTS BEGINS ********

The **Form_Load()** subroutine is called when the form loads.

```vb
Public Sub Form_Load()
    txtYr.MaxLength = 4
    mFlag = "F"
'Checking the value of the global variable 'gRprtType',
'to display a frame with appropriate data capture objects
    If gRprtType <> "Pass Book" Then
        frmShowRprt.Caption = "Monthly Statement"
        fraMnthStmt.Visible = True
        fraPassDate.Visible = False
        optRprtType(0).Value = True
    Else
        frmShowRprt.Caption = "Pass Book"
        fraPassDate.Visible = True
        fraMnthStmt.Visible = False
        optRprtType(1).Value = True
    End If
End Sub
```
'********* FUNCTIONALITY FOR THE FORM SPECIFIC EVENTS ENDS *********
'***

CHAP 07   CREATING REPORTS IN VB 6

```
'***************************************************************
'********* FUNCTIONALITY OF THE FORM's OPTION BUTTONS BEGINS ********
```
The **cmbAcctType_Click()** subroutine is called when the combo box listing account types get clicked.

```vb
Public Sub cmbAcctName_Click()
'Checking if the user has selected a different account type
    If cmbAcctName.Text <> mAcctType Then
        'Storing the value returned by PopNoCmd while populating
        'the combo box listing account numbers
        mAcctType = PopNoCmb(cmbAcctName.Text, cmbAcctNo)
    End If
End Sub
'********* FUNCTIONALITY OF THE FORM's OPTION BUTTONS ENDS *********
'***************************************************************


'***************************************************************
'********* FUNCTIONALITY OF THE FORM's OPTION BUTTONS BEGINS ********
```
The **optRprtType_Click()** subroutine is called when a report type is clicked.

```vb
Public Sub optRprtType_Click(Index As Integer)
'Checking if the option for Monthly Statement is clicked,
'to display frames with appropriate data capture objects
    If optRprtType(0) = True Then
        frmShowRprt.Caption = "Monthly Statement"
        fraMnthStmt.Visible = True
        fraPassDate.Visible = False
        optRprtType(0).Value = True
    Else
        frmShowRprt.Caption = "Pass Book"
        fraPassDate.Visible = True
        fraMnthStmt.Visible = False
        optRprtType(1).Value = True
    End If
End Sub
'********* FUNCTIONALITY OF THE FORM's OPTION BUTTONS ENDS *********
'***************************************************************
```

```
'*************************************************************
'******* FUNCTIONALITY FOR CHANGE EVENTS ON FORM FIELD BEGINS *******
```

The **txtSDate_KeyPress()** subroutine is called when the field for the Report's Starting date is changed.

```
Public Sub txtSDate_KeyPress(KeyAscii As Integer)
'Displaying the frame 'fraStrtDt' containing a MonthView control for
'the Report's Starting date
    fraStrtDt.Visible = True
'Clearing the Report's Ending date field
    txtSDate.Text = ""
'Placing the form cursor on a MonthView control to select the Report's
'Starting date
    mvwStrtDt.SetFocus
End Sub
```

The **txtEDate_KeyPress()** subroutine is called when the field for the Report's Ending date is changed.

```
Public Sub txtEDate_KeyPress(KeyAscii As Integer)
'Displaying the frame 'fraDate' containing a MonthView control for the
'Report's Ending date
    fraEndDt.Visible = True
'Clearing the Report's Ending date field
    txtEDate.Text = ""
'Placing the form cursor on a MonthView control to select the Report's
'Ending date
    mvwEndDt.SetFocus
End Sub
'******* FUNCTIONALITY FOR CHANGE EVENTS ON FORM FIELD ENDS *******
'*************************************************************


'*************************************************************
'******* FUNCTIONALITY FOR CALENDAR CONTROL's EVENTS BEGINS *******
```

The **mvwStrtDt_DateClick()** subroutine is called when form cursor moves away from the MonthView control capturing the Report's Starting date.

```
Public Sub mvwStrtDt_DateClick(ByVal DateClicked As Date)
'Setting the Text attribute of the Report's Starting date field
    txtSDate.Text = mvwStrtDt.Value
```

CHAP 07   CREATING REPORTS IN VB 6

```vb
'Hiding the frame 'fraStrtDt' containing a MonthView control for the
'Report's Starting date
    fraStrtDt.Visible = False
End Sub
```

The **mvwEndDt_DateClick()** subroutine is called when form cursor moves away from the MonthView control capturing the Report's Ending date.

```vb
Public Sub mvwEndDt_DateClick(ByVal DateClicked As Date)
'Setting the Text attribute of the Report's Ending date field
    txtEDate.Text = mvwEndDt.Value
'Hiding the frame 'fraEndDt' containing a MonthView control for the
'Report's Ending date
    fraEndDt.Visible = False
End Sub
'********* FUNCTIONALITY FOR CALENDAR CONTROL's EVENTS ENDS *********
'********************************************************************


'********************************************************************
'********* FUNCTIONALITY FOR THE FORM BUTTON's EVENTS BEGINS *********
```

The **cmdShow_Click()** subroutine is called when the button 'Show' is clicked.

```vb
Public Sub cmdShow_Click()
'Setting the flag 'mFlgGetRprt' to prevent the generation of the report
    mFlgGetRprt = "F"
'Checking if any mandatory fields are empty
    If Trim(cmbAcctName.Text) = "" Or Trim(cmbAcctNo.Text) = "" Then
        MsgBox "Select an Account type and number!!", vbCritical + vbOKOnly, _
                "Caution"
        Exit Sub
    End If
'Checking if the option for Monthly Statement is selected
    If optRprtType(0) = True Then
        'Checking the value returned by function MinLen called to validate
        'that the Year is four digits in length
        If MinLen(txtYr.Text, 4) Then
            'Checking the value returned by IsNumeric while scan the Year
            'field for non numeric characters
            If IsNumeric(txtYr.Text) Then
```

```vb
            'Checking the value returned by function CharFound called to
            'scan the Year field for a plus or minus sign
                If (Not CharFound(txtYr.Text, "+")) And (Not CharFound(txtYr.Text, _
                "-")) Then
                    'Setting the flag 'mFlgGetRprt' to allow the generation of
                    'the report
                        mFlgGetRprt = "T"
                        mFlag = "T"
                    End If
                End If
            End If
        'Checking the value of the variable 'mFlgGetRprt'
            If mFlgGetRprt = "F" Then
                MsgBox "Enter a four digit year format!!"
                Exit Sub
            End If
        Else
        'Checking if the fields that captures starting and ending dates are
        'empty
            If Trim(txtSDate.Text) = "" Or Trim(txtEDate.Text) = "" Then
                MsgBox "The Report's Starting or Ending dates cannot be left blank!!", _
                    vbCritical + vbOKOnly, "Caution"
                Exit Sub
            Else
            'Setting the flag 'mFlgGetRprt' to allow the generation of the
            'report
                mFlgGetRprt = "T"
                mFlag = "F"
            End If
        End If
    'Checking the value of the variable 'mFlgGetRprt'
        If mFlgGetRprt = "T" Then
            lblAcNo.Caption = cmbAcctNo.Text
            'Calling Connect2Db to open a connection with the database
            Call Connect2DB
            'Calling InsRec to insert records in the TempState table
            Call InsRec
            'Calling GetBalance to calculate closing balance
            Call GetBalance
            'Calling GetCurBal to calculate current balance
            Call GetCurBal
```

CHAP 07   CREATING REPORTS IN VB 6

```
'Calling GetClsBal to calculate current balance
    Call GetClsBal
    lblBal.Caption = mBalance
' Close the Recorset
    TempRs.Close
' Building an SQL query
    strSql = "SELECT * FROM TempState"
    TempRs.Open strSql, mConnection, adOpenKeyset, adLockPessimistic
    If TempRs.RecordCount > 0 Then
        ' Connect the Recordset to the DataReport
        Set rptStatement.DataSource = TempRs
        rptStatement.WindowState = vbMaximized
        rptStatement.Show vbModal
     Else
        MsgBox "No transaction during the period specified"
     End If
   End If
'Calling Unload to terminate the form's functionality
    Unload frmShowRprt
End Sub
```

The **cmdCncl_Click()** subroutine is called when the button 'Cancel' is clicked.

```
Public Sub cmdCncl_Click()
'Calling Unload to terminate the form's functionality
    Unload frmShowRprt
End Sub
'********* FUNCTIONALITY FOR THE FORM BUTTON's EVENTS ENDS *********
'******************************************************************


'******************************************************************
'******************** APPLICATION SUBROUTINE BEGINS ****************
```

The **FillCombo()** subroutine fills the cmbAcctNo combobox with all account numbers available in the Acct_Mstr table.

```
Public Sub FillCombo()
'Moving the recordset pointer on the first record
    AdodcMast.Recordset.MoveFirst
'While loop to go through all the records
    While Not AdodcMast.Recordset.EOF
        'Adding account numbers in the combobox
        cmbAcctNo.AddItem (AdodcMast.Recordset.Fields(0))
```

```
        'Moving the recordset cursor on the next reocord
        AdodcMast.Recordset.MoveNext
    Wend
End Sub
```

The **FillAcctType** fills cmbAcctName combobox with account types.

```
Public Sub FillAcctType()
'Adding account numbers in the combobox
    cmbAcctName.AddItem ("SB")
    cmbAcctName.AddItem ("CA")
End Sub
```

The **InsRec()** subroutine inserts all the transactions between specified dates and for the specific account number in TempState table.

This subroutine retrieves account holder's name and postal address information from the Acct_Mstr table for the specified account number.

All cash and cheque transaction between the specified dates for the specified account number are inserted in the TempSate table along with the personal information.

```
Public Sub InsRec()
    strSql = "SELECT cm.FName, cm.MName, cm.LName, cm.Addr1, cm.Addr2," & _
            "cm.City, cm.Pincode FROM Clnt_Mstr cm, Acct_Mstr am " & _
            WHERE cm.ClientId = am.ClientId1 AND am.AcctNo = " & _
            cmbAcctNo.Text & " AND am.AcctType='" & cmbAcctName.Text & ""
    AdodcMast.RecordSource = strSql
    'Refreshing a recordset
    AdodcMast.Refresh
'Checking if records have been retrieved in a recordset
    If AdodcMast.Recordset.RecordCount > 0 Then
        mFname = AdodcMast.Recordset.Fields(0)
        mMname = AdodcMast.Recordset.Fields(1)
        mLname = AdodcMast.Recordset.Fields(2)
        mAddr1 = AdodcMast.Recordset.Fields(3)
        mAddr2 = AdodcMast.Recordset.Fields(4)
        mCity = AdodcMast.Recordset.Fields(5)
        mPinCode = AdodcMast.Recordset.Fields(6)
```

```vb
        Else
            MsgBox "Account number does not exist!!"
        End If
    If mFlag = "T" Then
            'Calling GetMonth to get the months numeric value
            Call GetMonth
            mSdate = Format(mMonth & "/01/" & txtYr.Text, "mm/dd/yy")
            mEdate = Format(mMonth & "/" & mLDate & "/" & txtYr.Text, "mm/dd/yy")
        Else
            'Formatting dates and storing into the variables
            mSdate = Format(txtSDate, "mm/dd/yy")
            mEdate = Format(txtEDate, "mm/dd/yy")
        End If  strSql = "SELECT * FROM Trans_Mstr WHERE TransDate Between #" & _
                mSdate & "# AND #" & mEdate & "# AND CashTrans=True " & _
                "AND AcctNo=" & cmbAcctNo.Text
        AdodcMast.RecordSource = strSql
    'Refreshing a recordset
        AdodcMast.Refresh
    'Checking if records have been retrieved in a recordset
        If AdodcMast.Recordset.RecordCount > 0 Then
        mCount = AdodcMast.Recordset.RecordCount
            For i = 1 To mCount
            'Adding a blank record in a recordset
                TempRs.AddNew
            'Transferring variable value into a recordset field
                TempRs.Fields(0) = mFname
                TempRs.Fields(1) = mMname
                TempRs.Fields(2) = mLname
                TempRs.Fields(3) = mAddr1
                TempRs.Fields(4) = mAddr2
                TempRs.Fields(5) = mCity
                TempRs.Fields(6) = mPinCode
                TempRs.Fields(7) = AdodcMast.Recordset.Fields(2)
                If AdodcMast.Recordset.Fields(3) = "D" Then
                    TempRs.Fields(9) = AdodcMast.Recordset.Fields(5)
                Else
                    TempRs.Fields(8) = AdodcMast.Recordset.Fields(5)
                End If
                TempRs.Fields(13) = AdodcMast.Recordset.Fields(0)
```

```vb
        'Updating a recordset
            TempRs.Update
            AdodcMast.Recordset.MoveNext
        Next
    End If
    strSql = "SELECT tm.TransDate, tm.TransAmt, tm.TransType, cd.Payee, " & _
             "cd.ChqNo, tm.TransId FROM Trans_Mstr tm, Trans_Dtls_Chq cd " & _
             "WHERE tm.AcctNo=" & cmbAcctNo.Text & " AND tm.TransDate
             Between #" & mSdate & "# AND #" & mEdate & _
             "# AND tm.CashTrans=False AND tm.TransId=cd.TransId"
    AdodcMast.RecordSource = strSql
'Refreshing a recordset
    AdodcMast.Refresh
    mCount = AdodcMast.Recordset.RecordCount
'Checking if records have been retrieved in a recordset
    If AdodcMast.Recordset.RecordCount > 0 Then
    mCount = AdodcMast.Recordset.RecordCount
        For i = 1 To mCount
            TempRs.AddNew
            TempRs.Fields(0) = mFname
            TempRs.Fields(1) = mMname
            TempRs.Fields(2) = mLname
            TempRs.Fields(3) = mAddr1
            TempRs.Fields(4) = mAddr2
            TempRs.Fields(5) = mCity
            TempRs.Fields(6) = mPinCode
            TempRs.Fields(7) = AdodcMast.Recordset.Fields(0)
            If AdodcMast.Recordset.Fields(2) = "D" Then
                TempRs.Fields(9) = AdodcMast.Recordset.Fields(1)
            Else
                TempRs.Fields(8) = AdodcMast.Recordset.Fields(1)
            End If
            TempRs.Fields(10) = AdodcMast.Recordset.Fields(3)
            TempRs.Fields(11) = AdodcMast.Recordset.Fields(4)
            TempRs.Fields(13) = AdodcMast.Recordset.Fields(5)
            TempRs.Update
            AdodcMast.Recordset.MoveNext
        Next
    End If
End Sub
```

The **GetBalance()** subroutine calculates the opening balance of an account on the start date of the dates specified.

```
Public Sub GetBalance()
    mBalSql = "SELECT SUM(TransAmt) FROM Trans_Mstr WHERE " & _
              "Trans_Mstr.TransType = 'D' AND Trans_Mstr.AcctNo = " & _
              cmbAcctNo.Text & " AND Trans_Mstr.TransDate < #" & mSdate & "#"
    TempBal.Open mBalSql, mConnection, adOpenKeyset, adLockPessimistic
    If TempBal.RecordCount > 0 Then
        mDeposit = TempBal.Fields(0)
        If IsNull(mDeposit) Then
            mDeposit = 0
        End If
    End If
    TempBal.Close
    mBalSql = "SELECT SUM(TransAmt) FROM Trans_Mstr WHERE " & _
              "Trans_Mstr.TransType = 'W' AND Trans_Mstr.AcctNo = " & _
              cmbAcctNo.Text & " AND Trans_Mstr.TransDate < #" & mSdate & "#"
    TempBal.Open mBalSql, mConnection, adOpenKeyset, adLockPessimistic
    If TempBal.RecordCount > 0 Then
        mWithdraw = TempBal.Fields(0)
        If IsNull(mWithdraw) Then
            mWithdraw = 0
        End If
    End If
    TempBal.Close
'Calculating opening balance
    mOpBalance = mDeposit - CInt(mWithdraw)
End Sub
```

The **GetCurBal()** subroutine calculates the account balance after each transaction between the specified dates.

```
Public Sub GetCurBal()
    strSql = "SELECT * FROM Trans_Mstr WHERE TransDate Between #" & _
             mSdate & "# AND #" & mEdate & "# AND AcctNo=" & cmbAcctNo.Text
    AdodcMast.RecordSource = strSql
'Refreshing a recordset
    AdodcMast.Refresh
```

```vb
            If AdodcMast.Recordset.RecordCount > 0 Then
                AdodcMast.Recordset.MoveFirst
                mTransId = AdodcMast.Recordset.Fields("TransId")
                mCount = AdodcMast.Recordset.RecordCount
                mCurBal = mOpBalance
                For i = 1 To mCount
                    mTrack = AdodcMast.Recordset.Fields("TransId")
                        If AdodcMast.Recordset.Fields("TransType") = "D" Then
                            mCurBal = mCurBal + AdodcMast.Recordset.Fields("TransAmt")
                        Else
                            mCurBal = mCurBal - AdodcMast.Recordset.Fields("TransAmt")
                        End If
                    strSql = "UPDATE TempState SET Balance = " & mCurBal & _
                        " WHERE TransId = " & mTrack & " "
                    TempBal.Open strSql, mConnection, adOpenKeyset, adLockPessimistic
                    AdodcMast.Recordset.MoveNext
                Next
            End If
        End Sub
```

The **GetClsBal()** subroutine calculates the closing balance of an account till date.

```vb
Public Sub GetClsBal()
    mBalSql = "SELECT SUM(TransAmt) FROM Trans_Mstr WHERE " & _
             "Trans_Mstr.TransType = 'D' AND Trans_Mstr.AcctNo = " & _
             cmbAcctNo.Text & ""
    TempBal.Open mBalSql, mConnection, adOpenKeyset, adLockPessimistic
    If TempBal.RecordCount > 0 Then
        mDeposit = TempBal.Fields(0)
    End If
    TempBal.Close
    mBalSql = "SELECT SUM(TransAmt) FROM Trans_Mstr WHERE " & _
             "Trans_Mstr.TransType = 'W' AND Trans_Mstr.AcctNo = " & _
             cmbAcctNo.Text & ""
    TempBal.Open mBalSql, mConnection, adOpenKeyset, adLockPessimistic
    If TempBal.RecordCount > 0 Then
        mWithdraw = TempBal.Fields(0)
        If IsNull(mWithdraw) Then
            mWithdraw = 0
        End If
```

```vb
        End If
        TempBal.Close
'Calculating balance
        mBalance = mDeposit - CInt(mWithdraw)
End Sub

Public Sub Connect2DB()
    Set mConnection = New ADODB.Connection
'Indicating the oledb provider to Bind the provider to Access batabase
    mConnection.Provider = "Microsoft.Jet.OLEDB.4.0; Data Source = " & App.Path & _
                            "\Database\Bank.mdb"
'Opening up the connection
    mConnection.Open
    mSql = "SELECT * FROM TempState"
    Set TempRs = New ADODB.Recordset
    TempRs.Open mSql, mConnection, adOpenForwardOnly, adLockPessimistic
    Set TempBal = New ADODB.Recordset
End Sub

Public Sub GetMonth()
    Select Case cmbMnth.Text
        Case "January"
            mMonth = "01"
            mLDate = "31"
        Case "February"
            mMonth = "02"
            mLDate = "28"
    'Checking if the year is a leap year
            If ReturnMod(txtYr.Text, 4) = 0 Then
                mLDate = "29"
                If ReturnMod(txtYr.Text, 100) = 0 Then
                    mLDate = "28"
                    If ReturnMod(txtYr.Text, 400) = 0 Then
                        mLDate = "29"
                    End If
                End If
            End If
        Case "March"
            mMonth = "03"
            mLDate = "31"
```

```vb
        Case "April"
            mMonth = "04"
            mLDate = "30"
        Case "May"
            mMonth = "05"
            mLDate = "31"
        Case "June"
            mMonth = "06"
            mLDate = "30"
        Case "July"
            mMonth = "07"
            mLDate = "31"
        Case "August"
            mMonth = "08"
            mLDate = "31"
        Case "September"
            mMonth = "09"
            mLDate = "30"
        Case "October"
            mMonth = "10"
            mLDate = "31"
        Case "November"
            mMonth = "11"
            mLDate = "30"
        Case "December"
            mMonth = "12"
            mLDate = "31"
    End Select
End Sub

'The ReturnMod() subroutine is called to get the Remainder
Public Function ReturnMod(ByVal mDvdnt As Integer, mDvsr As Integer)
    mDvdnt = Trim(mDvdnt)
    mDvsr = Trim(mDvsr)
    ReturnMod = Abs(mDvdnt - (Round(mDvdnt / mDvsr) * mDvsr))
End Function
'****************************************************************
'******************* APPLICATION SUBROUTINE ENDS ****************
'****************************************************************
```

PROJECT SOURCE CODE FOR rptStatement.dsr

Option Explicit

```vb
'Creating object variables for later use
Dim mAcctNo, mAcctType, mName, mAdd1, mAdd2 As String
Dim mCity, mPinCode, mSdate, mEdate, mBalance As String
Dim mOPBal, strSql As String

Public Sub DataReport_Initialize()
'Calling GetCriteria subroutine
    Call GetCriteria
    If frmShowRprt.mFlag = "T" Then
        rptStatement.Sections("Section4").Controls("lblSDate").Visible = "False"
        rptStatement.Sections("Section4").Controls("lblEDate").Visible = "False"
        rptStatement.Sections("Section4").Controls("lblTo").Visible = "False"
        rptStatement.Sections("Section4").Controls("lblHead").Caption = "STATEMENT _
            FOR THE MONTH OF " & frmShowRprt.cmbMnth.Text & " " & _
            frmShowRprt.txtYr
    End If
End Sub

Public Sub GetCriteria()
'Assigning values to the string variables
    mAcctNo = FrmSelect.lblAcNo.Caption
    mAcctType = FrmSelect.cmbAcctName.Text
    mName = FrmSelect.TempRs.Fields("FName") + " " + _
            FrmSelect.TempRs.Fields("MName") + " " + _
            FrmSelect.TempRs.Fields("LName")
    mAdd1 = FrmSelect.TempRs.Fields("Addr1")
    mAdd2 = FrmSelect.TempRs.Fields("Addr2")
    mCity = FrmSelect.TempRs.Fields("City")
    mPinCode = FrmSelect.TempRs.Fields("PinCode")
    mSdate = Format(FrmSelect.txtSDate.Text, "DD/MM/YYYY")
    mEdate = Format(FrmSelect.txtEDate.Text, "DD/MM/YYYY")
    mBalance = FrmSelect.lblBal.Caption
    mOPBal = FrmSelect.mOpBalance
```

```vb
    'Assigning values to the report controls
       rptStatement.Sections("Section4").Controls("lblAcType").Caption = mAcctType
       rptStatement.Sections("Section4").Controls("lblAcNo").Caption = mAcctNo
       rptStatement.Sections("Section4").Controls("lblSDate").Caption = mSdate
       rptStatement.Sections("Section4").Controls("lblEDate").Caption = mEdate
       rptStatement.Sections("Section3").Controls("lblClBal").Caption = mBalance
       rptStatement.Sections("Section4").Controls("lblName").Caption = mName
       rptStatement.Sections("Section4").Controls("lblAdd1").Caption = mAdd1
       rptStatement.Sections("Section4").Controls("lblAdd2").Caption = mAdd2
       rptStatement.Sections("Section4").Controls("lblCity").Caption = mCity
       rptStatement.Sections("Section4").Controls("lblPinCode").Caption = mPinCode
       rptStatement.Sections("Section4").Controls("SDate").Caption = mSdate
       rptStatement.Sections("Section4").Controls("OpBal").Caption = mOPBal
End Sub

Private Sub DataReport_Terminate()
    'Close the recordset
       FrmSelect.TempRs.Close
    'Building an SQL query
       strSql = "Delete * from TempState"
       FrmSelect.TempRs.Open strSql, FrmSelect.mConnection, adOpenKeyset, _
                    adLockPessimistic
End Sub
```

PROJECT SOURCE CODE FOR rptAccHolderInfo.dsr

Option Explicit

```vb
'Creating object variables for later use
Dim mConnection As ADODB.Connection
Dim mRs As ADODB.Recordset
Dim mStr, mStr1, mStr2, mStrSql As String

Public Sub DataReport_Initialize()
'Calling Connect2DB to open a connection to the database
  Call Connect2DB
    mStr = "SELECT Clnt_Mstr.ClientId, ([Clnt_Mstr].[FName]) & ' ' & " & _
        "([Clnt_Mstr].[MName]) & ' ' & ([Clnt_Mstr].[LName]) AS CustName, " & _
        "Clnt_Mstr.Addr1, Clnt_Mstr.Addr2, Clnt_Mstr.City, Clnt_Mstr.Pincode, " & _
        "Clnt_Mstr.DOB, Acct_Mstr.AcctNo, Acct_Mstr.AcctType, " & _
        "Acct_Mstr.IntroAcct, (Clnt_Mstr_1.FName) & ' ' & " & _
        " (Clnt_Mstr_1.MName) & ' ' & (Clnt_Mstr_1.LName) AS IntroName " & _
        "FROM Clnt_Mstr INNER JOIN (Acct_Mstr INNER JOIN Clnt_Mstr AS " & _
        "Clnt_Mstr_1 ON Acct_Mstr.IntroId = Clnt_Mstr_1.ClientId) ON " & _
        "Clnt_Mstr.ClientId = Acct_Mstr.ClientId1 ORDER BY AcctNo"
    mStr1 = "SELECT Clnt_Mstr.ClientId, ([Clnt_Mstr].[FName]) & ' ' & " & _
        " ([Clnt_Mstr].[MName]) & ' ' & ([Clnt_Mstr].[LName]) AS CustName, " & _
        "Clnt_Mstr.Addr1, Clnt_Mstr.Addr2, Clnt_Mstr.City, Clnt_Mstr.Pincode, " & _
        "Clnt_Mstr.DOB, Acct_Mstr.AcctNo, Acct_Mstr.AcctType, " & _
        "Acct_Mstr.IntroAcct, (Clnt_Mstr_1.FName) & ' ' & " & _
        " (Clnt_Mstr_1.MName) & ' ' & (Clnt_Mstr_1.LName) AS IntroName " & _
        "FROM Clnt_Mstr INNER JOIN (Acct_Mstr INNER JOIN Clnt_Mstr AS " & _
        "Clnt_Mstr_1 ON Acct_Mstr.IntroId = Clnt_Mstr_1.ClientId) ON " & _
        "Clnt_Mstr.ClientId = Acct_Mstr.ClientId2 ORDER BY AcctNo "
    mStr2 = "SELECT Clnt_Mstr.ClientId, ([Clnt_Mstr].[FName]) & ' ' & " & _
        " ([Clnt_Mstr].[MName]) & ' ' & ([Clnt_Mstr].[LName]) AS CustName, " & _
        "Clnt_Mstr.Addr1, Clnt_Mstr.Addr2, Clnt_Mstr.City, Clnt_Mstr.Pincode, " & _
        "Clnt_Mstr.DOB, Acct_Mstr.AcctNo, Acct_Mstr.AcctType, " & _
        "Acct_Mstr.IntroAcct, (Clnt_Mstr_1.FName) & ' ' & " & _
        " (Clnt_Mstr_1.MName) & ' ' & (Clnt_Mstr_1.LName) AS IntroName " & _
        "FROM Clnt_Mstr INNER JOIN (Acct_Mstr INNER JOIN Clnt_Mstr AS " & _
        "Clnt_Mstr_1 ON Acct_Mstr.IntroId = Clnt_Mstr_1.ClientId) ON " & _
        "Clnt_Mstr.ClientId = Acct_Mstr.ClientId3 ORDER BY AcctNo "
```

```vb
'Building an SQL query and assigning it to mStrSql
    mStrSql = mStr & " UNION " & mStr1 & " UNION " & mStr2
    mRs.Open mStrSql, mConnection, adOpenKeyset, adLockPessimistic
'Assigning the Recordset as a data source to the DataReport object
    Set rptAccHolderInfo.DataSource = mRs
End Sub

Public Sub Connect2DB()
    Set mConnection = New ADODB.Connection
'Binding an OLEDB provider for the Access database
    mConnection.Provider = "Microsoft.Jet.OLEDB.4.0; Data Source = " & App.Path & _
                            "\Database\Bank.mdb"
'Opening up the connection
    mConnection.Open
    Set mRs = New ADODB.Recordset
End Sub
```

Chapter 07

Self Evaluation

In This Chapter We Learned:

- **Crystal Reports**

- **Microsoft Data Reports**

- **Understanding Microsoft Data Report**
  The Report Header section
  The Page Header section
  The Detail section
  The Page Footer section
  The Report Footer section
  Separating the Label and Textbox

- **Project Source Codes**
  frmShowRprt.frm
  rptStatement.dsr
  rptAccHolderInfo.dsr

Chapter 08

Basics Of Project Management And Quality Assurance

In This Chapter:

- **An Introduction To Project Management**

- **The Project Management Process**
  Beginning A Software Project
  Measures And Metrics
  Estimation
  Risk Analysis
  Project Scheduling
  Project Tracking And Control

- **The Quality Assurance Process**
  Examples Of Aesthetic Standards

- **Standards For Master Data Entry Forms**

- **Checklist For Master Data Entry Form Aesthetics**

- **Non-Conformities Of The Master Data Entry Form**

8. BASICS OF PROJECT MANAGEMENT AND QUALITY ASSURANCE

An Introduction

Since this is a book on projects it would not be complete without a reference to project management and quality assurance basics. All to often projects fail (or are not profitable) because there was no attention paid to either project management techniques or quality assurance techniques.

Most young project developers seem to believe that applying both project management and quality assurance to a project requires access to a lot of resources, experience and skill. Possibly this is because those developing software projects for the first time in their careers do not have any exposure to either of these two domains and because they want to quickly get their hand dirty by writing code.

This approach to project development is a **recipe for disaster**. If a **sure fire, guaranteed** way is required to ensure that a project comes in **over budget on all counts**, time, money, quality of deliverables and so on, start a project without applying sensible basic project management **and** do not apply any quality assurance to the project's deliverables.

When project management techniques are applied to any project, project developers get an absolutely clear idea of what**:**
- Responsibilities have been taken on
- The kind of skills required to meet those responsibilities
- The infrastructure required to execute the project
- The time frame required to complete all the project deliverables

When quality assurance techniques are applied to any project, project developers get an absolutely clear idea of what**:**
- Are the minimum standards maintained across **all modules** of the project
- Based on this what should be a **standards checklist** given to each programmer
- How non conformity reports are created and documented
- How code blocks are corrected to ensure an even set of standards across the project

Project management techniques helps ensure that a project will come in on time and within spec. Quality assurance ensures that each module of the project has a uniform level of quality maintained in its code spec. This level of quality ensures the robustness of a project, especially when it is scaled upwards quickly and guarantees that code maintenance will not be the nightmare that it often is.

Project management is the first domain dealt with. Its basics are laid out, simple common sense will help in implementing them.

THE PROJECT MANAGEMENT PROCESS

Software project management is the first layer of the software engineering process. It is best described as a layer, rather than steps or activities because it overshadows the entire project development process from start to finish.

In order to complete a software project successfully, the software development house has to understand the:
- Global scope of work to be done
- Risks to be mitigated
- Resources required
- Individual tasks to be accomplished
- Milestones to be tracked
- Effort costs
- Schedule to be followed to develop the system within a strict, pre-determined, time frame

Project management provides this kind of all encompassing, product development understanding, to a software development house.

Project management **begins** much before any coding work starts and must **continue** while the software product is being developed and **terminates** only when the software is finally delivered to the client.

Because project management is so important to any project, the following provides an overview of the key elements of software project management.

CHAP 08 — BASICS OF PROJECT MANAGEMENT AND QUALITY ASSURANCE

Beginning A Software Project

Before a software project is planned, its **objectives and scope** should be established. Alternative solutions to the software development exercise should be investigated, the company's technical, management and manpower constraints must be identified.

Caution

Without this information it is **impossible** to make a reasonable and accurate costing of the software project.

Objectives identify the overall goals of the project but **do not** consider how these goals are going to be met.

Scope identifies the **primary functions** that the software must accomplish.

Once a project's objectives and scope have been identified the following is usually carefully evaluated:
- Risks that will have to be mitigated
- Resources required
- Individual tasks to be accomplished
- Milestones to be tracked
- Effort costs
- Schedule to be followed to develop the system within a strict, pre-determined, time frame

The knowledge gained by using this formalized approach empowers project managers to choose the **best** path to project completion, given the constraints imposed by:
- Delivery schedules and deadlines
- Budgetary restrictions
- Personnel availability
- Technical interfaces

And a host of other factors.

Measures And Metrics

As in any technical endeavor, measurement and metrics help define and understand the technical processes that go into developing a software product. Each such process must be measured in an effort to improve it. Each such effort put into the project **increases** product quality.

Estimation

The **linch pin** around which a well-executed project is carried out is **planning.** When a software project is well planned, estimates of the required human effort (usually in person months), straight-line projections of time, infrastructure required (man and machines) is reasonably and carefully detailed. **Overall project costs** are then derived.

Caution

In many cases estimates are made using **past experience** as the only guide. This approach will **never give** an accurate estimate of what is required to complete a software project.

A number of estimation techniques have been developed for software development. Each method has its own strengths and weaknesses however all methods have the following common attributes**:**
- Project scope **must be** established in advance
- The project must be broken into smaller (but complete) pieces
- These are then estimated individually
- The estimates are then totaled up to estimate the global project cost

Tip

Many software managers apply a number of different estimation techniques, **usually as a crosscheck** to ensure the **accuracy** of the project's **estimate.**

Risk Analysis

Whenever there is any project to be developed there are areas of **risk**. A few of these can be quickly quantified as below**:**
- Are the needs of the client really understood
- Can the code base requiring implementation, be completed within / before the project's dead lines
- Are there any difficult technical (infrastructural, skill set, or otherwise) problems that have to be **overcome first** before the start of the project
- To what degree will the changes, specified **during** project development, cause the project to slip

Risk analysis is really important to software project development, regretfully many project managers simply do not bother to do any kind of risk analysis prior the start of software development.

To be able to **deal with** the element of risk in a software project be prepared to**:**
- Identify and document each element of risk in a software project
- Assess the degree of risk in each identified element
- Develop a plan to mitigate each identified risk
- Develop a plan to monitor risk mitigating methods

Project Scheduling

Every project **must have** a schedule that is carefully planned in advance. The schedule should be a **list of well-defined tasks** that when executed will lead to the project being completed. Each of the well defined tasks must have a time line defined within which the task must complete. Software project scheduling is no different from scheduling any engineering project.

- A set of project tasks are identified
- Interdependencies between tasks are established
- Effort and infrastructure required to carry out each task is estimated
- Finally people and resources are assigned

Project Tracking and Control

Once the project's development schedule is established, **tracking** and **control** activity commences. Each task described in the schedule is noted and tracked by a project manager. If any task falls behind schedule the P.M. can use a number of different solutions to help minimize task slippage or eliminate it such as**:**
- Work can be reassigned
- Machines and manpower increased
- Work can be sub-contracted under strict quality control
- Tasks can be re-scheduled or re-prioritized
- As a last resort the actual delivery commitments can be rescheduled to accommodate the problem that has developed.

The success of a software house is measured by the number of projects that are completed on time and within original cost estimates. Any project that goes into a time overrun must go into a cost overrun.

If a software house has provided a **safety margin** built into it's costing which absorbs some (or all) of the guesstimated overrun costs there will be no real harm done. If the client has to absorb these costs, then excellent justification must be provided.

In a large number of cases time slippage and thus cost overruns generally arise from project specifications being badly understood, not clearly documented, and/or being constantly changed by the client.

However, if the cost overrun **grossly exceeds** the safety margins built into the costing and has to be absorbed by the software house then the harm done to the software house is really **many fold**:
- A repeat order will not be forthcoming from the client
- The profits of the software house nose dive
- This makes the project development unviable
- This causes the software development house to down play the project's software development leading to an immense amount of client dissatisfaction.

In Conclusion

The success of **any business house** is established via its balance sheet. Its **running costs** subtracted from its **income** must indicate profit. The higher the profit the larger is the perceived success of a business house.

The success of a **software development** business house is evaluated largely along the same lines.

A healthy balance sheet generally reflects that excellent project management processes are in use and everyone involved in software product development understands its management processes with absolute clarity and actively contributes to keeping a project always running on time and within the specifications set prior commencement.

The more successful a software house, the more it is able to expand and develop its infrastructure, real estate, hardware, software, manpower, and so on. This expansion empowers the software house to offer an ever-expanding range of platforms and skills for clients to choose from.

This enables the software house to address its problem of attrition (**i.e.** turn round of staff) by being able to offer programming staff differing and challenging environments to work in. The result, satisfied staff which produce excellent quality of work. A below industry average in attrition always indicates a successful software house.

THE QUALITY ASSURANCE PROCESS

Reams and reams have been written about quality assurance. Here, a quick and dirty set of basic techniques, is described to get the basics of quality assurance in place.

A software project can be quickly (and broadly) divided into different sections, they are:
- Textual menus
- Toolbar menus
- Master data entry screens
- Master/Detail data entry screens
- Report generation data capture screens
- The actual system generated reports

Each of these sections has to be assigned to programmers with **explicit directions** in writing (often called programmers documentation) on how the section must be created.

Each section (**i.e.** Menus, Master Data entry screens, Master / Detail data entry screens, Report parameter screens and finally report formats) must have a set of standards defined so that **across the application** all Master data entry screens look, feel and **behave the same**. The same goes for each of the other sections described.

To achieve the same look, feel and behavior of Master data entry screens a set of standards that the programmers must adhere to need to be defined. The standards will fit the **aesthetics** of each Master data entry screen and the **code base** that lies below the Master data entry screen.

Examples Of Aesthetic Standards:

- All labels will have their text right aligned
- Label text will be immediately followed by a colon
- The Font used will be Times New Roman
- The Font size will be 8 pt
- The Font weight will be bold
- The Primary Key on the data entry form will have Dark Blue as the font color
- Text boxes when placed one below the other will have left edges aligned
- Text boxes when placed adjacent to each other will have centers aligned
- Text box font will be Sans Serif, Size will be 8 pt, weight will be normal

As described above, all the aesthetic standards of data entry forms whether Master or Master/Detail will be defined and documented. This document will become the **quality manual**, which should be made freely available to all programmers so that all who work on the project are completely aware of how to produce Mast and Master/Detail forms with **a uniform** look, feel and behavior.

Subsequently, these standards must be translated to a **checklist** and distributed to each programmer when their work is assigned.

It is the responsibility of the programmer to ensure that each item in the checklist is ticked (indicating that it is implemented) when their sections of the project are passed to the **Q**uality **A**nalysis team for a **QA** check or to the project leader for a QA check.

If the QA team / Project leader notices any nonconformities these are **carefully flagged** and the code base returned to the programmer who sent it in for QA.

A **sample set** of aesthetics for a Master form is shown in Table 8.1

STANDARDS FOR MASTER DATA ENTRY FORMS

Check For	Description
Form Title	All characters in **Sentence Case**
Form Title bar Icon	Set the Title bar icon as defined in the programmer docs
Form Background	Set to **Active Title Bar**
Data Capture Objects	All objects in Flat [**except Buttons & DropDown Listbox**]
Font Description for Data Capture Objects	Type - **MS Sans Serif**, Colour - **Black**, Size - **8 pts.**, Style - **Bold**
Font Description for Label Captions	Type - **MS Sans Serif**, Colour - **Black**, Size - **8 pts.**, Style - **Bold** TabStop – **False**

Table 8.1

Check For	Description
Icon of Toolbar Buttons	As defined in the programmers docs
Size of Toolbar Buttons	Button Height set to **400 twips**, Width set to **400 twips** [**except**] Navigation buttons Height and Width set to **300 twips**
Size of standard Command Buttons	Button Height set to **330 twips**, Width as required
Size of Command Buttons on DataGrid	Button Height set to **195 twips**, Width as required
Object Caption	Content of the Object Caption must be bound to the data that data entry object captures
Spellings of Object Caption	Based on the English Dictionary
Font Description for Frame Objects	Type - **MS Sans Serif**, Colour - **Blue**, Size - **8 pts.**, Style - **Bold**
Tool Tip for Data Capture Objects	For Data Capture objects begins with the word **Enter** [**except**] Checkboxes and Radio buttons begin with the word **Select**
Form Alignment	Center Aligned
Contents of Message Box	Informative and complete, bound strictly to application requirements
Tab Index For Form Controls	Tab Index order should be set according to the logical flow of how the data needs to be grouped and captured

Table 8.1 (Continued)

CHECKLIST FOR MASTER D/E FORM AESTHETICS

Project Name:	
Form Name:	

Sr.		FORM FOCUS AREA
1.	☐	Form Title Spelling and content is correct
2.	☐	Form Title bar Icon is as indicated in the programmers docs
3.	☐	Form Background is white
4.	☐	Data Capture Objects Appearance set correctly
5.	☐	Data Capture Objects Font, Name, Size, Weight set correctly
6.	☐	Labels Font, Name, Size, Weight set correctly
7.	☐	Toolbar Buttons (Icon) set correctly
8.	☐	Toolbar Buttons (Size) set correctly
9.	☐	Standard Command Buttons (Height) set correctly
10.	☐	DataGrid Command Buttons (Height) set correctly
11.	☐	Caption Content set correctly
12.	☐	Caption Spelling is correct
13.	☐	Frame Caption set correctly
14.	☐	Tool Tip for Data Capture Objects set correctly
15.	☐	Forms VDU Alignment as indicated in the programmers docs
16.	☐	Tab Index for Form Controls as per data entry requirements
17.	☐	Message Box contents as indicated in the programmers docs

Programmer's Signature   Auditor's Signature

Diagram 8.1

PRACTICAL VB 6 PROJECTS   CHAP 08

NON-CONFORMITIES OF THE MASTER DATA ENTRY FORM

Data Entry – Aesthetics

Form name	
Project Name	

The conditions **not** satisfied by the Master Data Entry Form are:

Sr.	FORM FOCUS AREA
1.	
2.	
3.	
4.	
5.	
6.	
7.	
8.	
9.	
10.	
11.	
12.	

Auditors Signature

Diagram 8.2

As can be seen a checklist bound to form aesthetics is given to each programmer as shown in diagram 8.1. As the programmer completes fulfilling each item its **check box** on the form is **ticked** indicating form standard compliance.

The form is then passed to the QA team / Project leader who then checks to ensure that everything is exactly as specified. If nonconformities are noticed the nonconformities form as shown in diagram 8.2 is filled in writing and the form returned to the programmer for standards compliance.

Similarly Menus, Master/Detail forms, Report parameter forms, and finally report formats must have their aesthetics defined and documented. A checklist must be created bound to each for the aesthetics defined. Finally, a nonconformities form created so that any nonconformities discovered can be documented in writing by the QA team / Project leader.

Once done, this must be passed back to the programmer who created the section being analyzed along with the appropriate section so that the standards defined from that section are actually applied to the project.

If a track is kept of the work being done by the programmers and the number of times (and why) their work is returned to them by the QA team / Project leader, all programmers who adhere to project standards will be identified.

Additionally, programmers who do not conform to the project standards set can be made accountable and responsible for shoddy, sub standard work and suitable corrective action applied so that the project has its aesthetics standards maintained.

In Conclusion

It's not too difficult to maintain standards across any project. A one-time effort must be made to define the aesthetic and code base standards that the company will adhere to.

Subsequently a set of simple forms need to be created using M.S. Word which will enable programmers to bind these standards to each project segment and allow the standards to be quickly and accurately checked.

INTRODUCING QUALITY TO CODEBASE

Having completed a look at bringing quality to a data entry form's aesthetics its time to take a quick look at simple but effective techniques that will bring quality to a form's code base.

Code maintenance is quite a nightmare. This is largely due to the fact that that there is little or no documentation being maintained about a form's code base. Sometimes a form's code base can be patched and re-patched so many times that the original functionality of the form is completely lost.

QA Techniques

Define **a structure** for the .frm file that every programmer must comply with. This will immediately bring a standard to the .frm file, otherwise each programmer will bring their personal touch to the .frm file which will make maintenance of the file a nightmare if the programmer leaves the company.

A Recommended Structure For A .frm File

The Option Explicit Section

In this section every variable used in the program will be declared. Variable naming conventions need to be followed, such as:

Variable Type	Naming convention
Global variables	g_varname
Memory variables	m_varname
Object variables	obj_varname
Record Sets	rs_recordset name
Connections	cn_Dbname

And so on.

There should be no variable declared and used outside the Option Explicit section.

The Form Opening Section

The code that executes in the **form open event** must follow immediately after the Option Explicit section in the .frm file.

The Database Connection Section

The code that sets up the connection to the database via appropriate middleware follows immediately after the codebase of the form's open event.

> Conceptually, once the VB form is opened and running in memory database connection /s can be opened. This facilitates the retrieval of a RecordSet from a database/table, which populates the form opened with business data appropriately.

The codebase that describes the database connection also includes appropriate SQL sentences to retrieve a RecordSet /s from database/table /s via the connection object spawned.

The Data Navigation Section

This section contains the codebase for the form's data navigation, command buttons (or tool bar buttons). **i.e.** First, Next, Prior, Last data navigation buttons. The code in the codebase section should also be First, Next, Prior, Last.

The Data Manipulation Section

This section contains the codebase for the form's data manipulation, command buttons (or tool bar buttons). **i.e.** View, Insert, Update, Delete, Save, Exit data manipulation buttons. The code in the codebase section should also be View, Insert, Update, Delete, Save Exit. The table's Read and Write operations segregated logically.

The Data Validation Section

This section of the .frm file will contain all the code required for validating business data captured in form objects. These code snippets get executed only when appropriate. The subroutines contained within this section are usually called from within the codebase of the data manipulation buttons.

There are two simple coding techniques used fairly universally. **One**, validate business data captured when navigating from one form field (**i.e.** data capture objects, such as Text boxes, Check boxes, Radio buttons, Text areas and so on) to another.

Two, let all the business data be captured first, then **on click** of the **Save** command button generic subroutine is called, that will one by one apply business rules to the business data captured in each of the form's data captured objects where appropriate, and validates their content.

It does not really matter which coding technique is used, the data validation codebase section should follow the data navigation and manipulation section in the .frm file.

Documenting The Codebase

Each section of the codebase must contain extensive remark statements interspaced between the lines of actual VB syntax. The remark statements explain the functionality of small sub-sections within the codebase. This will help a very great deal when the code is being modified in the future.

Remarks inserted within VB syntax must be short critically descriptive. They must make complete sense to anyone reading them not necessarily only to a programmer.

The VB code displayed throughout this material is liberally sprinkled with remarks and can be used as a model when developing any project in Visual Basic.

A sample of a structured .frm follows, this can be used as a model to create any VB project driven .frm files.

Option Explicit
'Setting up memory variables to be used later as necessary
   'Memvars used for setting up the connection to the Access database
   'Memvars used for setting up RecordSet objects for use with the connection
   'Memvars used with foreign Key manipulation of the details table

Public Sub Form_Load()
'Setting up the Data Grid attributes as per application requirements
   'Placing the form cursor on the View button of the master section of the d/e form
   'Disabling the Master section navigation buttons
End Sub

'***** DATA NAVIGATION SUBROUTINES FOR THE MASTER SECTION BEGINS ******

Private Sub cmdViewMast_Click()
   'Entering into View mode
End Sub

Private Sub cmdFirstMast_Click()
   'Moving to the first record in the recordset
End Sub

Private Sub cmdPrevMast_Click()
   'Moving to the previous record in the recordset
End Sub

Private Sub cmdNextMast_Click()
   'Moving to the next record in the recordset
End Sub

Private Sub cmdLastMast_Click()
   'Moving to the last record in the recordset
End Sub

'***** DATA NAVIGATION SUBROUTINES FOR THE MASTER SECTION ENDS *******

PRACTICAL VB 6 PROJECTS

'**** DATA MANIPULATION SUB ROUTINES FOR THE MASTER SECTION BEGINS **

```
Private Sub cmdInsMast_Click()
End Sub

Private Sub cmdUpdtMast_Click()
End Sub

Private Sub cmdDelMast_Click()
End Sub

Private Sub cmdSaveMast_Click()
    'Check to see if there is any record to save
    'd/e validations are done here
    'Validating the recommendors account number
    'Validating the recommendors first name
    'Validating the recommendors last name
    'Validating the account holders first name
    'Validating the account holders last name
    'Creating an empty record in the MasterRS recordset
    'Moving the new primary key value from mnewActNo to AcctNoRS Recordset
End Sub


Private Sub cmdExitMast_Click()
    'Removing the d/e form from the computer's memory
End Sub
```

'**** DATA MANIPULATION SUB ROUTINES FOR THE MASTER SECTION ENDS ******

'*********** APPLICATION's GENERIC SUBROUTINES BEGIN   **************

```vb
Public Sub ClrFrmFlds()
    'Clearing the Form's data controls and readying the form for data entry
End Sub


Public Sub Form2RS()
    'Moving Data from form controls to the New Record in the Recordset
End Sub

Public Sub PopFormFlds()
    'Binding a form text_item to a field in the recordset
    'Ensuring that the loading of a text_item does not throw an error
        'even if a recordset field is Null
End Sub


Public Sub Opt_Current_Click()
    'Assigning the value of the radio button text to the TxtAcctType text box
End Sub


Public Sub Opt_Saving_Click()
    'Assigning the Radio button Text to the TxtAcctType text box
End Sub


Public Sub LockCtrls()
    'Setting the Text boxes to a unique background color and font weight
    'Disabling the Account Type and Account Number text boxes to prevent
        'their contents being changed
End Sub
```

```vb
Public Sub cmdBkup_Click()
    'Backing up the MS Access Database
End Sub


Public Sub Link2DB()
    'Binding the Saving Bank form to a database using ADO and an OLEDB provider
        'to VIEW data in the database
    'Creating the ADODB connection object in memory
    'Indicating which OLE DB provider to use binding the provider to the Access database
    'Opening the BankMasterCN Connection to the database
    'Creating a new SavAcctMasterRS recordset object to hold the records retrieved
    'Making the SQL Query programatically replaceable when required
    'Retrieving records from the SavAcctMaster table via the BankMast Connection object
    'Specifying the Cursor type and Locking to be used
End Sub

Public Sub GetAcctId()
    'Picking up a new savings or current account number
    'Spawing an ADODB connection object in memory
    'Indicating which OLE DB provider to use and binding the provider to the
        'Access database
    'Opening the BankMasterCN connection to the database
    'Creating a new SavAcctMasterRS recordset object to hold the records retrieved
    'Firing a SQL query to retrieve the last accunt number assigned
    'Specifying the Cursor type and Locking to be used
    'Moving the value retrieved from the AcctNoRS Recordset to memory variable
    'Updating the value stored in newAcctNo to obtain the new bank account number
    'Assigning the new system generated account number to the form's data
        'control txtAcctNo
End Sub

Public Sub UnlockDBGContactInfo4VU()
    'Setting the Datagrid DGContactInfo's Add and Update attributes to
        'allow data capture
End Sub
```

```
Public Sub UnlockDBGContactInfo()
    'Setting the Datagrid DGContactInfo's Add and Update attributes to
       'allow data capture
End Sub

Public Sub LockDBGContactInfo()
    'Disabling the Datgrid
End Sub

Public Sub DisablDtls()
    'Disabling the Details section navigation buttons
End Sub

Public Sub EnablDtls()
    'Enabling the Details section navigation buttons
End Sub

Public Sub DisMastNavBtns()
    'Disabling the Master section navigation buttons
End Sub


Public Sub EnablMastNavBtns()
    'Enabling the Master section navigation buttons
End Sub

'************* APPLICATIONS GENERIC SUBROUTINES END **************
```

In Conclusion

The above is just an example of the logical flow of a .frm file. It indicates remark statements, which can be used within subroutines to document code snippets within the sub routine. Between these remark statements actual VB syntax will reside. Just this much is a huge leap forwards in bringing standards and QA to a VB project's code base.

Chapter 08

Self Evaluation

In This Chapter We Learned:

- **An Introduction To Project Management**

- **The Project Management Process**
  Beginning A Software Project
  Measures And Metrics
  Estimation
  Risk Analysis
  Project Scheduling
  Project Tracking And Control

- **The Quality Assurance Process**
  Examples Of Aesthetic Standards

- **Standards For Master Data Entry Forms**

- **Checklist For Master Data Entry Form Aesthetics**

- **Non-Conformities Of The Master Data Entry Form**

APPENDIX

APPENDIX

Both projects mentioned in this book, require a programmer to take the following steps prior the start of project coding.

- Adding all components (.ocx files) required by each project individually
- Adding all library references (.tlb and .dll files) required by each project individually

ADDING COMPONENTS AND REFERENCES TO A PROJECT

To add new component to a project, click **Project → Components** from the menu bar. Refer to diagram A.1.

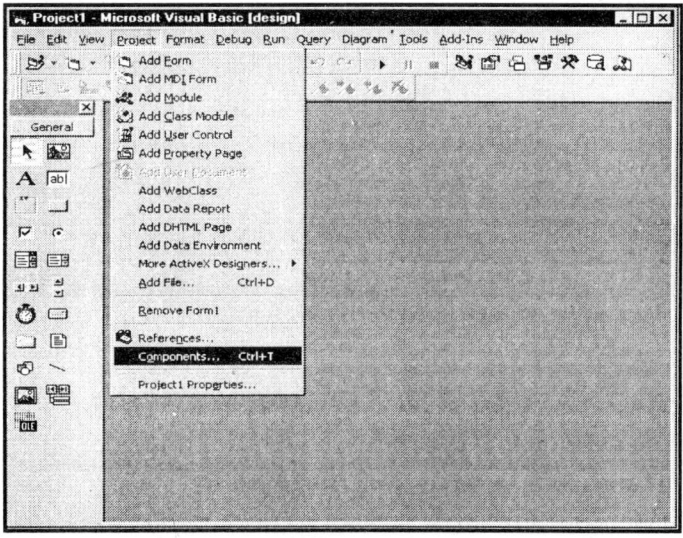

Diagram A.1

This will display a dialog box as shown in diagram A.2.

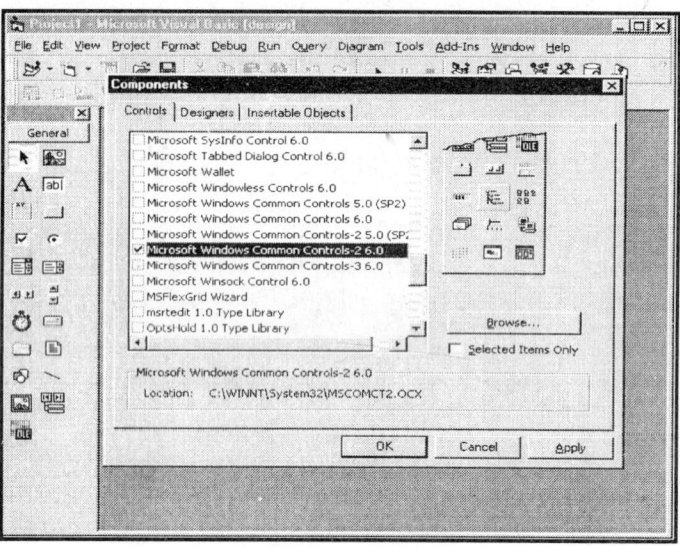

Diagram A.2

Select the required component by clicking on its check box (multiple components can thus be selected) then click **Apply**. Individual objects available in each new component will now be visible on the projects toolbar as shown in diagram A.3.

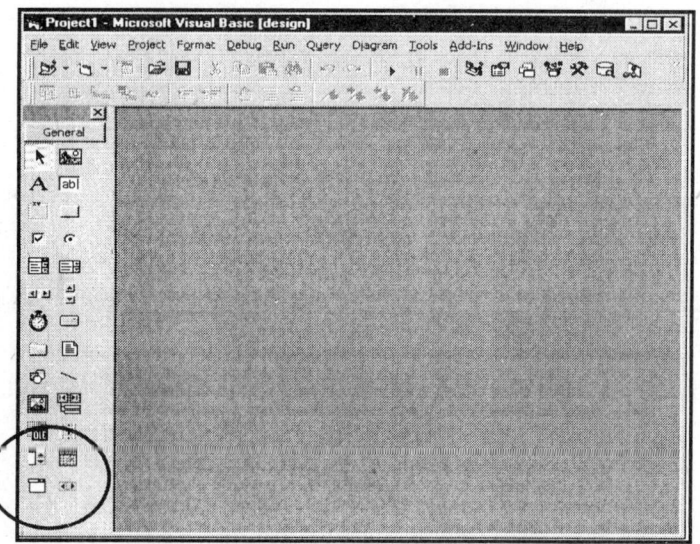

Diagram A.3

Appendix   ADDING COMPONENTS AND REFERENCES TO A PROJECT IN VB 6

To add new library reference to a project, click **Project** → **References** from the menu bar. Refer to diagram A.4.

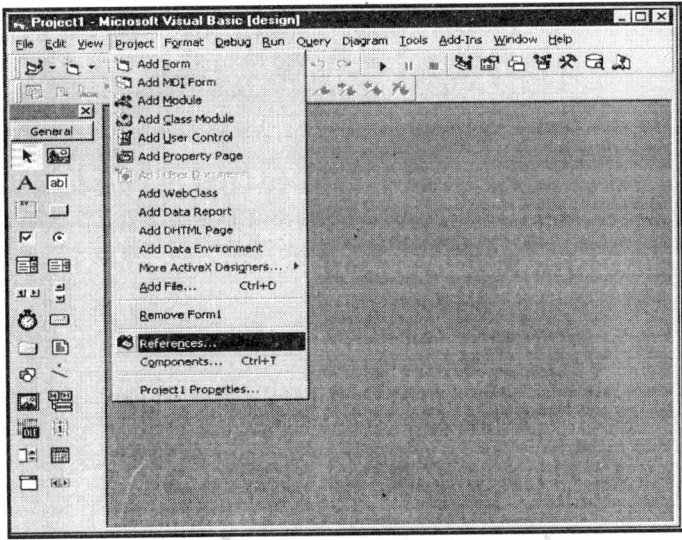

Diagram A.4

This will display a dialog box as shown in diagram A.5.

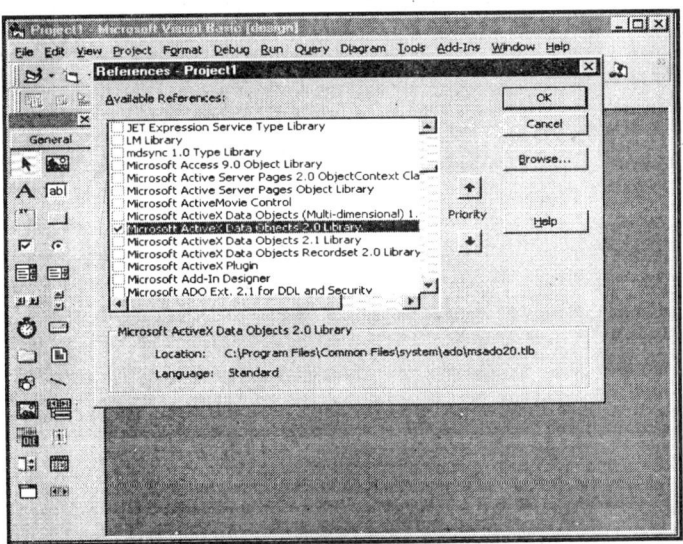

Diagram A.5

Click on the required checkboxes and then click **OK**.

INDEX

INDEX

3
32-bit ODBC driver 13

A
ActiveX Data Objects (ADO) 18, 20

C
Crystal Reports 342

D
Data Connector 344
DataField 351
DataMember 351

I
IDE 341
intrinsic controls 342

O
OLE DB 18
OLEBD 347

R
Report Designer 342
Report Extraction 341

S
System DSN 14

T
twips 342